Kinship and Continuity

Kinship and Continuity
Pakistani Families in Britain

ALISON SHAW
Brunel University, Uxbridge, UK

harwood academic publishers

Australia • Canada • France • Germany • India • Japan
Luxembourg • Malaysia • The Netherlands • Russia
Singapore • Switzerland

Copyright © 2000 OPA (Overseas Publishers Association) N.V. Published by license under the Harwood Academic Publishers imprint, part of The Gordon and Breach Publishing Group.

Amsteldijk 166
1st Floor
1079 LH Amsterdam
The Netherlands

British Library Cataloguing in Publication Data

A catalogue record for this book is available from the British Library.
ISBN: 90-5823-075-9 (hard cover)

For Jonathan, Helen, Kate and Adam

CONTENTS

MAPS

TABLES

FIGURES

PREFACE

This book is about the families of labour migrants who first came to Britain from rural Pakistan in the 1950s and 60s. It is based on research which I began in 1979 but it is the result not of a single project but of several periods of fieldwork. My initial research was towards a D.Phil. thesis in social anthropology and took me to Pakistan, where I spent seven months living in villages with relatives of families living in Oxford. The thesis that I completed in 1984 stressed the social and cultural continuities between Pakistan and Britain: it was an argument against prevailing assimilationist assumptions.

Towards the end of this formal research period, I began teaching Urdu to people such as teachers and health professionals whose work brought them into regular contact with Urdu and Panjabi speakers, and I had this audience in mind, as well as an academic one, when I revised the thesis for publication. *A Pakistani Community in Britain*, (Basil Blackwell, 1988) contained the anti-assimilationist argument of my thesis and was also written with the specific objective of addressing many of the assumptions that non-Pakistani readers might make about British Pakistanis.

In that book, I attempted to convey the dynamics of Pakistani *birādarīs* (kinship groups) 'from the inside', and the letters I have from time to time received from Pakistani students and English professionals suggest I achieved some success. Last summer, during a conversation about the local mosques, a Pakistani taxi driver mentioned to me a library book about the Pakistani community that his wife was reading for her PGCE course. "I only read the chapter on the mosques, because that is what I am interested in", he said, "but the author described it just how it is; she really got into people's heads, to know how they tick". I realized he was talking about my book and told him so. "You did a really good job", he said, "it portrays our community to a tee", adding, "Your Mum's famous!" as he turned to my children sitting in the back of the taxi.

Such remarks are flattering, of course, but they also draw attention to some of the problems with conducting anthropological research among people with whom the researcher must continue to live and work. Some of my Pakistani friends think that I should not have written about caste, for example, or about mosque disputes, because to discuss such issues might show a community vulnerable to racism in an unfavourable light. I have tried to balance my responsibilities to those who have shared aspects of their lives with me with my desire to write as objective and accurate an account as possible; I have also tried to show how issues which generate controversy, such as caste or Islamic sect, in fact reveal some of the dynamics of the Pakistani presence in Britain.

The present book builds upon and extends the analysis of *A Pakistani Community in Britain*, but it is not the same book. I have conducted fresh fieldwork, which included renewing contact with families I had not seen for some years. I have updated all of the chapters where appropriate. My earlier discussion of caste, kinship and marriage is substantially extended and now occupies two chapters. This book also includes an entirely new chapter containing previously unpublished material about attitudes to health and illness.

ACKNOWLEDGEMENTS

First, I must thank Adam Kuper for a lectureship at Brunel University that has provided the structure I needed for completing this new edition. On the domestic front, I am immensely grateful to Josephine Reynell, for our anthropological conversations over family suppers and childcare arrangements, to Mary Worrall for her practical and moral support, and of course to my husband and children. Parts of this book have benefited from being read by friends and colleagues. In particular, I thank Shakil Ahmed, Jonathan Flint, Ronnie Frankenburg, David Gellner, Norman Lawrence, Adam Kuper, Ian Robinson, Georgina Robson, Richard Tapper and Josephine Reynell for their comments. I would also like to acknowledge the students at Brunel University who attended my course on 'Britain's Ethnic Minorities' last autumn and read drafts of some of the chapters.

Since this book expands and updates an earlier book, I also wish to acknowledge previous debts to friends and colleagues who read part or all of various drafts, or who discussed some of the issues with me. Thank you to: Zahida Abbasi, Helen Adams, Nick Allen, Michael Carrithers, Jonathan Flint, Nikki Van der Gaag, David Gellner, Marion Molteno, James Noel, Caroline Roaf, Ralph Russell, Fozia Tanvir and Brian Todd, who drew the diagram on page 74. Edwin Ardener at the Institute of Social Anthropology in Oxford introduced me to social anthropology as an undergraduate and encouraged me to embark on the research for a D.Phil., for which I was initially supported by a three-year grant from the Social Science Research Council (UK).

Finally, I must acknowledge my permanent debt to the Pakistani families who welcomed me when I embarked on my research, who continue to welcome me into their homes and their lives and have given so generously of their time and hospitality. I have decided not to name anyone in particular here, because most of them would prefer not to be named and in any case the list would be very long. I remain deeply indebted to particular friends for lengthy discussions that considerably aided my analysis and interpretations. I have changed the names of everybody I know, and corrupted some family relationships in order to preserve confidentiality. I hope that those of them who read this book feel it does them justice, and that their descendants will see some value in it as a portrayal of a part of their social history.

A NOTE ON TRANSLITERATION

Here are approximations for pronouncing a few of the Urdu words that appear most frequently in the book:

> *birādarī* is pronounced something like 'biraaderi', with the emphasis on the first 'a' which is long, like the 'a' in 'father'.
> *lenā-denā* is pronounced something like 'layna dayna'.
> *baithak* is pronounced with the emphasis on the 'ai' which is like the 'ai' in 'air' and the 'thak' is pronounced something like 'tuck'.

I have used an approximate transliteration system, in which the consonants are close to those denoted by the English letters. For simplicity, I have not, for instance, distinguished the guttural 'gh' (as in *ghusal)* and the aspirated 'gh' (as in *ghī*); or the retroflex and dental 't', 'd' and 'r', or sounds which are nasalized. This transliteration does, however, note the difference between long and short vowels:

> a is short, like the 'a' in 'cat'
> ā is long, like the 'a' in 'father'
> i is short, like the 'i' in 'him'
> ī is long, like the 'ee' in 'keen'
> u is short, like the 'u' in 'put'
> ū is long, like the 'u' in 'rule'

For the remaining vowels, the approximate equivalents are:

> e, like the 'ay' in 'day'
> o, like the 'o' in 'hole'
> ai, is like the 'ai' in 'air', and
> au, something like 'awe'

INTRODUCTION

Provision of interpreters had always been a problem at the local community relations council, so when Mahboob volunteered to interpret for a family with a housing problem his services were much appreciated. Mahboob, who had come to England when he was eight years old, was then twenty and working with his father at the Austin Rover car factory in Cowley. Mahboob's evident diplomatic abilities and the ease with which he dealt with British bureaucracy led both the community relations council staff and myself to encourage him to leave the factory and apply to train as a social worker. Convincing him of the value of such a job was relatively easy: he appreciated the difficulties experienced especially by those of the first generation of Pakistani settlers in Britain, and spoke enthusiastically of how he would help them. The community relations council staff gave him their full encouragement, wrote him the best references they could devise, and spoke highly of him to the Polytechnic to which he eventually applied.

Six weeks after the beginning of term, I called into the shop that Mahboob's family had recently bought, and was served by Mahboob himself. 'Why,' I asked, 'are you working here? I thought you were supposed to be studying'. 'I've decided not to go,' he replied, 'I'm far too busy here in the shop.' This seemed to me a spurious reason, and I was surprised Mahboob could resort to it. I had expected more of him and I felt let down, both because he had, in my view, wasted an opportunity to escape from the factory work which offered no prospects, and because I believed he had given me an inadequate explanation for his decision to abandon the Polytechnic course.

As I talked more with Mahboob and his family, however, I began to realize that my disappointment arose from my own prejudices. It became clear that Mahboob had not been interpreting merely for pleasure, nor to improve 'community relations', nor even to help his fellow Pakistanis, though no doubt all these were part of the reason. Far more important

was the fact that those Pakistanis for whom Mahboob
translated felt in debt to him, and would repay this debt in
various ways that were advantageous to Maboob's whole
family. This was not a simple question of returning a favour,
but of initiating a process of exchange, called *lenā-denā*, that is
fully discussed in chapter 8. The community relations council
staff and I had seen Mahboob in isolation, as an individual
doing things for other individuals. This had never been
Maboob's perception, or that of the people for whom he
interpreted.

I also learnt that Mahboob's initial decision to go to the Polytechnic had not been made simply by weighing up the advantage
to his career or by considering his personal satisfaction. He also
had to take into account the extent to which attending the
Polytechnic would benefit his kinship group, or *birādarī*, both in
Oxford and in Pakistan. Many Oxford Pakistanis still view living
and working in Britain in much the same way as they, or their
parents, did when they first arrived here: that is, as a way to make
money to benefit the *birādarī*. In this case it happened that the
recently acquired shop needed looking after in the evening.
Mahboob and his family had reasoned that if Mahboob went to
college, the shop could not be kept open for so many hours and
thus money would be lost. Perhaps the calculation was misguided
as Mahboob's salary as a qualified social worker could have
provided more income than the shop, but neither Mahboob nor
his family thought so. Mahboob was therefore quite happy with
his decision and I was foolish to consider any other grounds for
his failure to take up the place on the course than that he was
busy in the shop.

My failure to understand Mahboob's motives was particularly
ironic given that this event occurred in 1984 just after I had
completed a doctoral thesis about the lives of Pakistanis in
Britain. Through an analysis of the migration and of
Pakistanis' intentions and priorities now that they are living in
Britain, I had concluded that many features of Pakistani
migrants' culture and social organization have survived rather
than disappearing: Mahboob's decision should then have come
as no surprise. My misunderstanding of Mahboob's reasoning
was for me a salutary reminder that even for a researcher who
thinks she knows a group of people well it is difficult to
abandon 'western' assumptions.

During the 1950s and 1960s, the first phase of substantial post-war south Asian and Afro-Caribbean migration to Britain, observers had commonly assumed that Pakistani and other minorities, like their Irish and Jewish immigrant predecessors, would inevitably become assimilated into the British social structure and adopt 'western' customs and values, however these may be defined[1]. From the 1970s onwards it was increasingly clear that this was a simplistic assumption. It is now obvious that Pakistanis settled in Britain have not adopted wholesale western lifestyles and values, despite the fact that at least some have achieved quite significant material and educational success[2]. What has occurred is perhaps better described as 'accommodation without assimilation'[3]. Part of the explanation for this situation lies in the dynamics of labour migration and of racial exclusion, which is sometimes expressed as outright racial hostility from white 'natives'. However, as I hope to show in this book, British Pakistanis are far from being the downtrodden victims of political, economic and social processes beyond their control. They have demonstrated great resiliance in adapting the structural and cultural resources at their disposal towards building and re-shaping their lives in Britain on their own terms[4].

Academics have discussed the ways in which groups of people use their social organization and cultural values to maintain their distinctiveness in relation to others, or to further common interests, in terms of the concept of 'ethnicity'[5]. They disagree, however, about what exactly 'ethnicity' means, and the academic disputes are complicated by the fact that terms such as 'ethnic', 'ethnicity' and 'ethnic minority' are now commonly used outside the academic world too. If I were to use the concept of 'ethnicity' as an analytical tool — even after discussing all its various usages[6] — I would risk giving ethnicity the status of an overall explanation for non-assimilation and would thus deflect attention away from how identities are constructed and how they change over time. There is plenty of ethnographic material in these pages that the energetic student could indeed use to illustrate or debate the value of the concept of ethnicity — and I return to this question in the concluding chapter — but this has not been my concern in this book.

I have tried to present an account of both continuity and change in the lives of Oxford Pakistanis with particular reference to the 'pioneer' generation who are predominantly from rural areas where their families own and work on the land. Living in an industrial city has confronted them with profound and dramatic contrasts, not just in living standards and styles of work and of education, but in ways of acting and thinking. Material changes have been accommodated quite easily, in Britain and in migrants' villages of origin in Pakistan, for, as I shall show, these are very much in keeping with migrants' original intentions to improve their socio-economic status. On the other hand, many beliefs and values and ways of acting and thinking have shown remarkable resiliance, even, contrary to my expectations, among the younger generation — the children and grandchildren of the pioneer migrants. The younger generations especially have confronted, questioned and re-interpreted previously taken-for-granted beliefs, values and practices, but they have not necessarily or in any simple way assimilated western beliefs and values.

The reasons for this are complex, but if I were to sum them up in one word, I would choose kinship: hence the title of this book. Kinship, with its obligations and dynamics, is a central theme in what follows. As chapter 1 shows, kinship provided the dynamic for migration in the first place, for migration was, and has long been, viewed as a means of furthering the interests of the *birādarī* or extended family. The kinship-based structure of the migration subsequently influenced the development of the Pakistani settlement in Britain, as chapter 2 demonstrates. Chapter 3 explores some of the dynamics of domestic and household organization, and demonstrates how *birādarī* interests underpin many of the changes that at first might look like evidence of weakening kinship ties. Chapters 4, 5 and 6 explore aspects of kinship through a discussion of marriage, which is the cornerstone of the perpetuation of the *birādarī*. Chapter 4 discusses the constraints of the caste hierarchy within which marriages are arranged, and chapter 5 looks at the deliberations, decisions and changing strategies of the marriage arrangers. This provides a background to the discussion in chapter 6 of young people's experiences of, and attitudes towards, arranged marriage. There is considerable debate about the process of arranged marriage, and parental interests continue to shape many marriage arrangements, but extreme dissent is relatively rare. While marriage is the corner-stone of the *birādarī*, producing children is essential to its reproduction; chapter 7 explores perceptions of health and illness in this context, with a particular focus on women's reproductive health. The remaining two chapters discuss aspects of Pakistani social life beyond the household and closest kin. One theme of chapter 8 is that some of the obligations and expectations of 'kinship' underlie the management of inter-household reciprocity; the principle of 'taking-giving' (lenā-denā) maintains existing social relationships but permits new ones to develop, lending a degree of flexibility to the concept of birādarī. Obligations towards kin and fellow villagers also play a part in shaping the more public politics of community representation and religious disputes that I discuss in chapter 9.

While kinship is a central thread running through the book, individual chapters take up other issues. In trying to view Pakistani migration and settlement in Britain as far as possible 'from the inside', I have attempted to shed light on some of the specific questions readers might have. Issues such as the position of women, the future of the second and now third generation who have grown up in Britain, and the nature of Pakistani community politics, for instance, are all particularly sensitive, overlaid by prejudice on the part of both English people and Pakistanis.

'Westerners' commonly assume Pakistani women are, as a general category, depressed and isolated in Britain, subordinate to men and confined to the home and childcare within their own communities and the victims of racism within British society at large. During my research, English people sometimes made remarks such as, 'I feel so sorry for the women; I would hate to be a woman in a society like that'. There is some truth in this picture, but such a wholly negative impression of Pakistani women's role is in many respects an inaccurate one. It is all too easily formed on the basis of most English people's contact with Pakistani women, which tends to be in situations where they are clients with language problems, such as at health centres or in D.H.S.S. offices. My own impression too at the beginning of the research was that Pakistani women had relatively little control over their new surroundings. I had intended to focus my research on the position of women and particularly of second generation Muslim girls brought up in a western society, among whom I expected there to be a extreme conflict between 'western' and 'Islamic' values. However, I soon realized that the position of women is much more complex than this.

For example, Amina, who joined her husband in Britain in the 1970s, hardly fits the general image of a dependent wife whose husband and family arranged her passage to a new country with a different language and strange customs. Having heard rumours that her husband had married an English woman, and fearing for her own and her children's future, Amina borrowed money for the fare and came with her children to England where she lived with the English wife until the latter left. Like many Pakistani wives, Amina now controls the day-to-day running of her household and is a daunting figure, while her husband, now a religious man, keeps a watchful eye over his children. From the 'outside' — at the doctor's surgery perhaps, where she struggles to communicate in her limited English or depends on the help of one of her children, Amina appears to have little control over her life, but from the 'inside' the picture is quite different.

English people tend to view Pakistani women out of the context of their family and community where, despite the structural and ideological constraints, they may in fact hold very strong positions. In three villages in Pakistan, each of the households in which I stayed was run by a middle-aged widow who supervised her unmarried daughters, her sons, daughters-in-law and their children in day-to-day household matters and influenced major family decisions about work and marriage. These women seemed larger than life, awe-inspiring and powerful. Later, however, when each of them came to England to visit their sons or daughters here, I was shocked at how frail, vulnerable and dependent they appeared. Of course, I was perceiving them in much the same way that Pakistani women are generally perceived, that is, out of context, in a social and physical environment where, outside the house at least, they are dependent on people normally under their authority.

Amina's story, told more fully in chapter 2, illustrates another generally overlooked feature of Pakistani women's position, which is that in certain respects their roles have been strengthened rather than weakened as a result of living in Britain. Many women like Amina have more direct practical control over their households in Britain than they would have had in Pakistan because they are free from the authority of a mother-in-law. They also exert a moral control that is peculiar to the new situation. Amina feared that her husband was 'going astray'; her joining him was a successful attempt to regain both moral and practical control. Some women see their roles in Britain quite explicitly in terms of maintaining and transmitting cultural and religious values and protecting their families from western influences, and while others may not admit this to be their aim, it is undoubtedly a result of their presence. It is to a large extent the women who are responsible for the distinctive structure and social life of the community today. Through networks of reciprocity, women evaluate one another and one another's households; women's status is thus not simply a function of whether they have roles independent of their families or paid work outside the home.

Another set of common western preconceptions concerns those Pakistanis who have grown up, or are growing up, in Britain. I have often been asked questions such as, 'What is happening to the next generation? Doesn't living in Britain and having English friends mean that Pakistani youngsters are rejecting their parents' culture, especially arranged marriages?' Usually behind such questions is the assumption that the second generation is torn 'between two cultures' — one which offers freedom and one which controls their activities and denies them basic liberties such a choice of marriage partner and career.

Most of us in an urban setting inhabit more than one social world, and Pakistanis are no exception. Young Pakistanis negotiate several social worlds — those of their parents and grandparents, those of their 'white' peers — at school, college, or the workplace — and that of their South Asian peers. For most of the time, they move successfully from one to the other. When there is conflict — and sometimes there is indeed bitter conflict, such as when an Asian girl runs away from home or elopes in order to escape an arranged marriage — this is not necessarily the inevitable result of living in Britain. While I was in Pakistan I was struck by the fact that sometimes young adults run away from home or elope in order to escape an arranged marriage; I began to realize that similar incidents in Britain are not solely or necessarily the result of being in England and being influenced by a different way of thinking, by permissive western values. They can also be the products of tensions and dynamics that are internal to the *birādarī* structure, played out in a Pakistani cultural idiom, while accommodating features of the new environment.

From a western viewpoint, an individual who fulfils her or his role within the family, *birādarī* and wider community does so at the cost of individual freedom. However, Pakistanis themselves, including the younger generation, do not necessarily prize individuality as highly as westerners do, and for many, the down-playing of individuality that is in effect required is more than offset by the advantages and satisfactions of fulfilling a role within the family, *birādarī* and community. Occasionally, of course, there is conflict between an individual's inclinations or convictions and their relatives' expectations; hence the elopements and other incidents that reach the press. But such incidents are not as common as the media's sensational reporting suggests; conflicts are often short-lived and only occasionally pose a fundamental or long-term threat to *birādarī* structure. At the same time, *birādarī*s are not static; conflict may entail questioning, challenging and gradual change, processes which arise from internal structural and ideological dynamics in response to changing socio-economic circumstances, rather than as passive responses to the western environment. As young Pakistanis themselves point out, many of the changes occurring within Pakistani families in Britain — the questioning of aspects of the arranged marriage, for instance — are also taking place in Pakistan, and these changes, while motivated at least in part by western values, are usually justified with reference to particular interpretations of Islamic values. Young adults often claim that such change is in fact proceeding more quickly in Pakistan, in certain areas at least, than among British Pakistanis, whom they consider more conservative because of their minority status.

Various aspects of Pakistani community politics have also, from time to time, been greeted with incomprehension or prejudice by the media or by local authorities. British politicians and bureaucrats often assume that a homogeneous Pakistani 'community' exists and that its interests can be 'represented' by one or two individuals, who are regarded as controlling extensive mafia-like kinship groups that operate as political units. In fact, Oxford Pakistanis comprise numerous different kinship groups that tend to compete with each other for access to status and resources. Where these groups overlap with statutory and voluntary agencies, 'leaders' or 'representatives' may indeed emerge and attempt to legitimize their position through the idiom of 'acting for their community'. The result quite often is internal and sometimes bitter conflict and division, in which allegiances are more shifting and fluid than is at first apparent, as individuals and groups attempt to consolidate their positions, in relation to their relatives and those they influence and to state-sponsored agencies. Chapter 10 explores some of the dynamics of this process.

These power struggles over access to resources have been an integral part of the process through which Pakistani Muslims have established their presence, not only in Oxford but also elsewhere in Britain. The negotiations involved reflect an increasing concern with questions of Islamic identity, concerns that, I have suggested elsewhere, have eclipsed the 'myth of return' as an ideology that to some extent protects *birādarī* interests[7]. These concerns have not arisen simply in the wake of responses to the publication of Salman Rushdie's *The Satanic Verses,* such as the Bradford book-burning in January or the Ayatollah Khomeni's *fatwa* against Salman Rushdie in February of 1989. While the Rushdie affair has no doubt heightened awareness of these issues at a national level, in local contexts, perceived threats to Muslim values were capable of mobilising a relatively cohesive Muslim response well before the Rushdie affair. In Bradford, which has a very substantial Muslim presence, the impulse towards Muslim co-operation and unity has had relatively early institutional form: the Bradford Council of Mosques has articulated collective Muslim interests since 1981, despite the ideological and *birādarī* divisions among Bradford's Muslims[8]. In Oxford, where Muslims are a small and internally divided minority, no single institution has, as yet, successfully overridden differences of sect, kinship and regional identity. There is also a profound class division between the vast majority of the city's Muslims, of predominantly Pakistani but also of Bangladeshi origins, and the Muslims who are linked with Oxford University. This division is currently represented through two quite separate proposals for building a mosque and an Islamic centre. The Muslim presence in Oxford has become established at least as much through differentiation as through consolidation.

How representative, though, is my analysis, based as it is on a relatively small-scale anthropological study? Oxford Pakistanis are indeed typical of the majority of British Pakistanis, in that most of them came to Britain directly from villages in Pakistan's Panjab province and from Azad Kashmir. Despite the local differences, for instance in employment opportunities, that give each settlement a distinctive character, the processes I describe for Oxford Pakistanis are broadly typical of Pakistani settlement elsewhere in Britain. Some of the main features of Pakistani settlement in Britain have parallels with, for example, the Bangladeshi Muslim settlement, while differing from those of some other South Asian groups — the urban origin, East African Asians, for instance. The diversity of Britain's South Asian population is striking, and represented in various ways in different British cities, as Roger Ballard's edited volume testifies[9]. In Oxford, Pakistani Muslims are the largest South Asian minority, but there are also Bangladeshi Muslims and Hindus, Panjabi Hindus and Sikhs, Panjabi Christians, and some relatively affluent, already urbanized East African Asians, whose ancestors left India two or three generations ago[10]. My account makes only passing reference to these other groups, each of which has its own distinct migration history, though in fact the presence of other South Asians is implicit and sometimes explicit in the account that follows.

Finally, to what extent is it possible to talk of a Pakistani 'community'? In the language of race relations and the media, the word community frequently suggests a homogeneous group with a common culture; this use of the term generally suits the political purposes both of the white majority and of 'community representatives' competing for access to resources[11]. Oxford Pakistanis themselves have many different identities. They are both British and Pakistani; they also have regional identities (see chapter 1); *birādarī* or caste identities (chapter 4); religious identities (chapter 9), and may belong to more than one distinctive linguistic group. The identity that matters, and whether it is more or less exclusive, is context-dependent. Yet Pakistanis themselves use the English word community in a variety of contexts. They speak of 'the Muslim community', for instance, when discussing plans to build a mosque, and of the 'Pakistani community' in relation to the other 'ethnic' groups — the Indians, the Bangladeshis, the Afro-Caribbeans — in the local council and at local community relations council meetings. They also use the word community to evoke their shared local history, to refer inclusively to Pakistanis who like themselves or their parents or grandparents came to Britain in the 1950s and 1960s as labour migrants from rural Pakistan and settled in Oxford. Men's experiences during the early years of settlement (see chapter 2) constitute a collective memory which conveys this sense of a shared past[12]. When I write of 'Oxford Pakistanis', it is to people of this background that I am referring, and not to those

Pakistanis of more privileged 'urban-educated' backgrounds, such as the professionals, academics and business people who have settled in more affluent parts of Oxford. In migrants' recollections, their shared history is also linked with a particular history of residence in the city, and while east Oxford was not the first main locus of Pakistani settlement in the city, and is not the only area where Pakistanis live, it is still where most Pakistanis reside. It is with this sense of community as shared local history that Oxford Pakistanis sometimes refer to Pakistanis who have recently moved to east Oxford from other parts of Britain as people 'from outside' and 'not from our community'. The following two chapters begin to provide the background for understanding how this sense of community has arisen.

NOTES

1. I use the problematic term 'western', in a general sense, in contrast to 'eastern', 'south Asian' or 'Islamic' (which are not, of course, interchangeable). This is in preference to 'British' or 'English', since defining these terms is perhaps even more problematic; 'British' of course includes ethnic groups such as the Afro-Caribbeans or Chinese who have their own particular viewpoints. I also use the terms 'English' or 'English people', which have an ethnic connotation, in a general sense (where others might have used the blanket term 'white') to denote British people of Irish, English, Welsh, Scottish heritages in contrast to 'Pakistani'.
2. Ballard (ed.), 1994.
3. Gibson, 1988.
4. For anthropological perspectives on South Asian migrants, see, for instance, Ballard, (ed.), 1994 and Gardner, 1995.
5. Barth, 1969; Cohen, 1969.
6. Eriksen, 1993; Banks, 1996.
7. Shaw, 1994, in Ballard (ed.), 1994.
8. Lewis, 1994 (a) in Ballard (ed.) 1994, p. 59 and p. 78. See also Lewis 1994 (b) for an excellent overview of the development of the Muslim presence in Britain.
9. Ballard (ed.), 1994.
10. See also Bhachu, 1985.
11. Baumann, 1996:14–15.
12. See also Werbner, 1980.

1 FROM PAKISTAN TO BRITAIN

The primary motive for Pakistani migration to Britain in the late 50s and early 1960s was socio-economic. Single or bachelor-status married men leaving wives and children in Pakistan came to Britain to earn and save money that would enable their immediate kin at home to settle debts, extend landholdings, build new houses, give larger dowries, start businesses and so on[1]. The economic 'pull' towards Britain was a powerful one, because wages for labouring jobs in Britain in the early 1960s were over thirty times those offered for similar jobs in Pakistan. In Mirpur, for instance, the average weekly wage was equivalent to approximately 37 pence; in Birmingham, a Pakistani's average weekly wage was £13[2].

Given this pecuniary motive, it is at first puzzling that most Pakistani migrants to Britain were from only a few particular areas in Pakistan. These areas are parts of the Panjab, the North West Frontier and Mirpur (see Map 1.1). Why did migrants not come to Britain from other parts of Pakistan, such as Baluchistan, which are in many respects poorer than the main regions of out-migration? Explanations usually mention the 'push' of pressure upon land, the high population density and the fragmentation of landholdings in these areas. This, however, is not the whole story for there are parts of India where population pressure on land is higher, but people have not emigrated in significant numbers. It is also clear that traditions of migration and local population movements have also helped shape migration from particular areas[3] and the regions represented by Pakistanis in Britain are no exception.

Britain's Pakistani Population

According to the 1991 U.K. Census, which included for the first time an explicit ethnic question, there are 476,555 Pakistanis in Britain who constitute 0.87% of Britain's population of nearly 55 million. The Census data identify Pakistanis as the third largest ethnic group in Britain[4]. In England, the largest Pakistani settlements are in West Yorkshire and the West Midlands

Map 1.1   Map of Pakistan

(see Map 1.2). Bradford, for instance, has a Pakistani population of some 49,000[5]. Birmingham, Leeds, Sheffield, Preston and, in Scotland, Glasgow also have a substantial Pakistani presence and there are smaller settlements further south in Aylesbury, Bristol, High Wycombe, Luton, Oxford, Reading, Slough and parts of London.

This settlement pattern to a large extent reflects the industrial labour shortages of the 1950s onwards in cities where industry was expanding. Britain exploited her historical links with India, Pakistan and the Caribbean by directly and indirectly recruiting labour from these countries and after 1962 by issuing work vouchers. The process brought workers to the

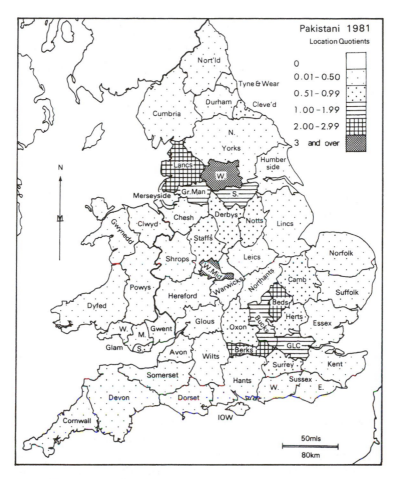

Map 1.2   Distribution of Pakistanis in England and Wales (Map reproduced from Vaughan Robinson, *Transients, Settlers, and Refugges: Asians in Britain,* Oxford Clarendon Press, 1986, p. 38, by permission of Oxford Univeristy Press.

Midlands manufacturing industries and to the West Yorkshire steel and the Lancashire textile industries. Subsequently, too, there were labour shortages in the south. It is not surprising, then, that Britain's Pakistani population is unevenly distributed, but what is less evident is that different areas of origin in Pakistan are also unevenly represented in different parts of Britain, as the somewhat piecemeal evidence from various local studies suggests (data on region of origin rarely enter public records).

Region of origin, like *birādarī*, or caste, is an important aspect of identity: Pakistanis distinguish themselves as 'Mirpuris' (from Mirpur), 'Jhelumis' (from Jhelum), and so on. Strangers usually first 'place' each other by asking about their region of origin in Pakistan, and then more specifically about their town or village; this process also provides one measure of social distance. Allegiances of kinship and village, which often influence participation in social activities, also in effect delineate broadly regional groups in the context of community politics and the mosques.

Evidence from the two largest British Pakistani settlements, those of Bradford and Birmingham, shows four main regions of origin:

1. Mirpur district in Azad Kashmir (disputed territory, here treated as part of Pakistan);
2. Attock (formerly Campbellpur) district, locally called the Chhachh (*sic*) area;
3. some villages in Nowshera sub-district, Peshawar; and
4. some villages in Rawalpindi, Jhelum, Gujrat (not to be confused with Gujarat state in India) and Faisalabad (formerly Lyallpur) districts[6].

These categories provide a general guide to the regional composition of Britain's Pakistani population as a whole, with Mirpur district probably accounting for the majority of British Pakistanis, but the relative proportions of different groups vary from one Pakistani settlement to another and each settlement has a distinctive regional character. My impression is that Mirpuris predominate in Birmingham, Bradford, Newcastle, High Wycombe and Bristol. People from Attock and Nowshera have a significant presence in Bradford and Birmingham. In Rochdale and Bristol, the main regional division is between Mirpuris from Azad Kashmir and Panjabis[7]. Mirpuris are not always the largest groups; in Rochdale, there are apparently more Panjabis than Mirpuris[8]. The relative strength of different Panjabi groups, such as Faisalabadis and Jhelumis, also varies from one settlement to another. Faisalabadis are a significant presence in Newcastle, Huddersfield, Rochdale, Glasgow and Dewsbury[9]. Jhelumis apparently form a substantial proportion of the Pakistani population of the London borough of Waltham Forest.

Oxford's Pakistani Population

How do Oxford Pakistanis fit into this picture? 1991 Census data for Oxford city give a Pakistani population estimate of 2,026, of which less than half were born outside the U.K. This may be an underestimate: my own estimate in the early 1980s was 1,930, of which the majority lived in east Oxford (Table 1.1). Many families have moved house within east Oxford since then, some have moved outwards further east and to other suburbs of the city, while a few 'new' Pakistani families have moved into east Oxford from other parts of the country. East Oxford remains the practical and symbolic focus of settlement; it is here that most of the Pakistani businesses are based, and where, on a prime site, the foundation stone for a purpose-built mosque was laid in 1997.

Oxford Pakistanis are of quite diverse regional origins. The general consensus, supported by my 1984 household survey (Table 1.1), is that Jhelumis are the largest group, while Faisalabadis, Mirpuris and people from Attock are also well represented, in roughly equal proportions. Each of these groups has certain distinctive characteristics such as their Panjabi dialect.

Many of the Faisalabadis were originally refugees from Jullundhur district (now in Indian Panjab) during the Partition of India and Pakistan in 1947, and their spoken Panjabi is closer to that of the Sikhs. People from Attock district bordering the North West Frontier province sometimes identify themselves as Pathans, like those from Nowshera in the North West Frontier Province, but their mother-tongue is a Panjabi dialect. 'True' Pathans are considered to be Pashtoo speakers of tribal (Afghan) origins. In a dispute which took place concerning the mosque, for example, a Panjabi group comprising people from many different districts of the Panjab was opposed by a so-called 'Pathan party' which included both Panjabis from Attock district and 'real' Pathans. Some Panjabis from Attock district have adopted the title 'Pathan' in Oxford, for it conveys a certain distinction and is associated with a respectable caste status, though their *birādarī*-based kinship organization is more characteristic of Pakistani Panjabis than of 'true' Afghan tribal origins.

APPROXIMATE SIZE AND DISTRIBUTION OF OXFORD'S PAKISTANI
MUSLIM POPULATION, 1979–80.

City of Oxford Polling District	No. of Pakistani Muslim households	No of persons
EAST OXFORD (including St. Clements)	207	1,387
WEST	28	188
SOUTH	27	181
REMAINING DISTRICTS	26	175
TOTAL	288	1,931

Note: This estimate was based on the city of Oxford electoral register for 1979–80.
I counted households whose occupants have Muslim names, excluding those I
considered to be Bangladeshis, Iranians, visiting Muslim academics and so on, and
adding 13 east Oxford households personally known to me whose occupants' names
were not on the electoral register. I made a population estimate by multiplying my
estimated number of Pakistani Muslim households by an 'average household size'
(of 6.7) that I calculated from a sample of 50 east Oxford households as follows:

No. in household	3 4 5 6 7 8 9 10 11
No. of households	1 6 4 14 9 7 5 3 1

These figures included the householder's children and other resident adults except
visiting grandparents and non-Pakistanis. The resulting 'average household size' is not, of
course, an average completed family size.

Table 1.1

Mirpuris comprise the fourth largest group in east Oxford,
whereas elsewhere in Britain Mirpuris often predominate,
sometimes, as in Oxford, forming separate settlements[10]. In
Oxford, the Osney settlement at the western end of the city was
distinctly Mirpuri, at least until the closure in 1982 of the
Mother's Pride Bakery where a substantial proportion of the
Mirpuri workforce had been employed since the 1960s. Since
then, Osney's Mirpuri settlement has declined; some families
have moved to other cities, some to east Oxford and some have
returned to Pakistan.

In the past ten years, there has been some residential mobility
around and into Oxford, but there is little evidence that the
relative proportions of these regional categories have substantially altered. Most of the newcomers are the brides and
grooms of young men and women brought up in Oxford; they
are usually close relatives of the families they have joined in

ANALYSIS OF REGIONAL, URBAN AND RURAL ORIGINS OF ADULTS IN 100 EAST OXFORD PAKISTANI HOUSEHOLDS, 1984.			
District (Rural)	No. of adults*	City (Urban**)	No. of adults*
Jhelum	64	Attock	1
Faisalabad	35	Peshawar	2
Attock	34	Karachi	4
Mirpur (Azad Kashmir)	30	Lahore	4
Nowshera (N.W.F.P)	10	Sialkot	1
Rawalpindi	9		
Gujrat	8		
Sahiwal	5		
Gujranwala	5		
Sargodha	3		
Total	**203**	**Total**	**12**

Notes:
* Usually this information pertains to the head of household and his wife, but where the households were joint, I recorded information on the background of the head of household's brother, sister-in-law, uncle etc. as well. In this way I accounted for a total of 215 adults, that is, about half of the adult Pakistani population of east Oxford. I excluded six wives — one Italian, one Yugoslavian, and four English.
** Urban denotes people whose families have been city dwellers for several generations.

Table 1.2

Oxford and tend to originate from the same village or region in Pakistan.

The Rural-urban Distinction

Some 95% of British Pakistanis are reportedly of rural origin, while the remaining 5% are from urban areas such as Karachi, Lahore, Peshawar, Rawalpindi and Sialkot[11]. Distinguishing migrants in this way is, of course, somewhat problematic, for it tends to reinforce the stereotype that 'urban' means 'educated' and 'rural' means 'uneducated' or 'illiterate'. It also obscures the considerable geographical, historical and social variation between migrants' backgrounds. Pakistan is itself in the process of urbanization, and many Pakistani families in Britain have recently moved, or partially moved, to the cities and these urban Pakistanis have relatives with whom they have close contact in the villages. In any case, all rural-origin Oxford

Pakistanis are now city dwellers, by virtue of their residence in Britain. So on what does being urban depend? Is it something more than the length of one's residence in a town? It is more instructive to look at what aspects a rural way of life and values persist in an urban setting, and how they may be re-worked, than to assume a fundamental distinction between 'rural' and 'urban'[12].

Among Pakistanis themselves, the connotations of being from a city or from a village can be very important, for many Pakistanis have their own prejudices in this respect. People from the cities tend to view themselves as superior to Pakistanis from the villages, regarding villagers as uneducated, ill mannered, crude and short tempered. Urban-origin Pakistanis in Bristol kept their distance from most other Pakistanis through their negative evaluation of village people as *jangli* (wild, uncultivated) and prone to fighting and gossiping[13]. In Oxford, where people who have been city dwellers for several generations comprise only 5.4% of the total such views persist regardless of 'actual' rural or urban origin. Pakistanis generally consider city people to be educated, 'better' and more 'respectable' than villagers, and they think an urban lifestyle is superior to a rural one. Individuals may say that they are from a city in Pakistan, but turn out to be from a village[14]. Indeed, such evaluations provided much of the force behind coming to England in the first place, and the process of improving one's status in Pakistan, through foreign-earned money, building a new house, starting a business and educating one's children may also involve moving to a city. Conversely, the trappings of an urban lifestyle — a large brick-built house, running water, etc. — are increasingly features of the rural landscape in Pakistan.

Two Main Regions of Out-migration

From a geographical point of view, the main areas of out-migration correspond to two regions, which are distinct in terms of their terrain, rainfall and agricultural prosperity. The first may be described by a line extending eastwards across the northern Pakistan from Nowshera subdistrict in the North West Frontier Province and Attock in the west of the Panjab, through Rawalpindi, Mirpur and Jhelum to Gujrat and

Gujranwala. Here, the terrain is generally rough and irrigation is difficult; agriculture is rainfall-dependent and only a limited range of crops can be cultivated. Much land lies fallow and male under-employment is high, with men looking to the cities or abroad for work. In the villages I visited young active men were mostly employed away from the land, in the cities, in the army or abroad. Those who did work on the land had long periods of inactivity. Many of the villages in these areas still lack electricity or paved roads.

By contrast, Faisalabad, Sargodha and Sahiwal, which lie in the plains at the heart of Pakistan's Panjab, are relatively prosperous districts. The villages generally have electricity and are accessible by paved roads, and many farmers have tube wells and tractors. The reason for the difference is the extensive network of canals and communal access to their waters. Efficient irrigation permits the cultivation of a range of crops including sugar cane and rice, which require a great deal of water, and makes possible two crop yields in one year. In the villages I visited, men worked the land throughout the year, sowing, harvesting and selling crops and maintaining the irrigation system. Men were also preoccupied with businesses of various types, such as chicken farms, ice factories or milk production. Faisalabad district is often called 'the bread basket of Pakistan' and Faisalabad city, well known for its textile manufacturing, is sometimes called 'the Manchester of the Panjab'.

Historically too the areas are very different. The long-settled northern rainfall-dependent districts were Muslim areas before the partition of India and Pakistan in 1947. The irrigated districts of the Panjab plains, by contrast, were arid waste-lands before settlement in the nineteenth century and the introduction of irrigation: these areas were, and sometimes still are, called the 'canal colonies'. They were colonised by Hindus, Muslims and Sikhs mainly from areas such as Jullundhur in what is now Indian Panjab. Then, at Partition, a great many of the original settlers of the canal colonies — sometimes entire villages of Hindus and Sikhs — returned to what is now Indian Panjab, while Muslims from India crossed the border into Pakistan. Muslims from Indian Panjab now comprise a substantial proportion of the population of the canal colonies.

While Partition itself may have predisposed people to migrate, for instance in order to compensate for lost land, this does not explain why people also emigrated from the northern region, which was not so directly affected by Partition. The experience of Partition is not in itself, then, a sufficient explanation for emigration, even from the areas most directly affected by it; we need to look further back, to the effects of traditions and experiences of migration in these different regions from before 1947.

Migration from the Northern Rainfall Districts

Historically and geographically speaking, the long-settled, rainfall-dependent northern region would also include Jullundhur, Hoshiarpur and other districts which were in the north-east of the Panjab before 1947 but are now in India, as well as districts such as Jhelum, Mirpur and Attock, which were formerly in the north-west of pre-Partition India. The region as a whole comprises long-settled farming districts, which over the years have suffered from the pressure of population on land and the fragmentation of landholdings (there is no system of primogeniture: a man's land is divided equally between his sons). In 1941, in parts of the Panjab there were over 800 people to the square mile[15]. Even after Partition, in 1951, one quarter of the landholdings in Jullundhur district were still less than one acre[16]. In many parts of pre-Partition Panjab there was also the problem of indebtedness to moneylenders[17]. Opportunities for improving one's lot were also limited because the land towards the north-west especially is relatively infertile, and so hilly and dissected by ridges that it is difficult to irrigate. These factors in themselves, of course, do not necessarily instil a desire to migrate, but during the nineteenth century a tradition of labour migration did develop in these areas and men would spend long periods away from their home villages in army and navy service, and later as labourers abroad.

The tradition of migration for service in the army developed because the British favoured particular Panjabi Muslim and Sikh castes, generally *zamīndār* (landowning) castes such as the Mughals, Jats and Rajputs, as sources of army recruits. The castes selected were those which had military traditions; the British believed that only certain 'races' (or castes) had military capacity[18]. Over half of the Indian army was drawn from the Panjab and during the first world war the Panjab with a population of 20 millions, provided 350,000 combatants, while Bengal, with a population of 45 million, supplied only 7,000[19].

The Royal Indian Navy also drew Panjabis as recruits, especially from the north-east and districts such as Campbellpur (now Attock) and Peshawar in the North West Frontier Province. From Kashmir, another tradition of migration developed, this time for work in British steamship companies. Mirpuris from Azad Kashmir were a major source of recruits into the merchant navy[20]. During the last quarter of the nineteenth century the Panjab also supplied labour for the construction of railways in the Panjab, Sind, Baluchistan and the North West Frontier. Later, in the first decade of the twentieth century, some 25,000 Panjabis were indentured as labourers for the building of the Kenya-Uganda railway[21]. The family structure made this kind of migration possible, for a man could leave his wife and children in the care of parents during his absence. Indeed, migrants' families actually encouraged this kind of migration, in which a man spent time away from his family earning a living that would benefit his immediate kin at home. It is likely that a similar view was taken of army and navy service and labouring abroad.

Settlement of the Canal Colonies

A different kind of migration from the rainfall-dependent north occurred at the end of the nineteenth century and during the early twentieth century. The British began a scheme of irrigation and settlement in the barren Bari Doab, the area of land between the Chenab and the Ravi rivers in Southern Panjab, which was often referred to as 'the Bar'. Canal colonies were developed at Lyallpur (now Faisalabad) in 1892, Sargodha in 1898 and at Montgomery (now Sahiwal) in 1912.

In 1880, the greater portion of the Panjab consisted of arid waste...this desert area was sparsely populated by nomad tribes of camel and sheep graziers. In order to open up some of these waste tracts, and at the same time to relieve the pressure on the land in highly populated areas elsewhere, Government took over these unclaimed

lands and embarked upon a scheme of colonization. The
country was first surveyed and divided into smaller
squares which...were standardized at 25 acres in all later
schemes...In the first colonies these squares were sold
for nominal sums, chiefly in small blocks to peasant
proprietors or given free to military pensioners. The
success of the first colonies was so great and the value of
land rose so rapidly that Government eventually adopted
the principle of auctioning the best lands to the highest
bidder. A large area in each colony was, however, set
aside for selected peasant proprietors who were allotted
one or two squares each on fixed terms; this enabled them
to acquire proprietary rights after paying for their land in
instalments in a stated number of years[22].

During the next 30 years, similar Government schemes encouraged the colonization of Sind and Multan. The colonizers were
hand-picked, often as the result of a physical inspection to sort
out those capable of agricultural labour from those who were
not. Furthermore, just as in the selection of army recruits, particular castes were favoured, but in this case men were drawn
'only from the best agricultural tribes'[23]. The Jat Sikh was
most favoured, as reliable and hard-working, while 'the Arain,
the prince of market gardeners, was his only rival'[24]. A memo
of a settlement officer for Amritsar describes in detail one such
inspection:

> Thus, the original crowd of applicants would be reduced
> to a band of men all connected by common descent, all
> physically fit to take up a new life in a new country under
> considerable difficulties, all hard up for land but with
> sufficient resources to start them[25].

Another reason for the careful selection of colonists was to
keep a check on those families that would try to secure more
than one square (each square was of 25 or 27.5 acres) by
putting forward more than one representative[26].

There is little doubt that the migrants themselves saw the move
to the canal colonies as a form of investment. For many peasant
proprietors the offer of squares of land to be bought at nominal
sums held the promise of improving one's lot at home.
Colonists maintained links in the home areas, often leaving

their women and children there for the first few years at least and returning home periodically, bringing their savings with them. The impact of the canal colonies on the home areas in the Panjab was profound:

> From Amritsar alone over 100,000 have migrated to the Bar, and in all the surrounding districts, if a cultivator has a pukka (*sic*) house, or better cattle than his neighbour, or a deposit in his village bank, or is using improved seed, it is ten to one that he has colony ties or has made money abroad. Even before the war, the Lyallpur colony (*now Faisalabad*) used to remit over twenty lakhs (*a lakh is a hundred thousand, and here refers to rupees*) a year[27].

Another effect of colonization was that those who failed to obtain land in West Panjab made repeated efforts to get to other parts of the world under the British flag (as contract labourers etc.)[28].

Colonization also seems to have had the general effect of generating restlessness and a desire for social advancement, which influenced the later migration to Britain. Saleem, an Arain, from a village in Faisalabad district, in describing his family's experience of colonization, first of Faisalabad and later of Multan, perceive his own migration to Britain as but a continuation of this trend:

> My grandfather, Anwar, and his brother, Ahmed, moved from Gurdaspur in the Panjab that is now in India to Lyallpur (now Faisalabad) during the 1890s when the Government was colonizing the area. But Ahmed could not settle in Lyallpur, made frequent trips back to Gurdaspur and eventually returned permanently. Then in 1910, he decided to join my grandfather and settle in the canal colonies. But by then his share of the 37 acres that had been allocated to the two brothers had been sold to someone else, so he returned to Gurdaspur. In 1930, Ahmed again moved from Gurdaspur. This time he went to Bahawalpur state in Multan district on another Government settlement scheme. This scheme allowed the debt for land bought at the rate of 250 Rs. to be paid off in 25 years. But Ahmed's wife and children did not want to move, so they stayed in Gurdaspur.

Ahmed persuaded one of my cousins — my grandfather had 2 sons and seven grandsons — to join him. Then Ahmed's own family — his wife, children and other relatives — joined him as refugees in 1947. So you see, of the 18 acres my grandfather bought from the Government, just over one acre was due to fall to me. That's why my father encouraged and paid for me to go to England — he wanted our family to buy more land again. My father also paid for the son of a man who used to be his servant, a Kumhar by caste, to go to England. He came with me, but settled in Rochdale, not Oxford. Now I have helped my elder brother to buy another 25 acres.

Migration from the densely populated north thus followed a tradition of army and navy service abroad, and was to some extent a response to the limited agricultural prospects offered by the difficult terrain in this long-settled region. In contrast, migration from the canal colonies followed a tradition of internal colonization, in which the original impetus was the promotion of agricultural prosperity. In both regions, the experiences of migration have had the effect of instilling in Panjabis the desire and the confidence to seek their fortunes abroad and to work for money that would assist them in improving their status at home[29].

It is also possible, as Roger Ballard suggests in relation to the contrast between Jullundri Sikhs and Mirpuri Pakistanis in Britain, that contrasting socio-economic features of the two main regions of Pakistani out-migration have had a differential impact upon migrants' subsequent socio-economic and educational success, in Britain and in Pakistan. There remains, today, a striking contrast between agriculturally and industrially prosperous Faisalabad in southern Panjab, with its infrastructure of railways, roads and irrigation canals built during British rule, and 'economically stagnant' Mirpur in the north, which has lacked such investment. There is some evidence that Faisalabadis living abroad have made considerable investment 'at home', in various forms of business and in agricultural development, while there is less evidence of such large-scale investment in Mirpur[30]. The relationship between migrants' regions of origin and their socio-economic success in Britain and in Pakistan would warrant further research.

Chain Migration

Even from the areas of out-migration, however, not every-one subsequently came to Britain. I found that while almost every person within one village might, with justification, claim to have some relatives who have gone abroad, in an adjacent village few people, if any, might have migrated. The explanation for this lies in the social structure of the migration itself, in a process which has been described as 'chain migration'[31].

> What is implied in the term is this: relatives contribute cash for the migration of one man, who finds work in Britain; from his savings he 'sponsors' the migration of another kinsman. Subsequent savings on the part of these two enable further kinsmen to migrate, and thus the 'chain' develops. Generally, the earlier migrants help the later ones with housing and finding jobs, and thus related men from the same areas in Pakistan tend to cluster in Britain[32].

It is in principle possible to account for virtually the whole Pakistani population of Oxford by tracing chains of migrants. I found that, for example, all thirty-five adults from Faisalabad enumerated in my 1984 analysis of regional origin (Table 1.2) could be linked into two chains of migration, one from two adjacent villages, numbers 203 and 211 (so-called following the numbering system that dates from the colonization of the area), about twelve miles from a small town called Samundri (off the main road to Kamalia, some twenty miles south of Faisalabad city), the other from a village about twenty miles from there. The Samundri post office clerk told me that people had also gone to Huddersfield, Rochdale and Glasgow, from villages number 212, 471, 477 and 482, all in the same locality, whereas from other adjacent villages no one has migrated. Several people in village number 203 joked that almost everyone in the village now lives, or has some relative, in Huddersfield, and that almost everyone from village 477 and 482 has moved to, or has kin in, Glasgow. Most men in the Oxford 'Samundri' chain detailed here (Table 1.3), if not actually related, were of the Arain caste, while others were friends from the same village or the adjacent village:

A CHAIN OF MIGRATION FROM FAISALABAD

Now in Oxford	Links between Migrants	Caste	Village	First settled	Moved to
–	Pioneer X	Arain	1	Glasgow pre 1947	
–	3 relatives of X	Arain	1	Glasgow 1950s	
Saleem	His father, a relative of X	Arain	1	Glasgow Jan 1958	Oxford 1959
–	Saleem's father's servant	Kumhar	1	Glasgow Jan 1958	Rochdale 1958
Safdar	Friend of Saleem	Arain	1	Glasgow Nov 1958	
Jabar	Relative of Saleem's father's servant	Kumhar	1	Glasgow Nov 1958	Oxford 1959
Farook	Friend of Safdar	Arain	2	Glasgow Nov 1958	Oxford 1959
Ijaz	Farook's wife's brother.	Arain	2	Glasgow 1958	Oxford 1959
Sarwar	Farook's friend	Nai	2	Glasgow Nov 1958	Oxford 1959
Zahoor	Saleem's cousin	Arain	1	Oxford 1962	
Gafoor	Farook's brother	Arain	2	Oxford 1962	
Aslam	Zahoor's brother	Arain	1	Oxford 1963	
Hurmat		Jat	2	Oxford 1964	
Habib	Farook's brother	Arain	2	Oxford 1964	
Izhar		Rajput	2	Oxford 1965	

Table 1.3

The first link in this chain was a man in government service during and following the settlement of the canal colonies (this was apparently unusual in an area where most men were farmers). He had gone to Glasgow before Partition. He helped three of his relatives to migrate in the early 1950s. Saleem (see pp. 25–6 above) told me that his father was distantly related to this first migrant and therefore decided to send Saleem and a 'servant' to Glasgow in 1958. Towards the end of that year, Jabar, a relative of Saleem's 'servant', went from Saleem's village to Glasgow, along with four men from an adjacent village: Safdar (Saleem's friend and fellow Arain), Farook (Safdar's brother's daughter's son), Ijaz (Farook's wife's brother) and Farook's friend Sarvar. In early 1959 Saleem visited Oxford on his first leave and brought all of these men except Safdar to Oxford. Saleem subsequently sponsored his cousin Zahoor's migration in 1962 and Zahoor in turn sponsored his brother's migration. Farook then called two of his younger brothers, Gafoor and Habib. By 1964, three brothers and a brother-in-law were living in Oxford.

The remaining eleven Oxford Faisalabadis are of the Dogor caste and can be accounted for in terms of another chain of close kinsmen. The first migrant in this chain was an ex-serviceman who went to Newcastle in 1957 and moved to Oxford in 1958. His sister's husband, to whom he sent money for the fare, joined him in 1959, two brothers came to Britain in 1962, a third brother in 1964 and his eldest brother in 1965. Each brother had in turn contributed to the migration of the next; obligations to kin had played a major role in shaping this chain.

Similar processes account for most of the other regional groups. The first man in a chain that developed from several adjacent villages in Mirpur was Sadiq, a seaman who had deserted from a merchant ship in 1937. He lodged with several fellow Mirpuri seamen in a Welsh household in Cardiff for a number of years, and worked as a labourer. During this time, he heard via a fellow seaman living in Cardiff who had relatives in Newcastle that a cousin and an old friend from his village, both also ex-seamen, were together trying to make a living from door-to-door peddling in Newcastle. Sadiq wrote to this cousin and all three agreed to try their luck southwards and inland. They came to Oxford in the late

1940s, but were unable to make a living from door-to-door peddling and Sadiq's friend returned to relatives in Newcastle. The cousins remained in Oxford, living with an Irish family, and in 1955 Sadiq obtained work with the City of Oxford Motor Services, who were employing New Commonwealth immigrants as conductors and cleaners from about that time. This enabled Sadiq to finance the migration of his brother in 1956 and in 1957 the three men bought a house in Osney in west Oxford. This house became the first stop for five other close relatives whose migration Sadiq and his cousins had sponsored, and also for fellow villagers. One of these fellow villagers was another ex-serviceman who wrote to Sadiq in 1957, arrived in Oxford in 1959, lodged in Osney, found work, with Sadiq's help, with British Rail, bought his own house in Osney in 1961 and sponsored the migration of several of his relatives.

Influence of Immigration Laws

Until 1962, as British subjects under the 1948 British Nationality Act, Pakistanis could enter Britain without restriction. The threat of immigration controls just before the Commonwealth Immigrants Act 1962 was passed quite clearly prompted a dramatic increase in the rate of immigration. 50,000 people entered Britain in the eighteen months before the 1962 Act was enforced, compared with 17,000 who entered between 1955 and 1960[33]. The process was given added impetus in 1960, when the Pakistan Government embarked upon constructing a hydro-electric dam at Mangla, in Mirpur district, which would submerge about 250 villages[34]. In 1961, in a move intended to compensate Mirpuri villagers who had been dispossessed of land by the construction of the dam, the Pakistan Government withdrew restrictions on emigration and promoted the migration of 5,000 people[35].

Certainly, one effect of the threat of controls, publicised to their advantage by travel agents, was that some men migrated who otherwise might not have done. Several men related stories about corrupt travel agents who extracted fees from prospective migrants with tales of the fortunes to be made in England and then disappeared[36]. It is also true that men were drawn from a wider range of districts and class and caste categories than in the first phase of migration: most of the small number of urban origin migrants in Oxford came to Britain at this time. However, while the threat of controls did encourage some men to migrate who might not otherwise have done, this did not alter the fact that most migrants came to Britain as labour migrants intending to better themselves at home, and because, in most cases, they had prior contacts in Britain. The threat of controls mainly accelerated this process.

The construction of the Mangla dam undoubtedly accelerated Mirpuri migration to Britain, but not all of the Mirpuris who came to Britain at this time had been affected by the dam, and not all of those displaced by the dam chose to come to Britain. Mirpuris who came to Britain in this migration did so because they had prior contacts, relatives or friends who encouraged them to emigrate[37]. Others preferred, instead, to take up Government offers of land elsewhere in Pakistan. Some, for instance, moved to a village in Sahiwal district, in which people displaced by the building of the Mangla dam are still referred to locally as *dammi log* (people of the dam) and live in a new separate settlement adjacent to the main village.

After the 1962 controls, a slightly different type of migrant was included in the migration. These were urban-origin men from white-collar occupations and some college students who applied for vouchers only half-seriously on the encouragement of friends. One of these men was Saeed, a former student in Sahiwal:

> I applied for a visa to go England in 1962 and got it in 1963. I had started an advanced science course (FSC) at school, but it was getting difficult and my friends had started going to England as an alternative. They said, 'Why don't you come too? After two years there you will be rich'. I was young then, about nineteen. I didn't know any better, so I went.

Yet the pattern of migration from particular areas remained essentially unaltered, partly because a man's emigration still depended upon prior contacts in Britain and also because the controls themselves institutionalised a preference for certain types of people. The 1962 controls introduced three categories of work voucher, issued in a limited number each year. The first two were for people with specific jobs to come to and for people with particular skills and qualifications, the third was for people with no definite employment prospects. In this third category, preference was given to men who had served in the armed forces during the Second World War, a preference which reinforced the pattern of migration from the districts with traditions of army and navy service.

The regional and local specificity of migration also continued because the desire to improve status through foreign-earned remittances grew in precisely those villages in which families with men working abroad were perceived to be already reaping the benefits. This was the case in Amjad's village, for instance. Amjad is of the Gujar *zamīndār* (landowning) caste from a village in Jhelum district. Traditionally, the Gujars from his and the surrounding villages had served in the army, and Gujars and other *zamīndār* status ex-servicemen had provided the initial contacts in England for subsequent migrants who had been working in and remitting money from England since about 1950. However, by 1961 a majority of the emigrants in U.K. were in fact men from the village service castes who were seeking to improve their status in relation to the *zamīndār*s in the village. In comparison, relatively few of the Gujars had migrated, perhaps by being in traditionally dominant position in this village (as landowners and ex-servicemen) they had not felt the same desire to emigrate, earn and save to improve their status locally. However the benefits of migration were soon visible in the village, in the form of large two or three storey brick and mortar houses, or conspicuously displayed goods 'from abroad' such as refrigerators, air conditioners, electric fans, tape recorders, televisions, and machine-made silky fabrics, which are preferred to local cotton. These goods, symbols of migrants' claims to new status, were ones that those who had not migrated began to covet. Ironically, the desire to migrate grew just as the controls on immigration to Britain were being enforced and were to become more stringent. In this context, Amjad said, it would have been absurd for a man who qualified for a voucher to reject the opportunity to go abroad. In fact, he said, the decision was made for him: he

had been unwilling to go abroad but succumbed to pressures
from his wife and mother:

> In 1962 I'd left the army and was looking for a job. A
> man at the employment exchange told me of a vacancy
> for someone with my qualifications in the Water and
> Power Development Authority (WAPDA) and also of a
> job in England, suggesting that I apply for the job in
> England because it offered much better pay. I said I didn't
> want to leave my family because I'd been away from them
> long enough in the army. The man laughed at me, and
> said I was very foolish not to go to England. In my village
> my brother said the same thing. Then I went with my wife
> to the fields to harvest lentils. Some women were working
> in the next field and made fun of my wife, 'What's a man
> with your husband's qualifications doing picking lentils?
> Can't he get a job in town? What's wrong with him?' My
> wife replied, 'He's going to England.' The women were
> silenced and amazed at this reply. So I had to go, didn't I?
> I sent off my application and three weeks later two letters
> arrived, one from WAPDA offering me the job, and one
> from England enclosing the employment voucher. I asked
> my mother what to do (my father was dead) and she told
> me to go to England to earn some money so that we all
> might live a better life.

When he arrived in England in 1962, Amjad lodged with a
cousin, another ex-soldier who had come to England a few
months previously on the same type of work voucher. This man
had, in his turn, first lodged with a man from one of the
village's service castes who had come to England during
the pre-controls phase of migration.

As in Jhelum district with its tradition of army service, so in
Attock district, particular villages with traditions of navy service
were well represented in Britain after 1962. One chain
developed from a village near the town of Hasan Abdal, after
Zafar, his cousin and his cousin's brother, all of whom had
served in the Navy, decided to apply for work vouchers. These
three men — Zafar with his wife and children — were staying
with relatives in Karachi when they heard that jobs for
ex-servicemen were available in Britain. Zafar had retired at the
age of forty from the Royal Indian Navy, so he applied for and

obtained a voucher from the Karachi High Commission and returned with his family to the village for a few months before departing for Britain in 1962, using some of his 8,000 rupee retirement pension towards the fare. In the months before his departure, Zafar recalled:

> I had nothing to do in the village, and other men in the village were very interested that I was about to go to England. Yasin, for one. He had also retired from the navy, and was struggling to make a living out of shopkeeping. He asked me for details of how to apply and I gave him my spare voucher application form. This was very generous of me. Some men used to sell these forms at high prices to innocent villagers. I also took Yasin to Rawalpindi, paid for his train fare there and back and for our hotel food and helped him complete his application. Yasin's voucher arrived before I left for England, so when he asked me to, I went with him to Rawalpindi again, to help him obtain a passport and to tell him what to say in his interview. Yasin arrived in England shortly after I did in 1962, and he arranged for his brother Mukhtar to come to England in 1964.

The general effect of the post-1962 restrictions on immigration was thus to reinforce the pattern of emigration from particular villages within areas of out-migration that had already been established before the controls, and in many cases can be traced back to service in the British army and navy. The links of kinship and village that shaped the process of chain migration continued to influence patterns of employment and residence in Oxford, patterns of investment in Pakistan and, in many cases, the direction of marriage preferences. The rest of this book explores these processes, considering, first, how the presence of kin and fellow villagers in Britain and their migrants' links with kin in Pakistan continue to influence migrants' experiences of and attitudes towards life in Britain.

NOTES

1. See, for instance, Dahya, 1972–3:30.
2. Rex and Moore, 1967:119–20.

3. See, for instance, Aurora, 1967:25 (on Sikh migration from Indian Panjab); Jeffery, 1976:46 and Taylor 1976:16–17.

4. The 1991 Census identified over 51 million 'Whites', a 'Black' population (subdivided as 'Black-Caribbean', 'Black-African' and 'Black-Other') of 920,540 people and four 'Asian' categories of which the Indian and Pakistani were the largest, numbering 840,255 and 476,555 respectively. On the demographic and other implications of the 1991 census see Coleman and Salt (eds.) 1996; for an analysis of the process and implications of including the 'ethnic question' see Ballard, 1996(a), 1997.

5. Simpson, 1997:89–107.

6. Adapted from B. Dahya, 1972–3:25.

7. M. Anwar, 1979; P.M. Jeffery, 1976.

8. In a Rochdale study, Panjabis comprise 67% and Mirpuris number 29% of 371 households (Anwar, 1979).

9. In a Newcastle study, the biggest single group of Pakistani Panjabi fathers came from Lyallpur district (Taylor, 1976:15). Scott (1972–3) shows that a 'considerable number' of a sample of 100 men 'came from canal colony settlements in the Lyallpur District' (now Faisalabad). Similarly, Anwar (1979) shows that in Rochdale too, Faisalabadis form by far the largest single Panjabi group with adjacent areas like Sahiwal and Bahwalpur also represented. In Glasgow and Dewsbury too, Faisalabadis form a distinctive regional group.

10. For example, in Rochdale (Anwar, 1979:44).

11. Dahya, 1972–3; also see Saifullah-Khan 1976(a) and Anwar 1979.

12. See also Vatuk, 1972.

13. Jeffery, 1976:130.

14. Negative connotations of 'villager' might explain why a substantial proportion of the fathers in Taylor's study (1976) said they were from the cities. 'Villager' also sometimes connotes low caste, and, occasionally moving to the city enables people of low caste status to change their caste identity.

15. Davis, 1951, map 8, p. 19.

16. Aurora, 1967:26.

17. Darling, 1928.

18. Davis, 1951:131; Aurora, 1967:28.

19. Davis, 1951:131; Darling, 1949:336. See also Taylor, 1976:16.

20. Hiro, 1971:121–2. Also see Taylor, 1976, p. 16.

21. Aurora, 1967:28.

22. Davis, 1951:119–20.

23. Darling, 1928:133.

24. Darling, 1928:136.

25. Darling, 1928:134.

26. Darling, 1928:133.

27. Darling, 1928:143. Ironically, the Sikhs who had comprised a large proportion of the original settlers returned to their areas of origin during the massive exchange of population between east and west Panjab at Partition. Some of those who had retained links with their villages of origin during colonization returned in 1947 to their old villages where they still had relatives. See Nair, 1961 and Rai, 1965:121.

28. Aurora, 1967:29.
29. This past experience of migration lies behind the Panjabi 'frontiersmen mentality' described by Aurora (1967:27–34); Nair considers that Panjab's unsettled political history has made Panjabis one of the least 'rooted' people in India (1961:112).
30. Ballard 1983; Ballard 1990.
31. See Dahya, 1973:253; Jeffery 1976 and M. Anwar 1979.
32. Jeffery, 1976:48. Her summary is based on Dahya, 1973.
33. Rose *et al.*, 1969:83.
34. Rose *et al.*, 1969:59.
35. Saifullah-Khan, 1977:66–68.
36. See also Deakin, 1970:46 and Aurora, 1967:42–43.
37. Saifullah-Khan, 1977:67.

2 THE PROCESS OF SETTLEMENT

The history of Pakistani settlement parallels that of some other South Asian groups in Britain, such as the Panjabi Sikhs and the Bangladeshi Muslims, in that wives and children came to Britain some years after the pioneering bachelor-status migrants of the 1950s and 1960s[1]. The beginning of 'family reunion' in the late 1960s and early 1970s quite clearly signaled in a new era in which the earlier all-male settlement would be transformed. What is puzzling, however, is why Pakistani women and children should have come to Britain at all. If migrants viewed living and working in Britain as a means of improving their lifestyle in Pakistan, why should they risk *izzat* (honour, respect) by exposing their wives and daughters to the influences of a society which does not value purdah and female modesty? Why should they incur extra living expenses by bring wives and children to Britain, leaving less money to remit to Pakistan?[2].

It is possible that the arrival of Pakistani wives and children in Britain indicates that migrants no longer viewed living in Britain as a means of improving their position in Pakistan. One explanation along these lines identifies the immigration controls as playing a decisive part, because from 1962 onwards it was increasingly difficult for adult men to enter Britain but men already here were entitled to be joined by their families. In other words, the creation of a permanently settled population from a transient one is, in this view, an unintended effect of immigration controls[3]. But does it necessarily follow that the presence of wives and children means that migrants or their families are committed to living in Britain permanently? And is there necessarily a causal connection between immigration controls and the creation of an apparently permanently settled immigrant population? The absence of controls or even the imposition of much tighter controls (as in the case of Turkish migrants to West Germany) is associated in other countries with a similar demographic result.

My analysis of the processes involved in the eventual transformation of the all-male settlement seeks to show how migrants have negotiated a way between the wider economic and political constraints upon migration and settlement and their own socio-economic aspirations and cultural values. By considering the views of relatives in Pakistan, of the male pioneer migrants and of the women who eventually joined them, I suggest that migrants were not merely pawns in the game of international labour migration but neither were they fully independent agents. They made decisions and acted with reference to both their own aspirations and values and the wider socio-economic and political forces that have constrained their lives.

The Early All-male Settlement

Relatives in Pakistan of men who came to Britain in the early 1960s often worried about the potentially corrupting influences of the British environment. Attitudes to Britain were, and often still are, deeply ambivalent. On the one hand, Britain was a rich country where a man could earn huge sums of money after only a few months' work; on the other hand, its inhabitants are lax in their moral standards, particularly their sexual morals. English people eat pork, the meat of a beast with no sexual shame, and drink alcohol to enjoy its intoxicating effects; both activities are forbidden in Islam. One prevailing myth was that every English man always carried a bottle of whisky with him and would encourage any newcomer to partake; another was that every English woman was sexually promiscuous and would try to seduce any Indian or Pakistani man out on the streets. Such myths were no doubt reinforced by the fact that most Pakistani men arrived in Britain during the decade of the mini-skirt and the contraceptive pill. Were there grounds for these fears, and if there were, how did migrants' relatives respond?

Lifestyles in the early years of all-male settlement tended to insulate men from many of the influences of the western environment, including the impact of racism. When a man first arrived in Britain, he generally went to a place where he had relatives, friends or fellow-villagers. A brother would join a brother, a son would join his father, a nephew would join an uncle, a villager would join a member of his wider kinship group or a fellow villager; this pattern recurs again and again in migrants' accounts of their arrival in Britain. Links established by chain migration also helped Pakistanis to find work when, in a climate of racial prejudice, the only employment available to them was in occupations that did not attract the white labour force. Having no particular roots in Britain, migrants moved around the country seeking work, usually in response to fellow migrants' reports of local labour shortages. Pakistani settlements in various British towns and cities therefore developed in relation to local work opportunities on the one hand and along the distinctive lines of kinship and village on the other, and Oxford was no exception.

A few Indians and Pakistanis had been employed in Indian restaurants in the city of Oxford for some time before 1955. Some pioneering settlers who had been door-to-door pedlars since the 1940s in South Wales, Glasgow and Newcastle had also come to Oxford as pedlars before 1950[4]. However, it was not until the mid 1950s, when there was simultaneously an opening for poorly paid unskilled and semi-skilled labourers in Oxford and an economic recession in the Midlands and the North, that Pakistanis came to Oxford in any significant numbers.

The first main phase of settlement of New Commonwealth immigrants in Oxford began in 1955 and was linked to the failure of a private bus company, the City of Oxford Motor Services, to attract indigenous labour. Bus conductors and cleaners were moving to better-paid jobs such as those offered by Morris Motors (later British Leyland and now the Rover Group) at Cowley. Local residents recalled that by 1955 the bus service in some parts of Oxford was almost at a standstill. In order to fill this vacuum, the Bus Company recruited twelve West Indian ex-servicemen from the Brixton employment exchange[5]. These twelve men were initially accommodated in a company hostel, but soon started to move out into lodging houses in the Jericho area as wives, girlfriends and other men arrived to join the first twelve. However, the Bus Company was not the only employer requiring labour at this time. Local English unskilled and semi-skilled labour was also being drawn away from British Rail, hospitals, several building firms and other small industries by the attraction of the relatively high wages being offered by the car industry in Cowley. The vacuum left was one that only 'coloured' workers were prepared to fill.

If circumstances in Oxford created a vacuum which immigrant labour filled, conditions elsewhere fuelled the influx of

Pakistanis to Oxford from about 1956 onwards. Accounts by Pakistanis who lived in the city at this time indicate that the most substantial number arrived between 1958 and 1959. The 1958 economic recession in the Midlands and the North, where West Indian, Indian and Pakistani immigrants were severely hit by unemployment, was an important factor behind this influx[6]. In the autumn of 1958 substantial numbers of Indians and Pakistanis came south to Birmingham, Slough and Oxford from places such as Bradford, Manchester, Rochdale and Sheffield which had been affected by the recession[7]. The men who came to Oxford at this time did so on the basis of personal contacts and recommendations. The Mirpuri ex-seamen who had been living in Oxford since the 1950s informed relatives and villagers in areas affected by the recession about work opportunities in the city. Similarly, Saleem, from a village in Faisalabad district, came to Oxford on the advice of friends and subsequently brought fellow villagers to the city:

> When I came to Britain in January 1958 I flew directly to Glasgow where a man from my village was living. I went to the employment exchange, got a green card but after four days nothing had turned up. The man I was staying with didn't help, so I decided to try my luck in Wolverhampton where another of my village friends was working. I stayed there for four months, because my friend was good to me, but again I couldn't get work. Then other Pakistanis told me that there was work in Oxford so I came here in July 1958 and in the first week got a job at a cement factory. During my first holiday in January 1959, I went to Glasgow, Wolverhampton and Rochdale to visit my friends. In Glasgow, I met five men from my village who had arrived from Pakistan two months before, and still hadn't got any work. Four of them came with me to Oxford and I helped two of them get work with me at the cement factory; the third got work at a dairy and the fourth got a job on a building site.

Migrants also tended to depend upon one another for accommodation, most of them lodging with fellow migrants rather than risking being turned away by local landlords. The houses occupied by Pakistanis in the late 1950s and throughout the 1960s were confined to a few particular areas of the city and to a few particular houses within these areas; migrants' accounts suggest that there were perhaps sixty Pakistanis in Oxford by 1960. The electoral register for 1960 records only four houses which had occupants with Muslim names, three in west Oxford (see map 2.1), the fourth the Moti Mahal restaurant in the city centre. These houses account for twenty-two people, nine of whom lived in the Moti Mahal restaurant[8]. However, men who were living in Oxford at this time mentioned eight other houses, two of which appeared on the electoral register of 1961. All of these except two (one in Boulter Street, St. Clements, in east Oxford, and one, which has since been demolished, in Paradise Square in St. Ebbes in the city centre) were in Jericho and in west Oxford.

Four of these houses were particularly notorious for their over-crowding and poor living conditions and attracted the shocked attention of local residents. One Sikh-owned house in Southmoor Road on the border of Jericho and north Oxford apparently accommodated between forty and sixty Indian and Pakistani Panjabis at one time. The extent of overcrowding may of course be exaggerated in Pakistanis' recollections of this period, but Aurora observed at first hand as many as thirty-five Indians sharing a single house in London[9]. Amjad was explicit about the conditions of the house in which he first lodged:

> I came straight to Oxford because I had a cousin here who arranged my accommodation. He lives in Cardiff now. We lived in a two-bedroomed house. There were seventeen of us living there, including myself, my cousin, Yunis from our village, who you know, and also Anwar from a village near ours. The rest were strangers to me. It was terrible living there. We slept two or three men to a bed and each bedroom had two or three double beds in it. People also slept on the stairs and even outside, in the garden, like we do in Pakistan in the hot season. The British Government should not have called us over here for work without telling us how to live and providing some facilities. I was all right because I had been in the army and had learnt some of the English ways, but the others did not even know how to use English bathrooms or toilets. No wonder our English neighbours disliked us. I saw a headline in the Daily Telegraph in 1963 that said, 'Pakistanis eat cats'. You know why they thought that?

During the week, for three months, we ate nothing but baked beans. After a day's work, all of us labouring on building sites, we were all too exhausted to cook a proper meal. Sometimes we would cook a meal at the weekends; we had to take turns making curry and *chapātī*s in fact, that's how I learnt to cook — but we rarely ate meat because there were no *halāl* butchers[10]. But occasionally, at the weekends we would cycle out to a local farm and buy a live chicken which we would slaughter the proper *halāl* way ourselves, and cook a decent meal. I suppose the dustmen who found the chicken skin and bones in the dustbin thought that we were eating cats.

Many of the houses that Pakistanis bought or lived in also lacked amenities such as hot water and bathrooms. Men living in such houses would use the public baths[11]. A few men, having arrived in Oxford and experienced or witnessed the conditions of these houses, opted to be more independent of fellow-migrants in their search for accommodation. Saleem, for example, lived in the notorious Sikh-owned house on Southmoor Road when he first arrived in Oxford in July 1958, but found the house so unbearably overcrowded that he left after two weeks. He said he did not wish to speak about the conditions of that house. He moved to an 'Indian' restaurant on Walton Street, but the Bengali proprietor charged such an extortionate rent (£5 a week, including only one meal per day) that Saleem left after three weeks. He spoke to the welfare officer at the cement factory where he was employed about his problems finding suitable accommodation. The welfare officer helpfully arranged rooms for Saleem in a hostel specifically for cement factory employees, and Saleem stayed in that hostel for two years.

Saleem, however, was not typical in this respect since most men remained living in multi-occupation lodgings for up to several years. Often they had little choice, for multi-occupation lodging enabled men to circumvent the discrimination that they encountered in seeking accommodation with white landlords and which forced prospective tenants back into houses owned or occupied by Pakistanis[12]. Migrants also sometimes chose to continue living in such conditions because despite the discomforts, multi-occupation lodging incurred fewer living expenses than renting a single room. A man who worked as many as

75 hours a week as a labourer, by taking all possible overtime, would have little time, energy or opportunity to do anything other than work; the houses in which the men lived were often no more than dormitories. Men working on night shifts would share beds with men on day shifts and further reduce their rent. In the early 1960s, a man could in this way earn between £12 and £18 a week, spend £2 per week on lodging and food and save the rest. By keeping expenses to a minimum, some men saved as much as £500 in one year. Apparently Indians in London were even able to save from their unemployment benefit and national assistance benefits when they were out of work[13]. Indeed, saving itself became a source of status among migrants. A man who saved large sums of money for the benefit of kin at home gained considerable status among the relatives and friends with whom he was living in Britain. On the other hand, if a worker saved less than £25 a year, he would be ashamed to admit this to others. There was therefore also a moral pressure from relatives and fellow villagers, which tended to ensure that migrants continued to live frugally, save and remit money home. To do otherwise would involve a loss of face.

Another reason for remaining in overcrowded lodging houses was that many migrants had a poor knowledge of English language, law and customs. As result they were dependent upon fellow migrants more fluent in English and experienced in dealing with English people and society (generally the ex-servicemen among the early settlers) for help with filling forms and finding work. This was particularly important in the prevailing climate of racial exclusion in which the range of jobs available to Pakistanis was in general limited to semi-skilled and unskilled work. Some employers, such as the Bus Company, operated a quota system restricting the number of Black and Asian employees. In several other firms, including Morris Motors at Cowley, Pakistanis were unable to get work at all because an unofficial colour bar was in operation until 1965.

Given this environment, it was vital that information about employment opportunities be passed on among relatives and fellow villagers who would actively assist one another in obtaining work. Men who could speak English reasonably well would negotiate the employment of their relatives and fellow-villagers.

A Mirpuri shop steward at the Osney bakery ensured that his relatives were employed at the same place: the effect was that bakery employees constituted one major kinship group in Osney and almost the entire work force at the bakery. Similarly, during the 1970s an outspoken Faisalabadi negotiated employment at British Leyland (formerly Morris Motors, now the Rover Group) in Cowley for a number of his relatives and friends.

On the whole, Pakistanis of the pioneer generation did not speak openly about racism in their recollections of this period. Sometimes, when prompted, they would relate racist incidents, sometimes exaggerating the bravado of their responses. Saeed, for instance, was called a 'fucking Paki' by a white workman and claims he hit him and that settled it. He went on to say:

> I had a clerical job and was in charge of white blokes and some didn't like that. Then there was one who would not look at me when he brought the books for checking — he would walk in with his head on one side. So I said, 'You do that again and I will knock you down'. He did it again, and I knocked him down. I went to the management, who told me that when men fight they are either sacked or transferred, and asked me what I wanted. So I was transferred, but stayed in that factory for nine years, because they liked my work. Now of course there are laws against this sort of behaviour, to protect the victims. Of course, all people have 'others' they don't like. You can tell when it is malicious. Sometimes it is just joking and should not be taken too seriously.

More formal welfare was provided by the Oxford Pakistan Welfare Association, founded in 1961, and by the opening of the mosque in Bath Street, St. Clements, in 1965. The Pakistan Welfare Association was co-founded by a Pakistani who has since moved to Birmingham and a Bangladeshi who subsequently became president of the Bangladesh Welfare Association when it was formed in 1971.

Both informal and formal welfare in effect countered tendencies towards assimilation in that men who needed assistance would go to fellow migrants or members of the Welfare Association rather than to outsiders. Relatives or friends would sometimes threaten to withhold assistance from men thought to be squandering their money or becoming too 'westernized'. In serious cases, the office holders of the Welfare Association, often regarded as capable of exerting moral influence simply by virtue of their office, would also be called upon. In one case, for example, the President of the Welfare Association and the *imām* (leader of prayers in the mosque) were summoned to settle a dispute concerning the money a man owed to a relative and a friend.

The same two co-founders of the Welfare Association played a major part in founding the mosque in 1965, by raising funds from fellow Pakistani Muslims (a category which until 1971 included east Pakistanis) for buying and converting an old warehouse into a mosque. Previously, work routines permitting, some men had met for Friday (*jum'ā*) prayers in an Indian restaurant in Walton Street. *Jum'ā*, the word for Friday, means 'the day of the congregation' and the Friday noon prayer is the main congregational prayer which men try to perform with fellow Muslims. The opening of the mosque in Bath Street, St. Clements (in east Oxford), provided a focus for regular worship, and in doing so, provided a symbol of unity and common purpose. This too exerted a form of moral control and had the effect of keeping men's activities in line with their original intentions.

Of course, men's involvement in the setting up of formal institutions such as the Welfare Association and the mosque often involved more than a concern to maintain religious and moral values. Simply holding such a position gave the office holders authority over and status in the eyes of fellow migrants and to some extent, in relation to 'English' society too. Since the founding of the first welfare association, rival welfare associations have flowered and perished, each generally short lived, with influence limited to a small circle of kin and villagers. Concerns for influence and status continue to fuel competition and disputes between leaders of rival welfare associations and mosques.

The Early 1960s

From the early 1960s, a number of changes in the factors that had originally contributed towards maintaining the tight structure of the early settlement started to weaken it. One of the first gradual but significant changes was transfer of the Didcot Central Ordnance Depot (C.O.D.) to Bicester brought new prospects of short-term work, which Pakistanis already living in Oxford informed relatives and friends in other British towns about. Migrants recalled that the C.O.D. provided two coaches to transport over eighty Pakistanis from St. Clements, in east Oxford, to Bicester and back daily.

The Bicester C.O.D. no longer has records of staff employed in the 1960s, but staff who worked there in the 1960s recalled a sudden influx of Pakistanis to Oxford over a period of about three months and that between 30 and 50 Pakistanis were employed at the C.O.D. in the early 1960s. Saeed, who came to Britain in 1962, was one of them:

> I came straight to Oxford. The Pakistani landlord in whose house I first lived is still my friend, although he now lives in Slough. My first job was labouring; I was so weak, because in Pakistan my father had worked on the land in our village so that I could study. I thought that job would kill me. Twice I left off work at midday rather than at 5 o'clock, because I thought that if I stayed on I would be dead. So of course I lost the job. I was unemployed for several months and thought seriously of returning home, but then I got a job at the Ministry of Defence depot in Bicester. It was a clean job. Because I could read and write English, I was soon promoted to store supervisor. In fact, when I applied for the promotion, the English men who also applied made jokes about the Pakistani who hardly speaks English but has ideas beyond his status. But they failed on the written test. As store supervisor, I had a responsible position and liked the job. I stayed on there for eight years, and only moved to the car factory because the pay there was double what was being offered at the depot.

Saeed was one of the few Pakistanis who continued to work at the C.O.D. after the transfer of the Didcot depot to Bicester had taken place; by the 1980s, only a few Pakistanis were still employed there. Most Pakistanis had worked there only on a short-term basis for a relatively low wage of between £6 and £7 a week. They then found work with the Post Office, the

hospitals and the Bus Company where earned between £10 and
£13 per week. During the 1960s, the quota for 'coloured' bus
drivers and conductors was gradually increased, following
pressure exerted by local voluntary organizations to end racial
discrimination by local employers. After the 1965 Race
Relations Act was passed, the quota was abandoned altogether.
Some men obtained work in foundries outside Oxford, at the
paper mill in Sandford, and at the Mother's Pride bakery in
Osney, which became a major source of employment (but the
bakery was to close in February 1982, and the paper mill in
January 1983). While some men moved from Oxford in
response to reports of work opportunities in other cities, two
Mirpuri kinship groups, one from Sheffield, the other from
Bradford, came to Oxford specifically to work at the Osney
bakery; one group settled in east Oxford; the other settled in
the Mirpuri area in Osney.

The most significant change in employment opportunities,
however, took place at the British Leyland (or 'B.L.', now
known as the Rover Group) car factory in Cowley. From after
the war until 1965, there had been an unofficial colour bar on
the employment of Black and Asian workers at B.L. Several
Pakistani men described an incident at B.L. that led to the end
of discrimination on the grounds of colour. The incident
involved a West Indian who had obtained work at B.L. in
1964, and was the first black to do so. White workers apparently refused to work alongside the West Indian until an
English convener, Bobby Fryer, told the white workers to
hand in their notice if they objected to working with a black.
The white workers gradually returned to work. Finally, a dep-
utation from the Oxford Committee for Racial Integration
successfully ended this form of discrimination at British
Leyland[14].

From 1965 onwards, West Indians and Pakistanis were
employed at British Leyland, at first for menial tasks as assem-
blers, painters, cleaners and storemen. Most of the Pakistanis
who were working at the C.O.D. in Bicester moved to British
Leyland at this time, not necessarily because they preferred the
type of work available, but because British Leyland offered
wages twice as high as those paid by the C.O.D. By moving to
British Leyland, Saeed for example, who had been a store super-
visor at the C.O.D., accepted a job as a semi-skilled labourer for

financial reasons. Similar economic considerations influenced Saleem's employment and residential history in Oxford:

> In 1960, after two years at the cement factory, I decided to leave. Because the hostel and factory were several miles from Oxford, I rarely met my friends and didn't like spending my evenings alone. I got a job with the Oxford University Press in Walton Street and lodged in an Indian house in the same street. The landlord of this house was a man I'd shared a room with in the Sikh household on Southmoor Road. Now he had his own house and an English wife. I worked for nine months with the O.U.P. but decided to leave because my friends said that the dairy (where I had helped two friends to find work) had better pay and working hours. I thought I would have my evenings free and work in the morning. I was embarrassed to say I wanted to leave the press. First I said the machinery was too noisy, so they moved me to a different department. But I left soon after, and then realized I'd made a wrong decision in leaving the Press, which was a clean place to work, because the dairy was wet and dirty and I badly injured my finger on a machine. Then, in 1966, when Pakistanis started getting work at British Leyland, I moved to B.L. and got lodgings in east Oxford. In 1967, my cousin, who was also working at B.L., and I bought our own house in east Oxford.

As work opportunities increased, the Pakistani settlement gradually dispersed from west and central Oxford towards the east and south of the city. According to migrants' recollections, by the mid-1960s there were about six Pakistani shops in east Oxford on the Cowley Road. There were a number of houses on St. Clements, James and Circus Streets in east Oxford (see map 2.1) occupied mainly by Jhelumi migrants, while houses in other east Oxford streets including several on Bullingdon Road contained mainly people from Gujar Khan, Rawalpindi and Attock. Most men moved eastwards, but some settled in south Oxford. Farook, in a village-based chain of migrants from Faisalabad (one of the men Saleem brought to Oxford from Glasgow), his brother-in-law Ijaz and his brother Gafoor moved out of lodgings and, pooling their resources, bought a house in south Oxford into which Farook's brother Habib subsequently moved.

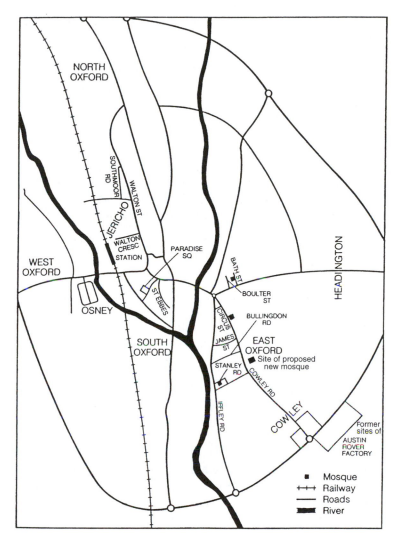

Map 2.1 Map of Oxford

This shift in the nucleus of the settlement is reflected in the number and distribution of Pakistani households recorded in the electoral registers of the mid-1960's. Health centre records also reflect this shift: GPs at the Jericho health centre recalled that 20% of the centre's patients were Asian (meaning South Asian) in the mid-1960s, but that the proportion declined from then on. The majority of 'Asians' are now registered as living in east Oxford.

Not everyone moved from west Oxford. A number of Mirpuri ex-servicemen, for example, who bought houses in Osney in the first phase of migration, continued to live there (the area is now predominantly Mirpuri), while their former non-Mirpuri tenants bought their own houses in east Oxford. The first Pakistani grocery, which opened in 1962, remained on Walton Crescent in Jericho until the mid-1970s (changing hands seven times), before being moved to the Cowley Road. The second Pakistani grocery, which opened on Walton Street in 1964, remained there until the 1980s. Nevertheless, the new nucleus of the settlement gradually consolidated in east Oxford.

One reason for the residential shift was that the increase in the numbers of Pakistanis who came to Oxford in the early 1960's created a shortage of available rented accommodation in Jericho and west Oxford. Landlords would give priority to their own relatives or fellow villagers in the allocation of rooms. At the same time certain parts of the old city centre, such as the old Victorian properties in Paradise Square in St. Ebbes which contained one particularly notorious multi-occupation Pakistani lodging house, were being demolished by the City Council's programme of slum clearance. Rather than move into a council house in accordance with slum clearance proposals, the Pakistani owners preferred to sell and buy a house elsewhere. The settlement dispersed in the direction of east and south Oxford mainly because cheap houses were available in these areas of the city. East and south Oxford had been officially described as 'stress' areas, overcrowded and lacking in modern amenities[15]. During the 1960s terraced houses lacking bathroom facilities and with outside toilets could be bought for between £3,000 and £4,000 in east Oxford. Many Pakistanis subsequently made use of City Council improvement grants, which were available from 1954 as part of the Council's urban renewal scheme to assist the improvement of owner-occupied properties in these areas.

The shift in the location of settlement coincided with a move from tenancy in multi-occupation lodging houses to owner-occupation. Typically, men who moved to east Oxford during the 1960s bought houses there, which they paid for outright.

The money was raised in several ways. Sometimes, by pooling their savings, relatives embarked upon joint enterprises in property ownership or shopkeeping at an earlier stage than was usually possible for an individual. Houses were often collectively owned though usually registered in the senior relative's name. Subsequently, as men decided to buy their own houses many of these joint arrangements ceased, the house being sold and shares apportioned out; sometimes this involved disputes over shares in the property.

Men also obtained interest-free loans from fellow migrants or former landlords and with money saved in rotating credit associations called *kametī*s. The principle of a *kametī* is that every week or month all the contributors to it pay a given sum, say £5, to the organizer and each week (or month) one person in turn receives the total, which, if there are 20 contributors, amounts to £100[16]. These methods of raising money enabled men to pay for their houses with cash rather than by taking out mortgages.

Men did not generally obtain mortgages on houses at this time. Firstly, property ownership demonstrated both independence from a landlord or patron and superiority to Pakistanis still dependent on landlords, unable to buy their own houses. Little or no status was attached to paying rent or living on 'borrowed money', and in the early 1980s few Pakistanis were council house tenants. A number of men, even then, owned four or five properties and property ownership remains a major indication of status. A second reason for outright cash purchase was that many men were unfamiliar with the procedure for acquiring mortgages. Many of those who obtained mortgages in the late 1960s said they would have done so earlier had they known how. They complained that some men who had bought houses with mortgages had withheld this information from fellow migrants who were tenants, in order to continue to make money from rent and to exploit their position as creditors. Some men may not have taken out mortgages on religious grounds, because according to Islamic law, the giving or receiving of interest is prohibited, the correct form of loan is that given or received without interest. (In theory, interest accrued on money kept in building societies or investment accounts should be given in alms to the poor and needy). However, men who obtained mortgages justify their actions by saying that they were financially compelled to borrow money on which they had to pay interest. Flexibility was probably the major reason for cash purchase, for a house paid for outright is a major investment that is easily capitalized. When a house was sold, the owner would have a lump sum that he could take back to Pakistan or invest quickly in another property or in a business. This remains a major reason for the emphasis on owner occupation and on completing mortgage payments on a house as soon as possible.

During the 1960's, the range of economic opportunities increased, the location of the settlement shifted and more men became house owners. Gradually, too, some migrants became less dependent on kin for welfare and assistance, more competent in spoken and written English and more familiar with procedures for obtaining mortgages, employment and welfare. Financial independence and competence in English brought status in the eyes of fellow migrants, especially as these qualities enhanced a man's ability to save money for remitting to Pakistan; they did not necessarily mean that a man was any less committed to this original purpose.

Yet adapting to life in Britain sometimes also involved less well-regarded changes, as some men 'succumbed' to the 'corrupting influences' of the British environment, just as their relatives had feared. Few men today would openly admit that they had English girlfriends or visited prostitutes or went drinking during their bachelor years in Britain, but migrants' account of their own, or, more accurately, each other's activities at that time and the rumours which abound suggest that these activities were fairly widespread. Several men spoke about the prostitutes who used to visit particular multi-occupation houses[17]. One man recalled how he asked a prostitute who had come to his lodgings how much money she wanted, gave it to her and told her to go away. Others were less scrupulous, but on the whole men's philandering was tolerated as long as it involved no commitment and was therefore not seen to be in conflict with migrants' original intentions.

Regular drinking and extravagant spending of money were, however, disapproved of, because they interfered with a man's ability to remit money to kin in Pakistan. A yet dimmer view was taken of a relationship with a girlfriend that appeared to be serious or long term; kinsmen and villagers would exert pressure to ensure that the man concerned would 'toe the line', by threatening to withdraw assistance, ostracism, or summoning the leader of a Welfare Association or the *imām*. Amjad was one of the men thus threatened:

> After a year or so of living in England, I became one of the lads, although it upset my cousin. I moved out of that crowded house we were all living in, and rented two rooms of my own in a boarding house in Cowley. I wanted to be more private and independent. I had a sports car at that time — one of those with a roof that opens up. The girls loved it; they used to hang around waiting for me. Then one girl got a bit serious — she was a good girl you know and I used to visit her parents, and her grandparents; they were good people and made me welcome. My cousin didn't like it at all, and my brother warned me, if I got serious, he'd write home. But Yunis from my village didn't bother — in fact, he was like me in those days. Don't say I told you. Eventually I married the girl, but by that time even my brother, who I'd helped come to England, wasn't speaking to me.

Mid-1960s: The Arrival of Women and Children

From about 1964 the transformation of the settlement was set in motion as wives, children and young brides began to join the men. Most wives of 'pioneer' migrants came to Oxford between five and fifteen years after their husbands, as table 2.1 illustrates:

CONTRASTING DATES OF ARRIVAL FOR MEN AND WOMEN IN TWO ADJACENT EAST OXFORD STREETS						
Year of entry	1956–60	1961–65	1966–70	1971–75	1976–80	TOTAL
Men	2	17	8	4	1	32
Women	0	3	9	6	12	30
						Table 2.1

This pattern of gradual and 'late' family reunion, reflected in the city of Oxford registers over this period, parallels the national picture[18]. In Oxford, wives and children have now joined the few men who in the 1980s were still waiting for their families. Today's outstanding immigration cases mostly concern the adult sons and daughters of pioneer migrants who are waiting to be joined by brides or bridegrooms from Pakistan.

The arrival of women and children does not, of itself, indicate a commitment to permanent or semi-permanent residence in Britain. Some men said that they wanted their families to benefit from the health facilities in Britain and their children to come 'for the education'; there is no doubt that education is a major consideration for many families. It is also possible that, by summoning their families, some migrants were trying 'to re-create the earlier situation of male-dominated chain migration within the constraints of immigration regulations' because 'bringing the whole family to Britain enables the man to ensure that he can be replaced by his son when he wants to return to Pakistan'[19].

As it became more difficult for adult men to enter Britain, some families adopted various strategies for bringing boys or young men into the country[20]. In several cases men brought over 'sons' who were in fact brothers' sons or other relatives' sons and in some cases boys' ages were inflated in order that they might qualify for entry unaccompanied by their mothers. This was after the 1965 regulation which continued to permit the entry of wives accompanying children under 16, but removed discretionary rights for children under 16 to join relatives other than parents and for children between 16 and 18 to join their fathers without being accompanied by their mothers. Habib explained why families were brought over in this way:

> The 1962 controls were supposed to stop us coming in, but they left loopholes because you could still bring in your son or a brother's son and say he was yours. The Government soon realized that this was a loophole and stopped it by saying that children had to come with their mothers. That is why we brought our wives over.

There is, however, little evidence of women returning to Pakistan permanently, which would be required to support this interpretation[21]. Pakistani men may have viewed calling their wives and children to Britain as a means of getting a second generation of male wage earners into the country, but why have the majority of Pakistani wives remained in Britain? By the late 1980s, many women had returned to Pakistan for at least one relatively short visit of several months' duration, sometimes leaving school-age children in Britain but taking their younger children with them. They did not, however expect to stay in Pakistan permanently, at least while their children were at school in Britain and only two women had returned 'permanently', one leaving a son in Oxford in the care of a daughter-in-law and the other returning to Pakistan with all her children. This pattern of short-term return visits, sometimes involving taking children out of school for several months, has continued. Parents may now also return their adolescent girls to Pakistan, during the high-school years, leaving school age or working sons in Britain, but these patterns do not represent the permanent departure of women.

Women's accounts of their migration to Britain have a different emphasis. The kin- and village-based structure of the settlement ensured that information about a man's activities in Britain eventually reached his relatives in Pakistan, through migrants' letters home or through conversations with migrants during their visits home. Senior kinsmen would then ensure that a man's activities in Britain did not permanently hinder him from fulfilling his obligations to his relatives, usually by arranging the marriage of a man who was a bachelor or by arranging that a married man be joined by his wife and children. The head of the household generally took the formal action this required, but women had a direct interest in ensuring that a man continued to fulfil his family obligations, for his failure to do so threatened their own social positions.

Amina, Amjad's wife told me that initially she did not believe the story spread by England-returnees and mentioned in letters from other villagers settled in Oxford that Amjad had married his English girlfriend. Eventually, however, a letter from Amjad's brother in London confirmed the rumour. Amina then resolved to go to England herself. She borrowed money for the fare from relatives (including Amjad's mother; his father was dead). She brought her children with her to Oxford and lived for almost a year in the same house as the English wife, who by then also had a child. Eventually the English wife left and the child remained with Amina. The English wife made one return visit to see her child, several years later, accompanied by the English man with whom she was living. Recalling the visit drew some scathing comments from Amina about the English woman's scruffy jeans, her slovenly ways, her loose morality and her lack of interest in her child. Amina is still suspicious of any English woman who visits her home. Although Amjad now expresses shame for his misdemeanour, and has strict attitudes towards the upbringing of his daughters, Amina feels she cannot entirely trust him and is reluctant to go back to Pakistan and leave her husband in England.

Several other married women stated explicitly that they had similar reasons for coming to Britain[22]. Zafar's wife Zahida said that when Zafar's remittances became irregular she became dependent on kin for financial support for herself and her children, she worried that her husband had married again, for she had heard that some men had done so. Other married women said that they came to England to ensure that their husbands did not forget their duties as husbands. All married women, even those who were not as explicit as Saleema or Zahida, said they thought a man and wife should be united after several years of separation. 'It's no good for a man to live alone', women would say, 'his wife should be there to cook *chapātī*s for him'. They also said that children need a father to discipline them. Even some of the single women whose marriages were arranged at this time realized and accepted that one of the motives behind the arrangement of their marriages was to keep a check on their husbands' activities. Several other young brides who came to England at this time echoed Imrana's recollections of her thoughts and feelings before her marriage to Ijaz:

> You want to know how I came to be living here? Well, you might not think so now, but when Ijaz was first here, he got into bad company and his uncle was not much better. It is not surprising really, men here on their own. And he was only 19 at the time. But soon his parents got to hear that he had an English girlfriend: at least, that's what some people from his village were saying. His parents were very worried. They had started to build a new house with the money he had been sending back. Other people got to know too, and his parents thought that because of it they would have trouble finding a girl for him to marry. A man's family loses

respect that way you know. So his parents came from their village in Jhelum to our city and spoke to my parents. Our families are the same caste — Pathans — but we are not relatives; my father had known his father for some time. They said their son was returning for the marriage. You know what they did? It was his mother's idea. They sent a telegram saying an uncle had died. It wasn't true, but it brought him home straight away. Before the marriage, women in our neighbourhood used to talk to me about what England was like. They said there was no control. Men drank alcohol and went with women and no one bothered. They also made remarks, not directly, but I knew, about my husband's behaviour, hinting at what sort of man he was. I don't know how they knew. Perhaps they were jealous that I was going to England. Anyway, it made me very frightened about the marriage and I could hardly eat for weeks before it. But I couldn't refuse this marriage. My parents had decided and were so proud to have a daughter going to England. I couldn't shatter their hopes. But since I've been here, as far as I know, my husband has been a good husband to me.

In most cases, the effect of the arrival of wives was that the relationships with English girls eventually if not immediately ceased. Amjad's English wife was not prepared to live as a co-wife, and no doubt Amina made her feelings about the situation clear during the year that they lived together. Several men and women said that most marriages or liaisons with English women ended because the women would not conform to the ideals expected of a Muslim wife; they were too independent. In one case, however, in which a Pakistani wife joined a husband married by Islamic law only (thus avoiding bigamy) to an English woman, an effect of the first wife's presence was that the English wife started to conform to the ideals expected of a Pakistani Muslim wife. She now wears the traditional Panjabi *shalwār-qamīs*, comprising baggy trousers and a long tunic top and covers her head with a *dupattā* (headscarf), behaves demurely in the presence of her husband's kin, avoids speaking to unrelated men and only leaves the house to go shopping or to visit the doctor. For this she wins a certain approval from other Pakistani women, including the co-wife. She is considered very respectable as a white woman who has rejected English ways and Christianity.

Even when a wife from Pakistan did not join a man who had an English girlfriend or wife, the arrival of Pakistani women and children exerted a moral pressure that often, in effect, broke up such relationships. In some ten or a dozen cases where marriages with English women have lasted, the couples tend to comprise a separate circle of friends, not entirely independent of the 'community', but nevertheless regarded as morally on the edge of it. Western women tend to be viewed as promiscuous and unfaithful, even when they have married Pakistani men; comments about an English wife's sexual history may be made in order to insult her husband.

So while men may mention the immigration restrictions or the advantages of the health service and educational system when explaining why their wives and children have come to Britain, women may mention the need to control men's behaviour and stress the 'morally conservative' effect of their presence in Britain. All in all, the advantages, from the point of view of men, of women and of their immediate kin in Pakistan, would seem by now to have outweighed the perceived risks of exposing Muslim wives and daughters to western culture. Yet, as we shall see, for some at least this remains a delicately balanced issue.

Employment and Residence: the Early 1980s to the Present Day

Women who came with their young children to join husbands in Britain were often alone during the working week and sometimes at night too. Their husbands worked mainly at British Leyland (now the Rover Group) in Cowley, the Bus Company and the Post Office. In 1984, of 135 men in three adjacent streets, 81.5% were employed. British Leyland, the largest single employer, accounted for 39% of those in work, while the Bus Company accounted for 12.7% and the Post Office for 9%. 13.6% of the employed men were either self-employed shopkeepers or worked in South Asian-owned shops. The rest of the employed men, with the exception of the *imām*, were engaged in a range of unskilled and semi-skilled occupations, as hospital porters, at British Rail, in the construction business and in other factories. The recession was already in evidence as the remaining 18.5% were unemployed[23].

Those in employment often worked long anti-social hours; some British Leyland employees regularly worked a fortnight of night shifts followed by a fortnight of day shifts, while others worked nights. Work for the Bus Company and the Post Office also involved long and irregular hours. Some men had more than one job. Saeed worked full-time during the day at British Leyland and part-time in a chip shop in the evenings and at weekends. Mehmood worked full time at British Leyland and then sold petrol in a service station until half-past nine every evening; his brother, working outside Oxford, also sold petrol when he returned home at the weekends. Farid worked full-time at British Leyland and in the family shop until nine o'clock most evenings. He shared the shop work with his brothers, both full-time bus drivers, and a cousin who worked in the shop during the day. Men spent little time relaxing at home and, whether employed or not, would be likely to spend any 'spare' time in the company of other men in the south Asian shops or in the mosque rather than at home.

It was, of course, usual for men to be away from home for long periods of time, for this has long been the case in rural Pakistan. In this respect, the domestic division of labour echoed the pattern typical of rural Pakistan; a man who works in the fields there may leave home early, returning home only at dusk. Also, as in rural Pakistan, men often did the grocery shopping in the evenings, after their return from work. In contrast with rural Pakistan, however, many newly-arrived Pakistani wives in Britain were isolated from close female kin in Pakistan, unable to speak English, reluctant to venture out, and dependent on their husbands in new ways[24]. Ideals of purdah also tended to constrain women's activities outside the home, for a man with a working wife would lose *izzat* (respect, honour). In Oxford at this time, the vast majority of Pakistani wives did not have any paid work outside the home. The few exceptions were mostly educated women of urban backgrounds, employed as teachers.

With the exception of some Pathan families who are reputedly the strictest observers of purdah, most women fairly quickly overcame their dependence on husbands for shopping or taking children to school, taking on these tasks themselves, accompanied by young children. Women tended to use the English super-markets and the weekly open-air market in the city centre, rather than the local Pakistani groceries, because there they ran less risk of meeting unrelated Pakistani men. They would also send older children on errands while a husband was at work or, if he worked nights, asleep.

The women in several shopkeeping families began to work on a fairly full-time basis, without pay, alongside their men in the family businesses, soon after their arrival in Britain. They regarded their work as an extension of women's work at home. It was, as Habiba said, 'like working in the fields in Pakistan', because it was 'for the family', not for someone else. Other women did paid work at home which included sewing *shalwār-qamīs* for other women, cooking *samosās* or *pakorās* for the local Asian shops or for catering companies, or 'homeworking', that is, low-paid piece-work such as sewing toys or quilted jackets and other clothes for local factories. A few young women in the 1980s had paid employment outside the home, but opinions were divided about whether this was desirable for Muslim women.

Considerations of purdah were uppermost in how Pakistani families viewed female employment, but it is worth remembering that Pakistani (and Bangladeshi) Muslim wives came to Britain later than other south Asian women, as the official dependants of their husbands, and at the close of the post-war boom when the labour market was in recession. Most were looking after pre-school children during the 1980s, and did not have the immediate support of a mother, mother-in-law or sister-in-law. Pragmatic considerations perhaps just as much as cultural constraints influenced women's experience of 'work' at this time.

Pakistani male unemployment has increased significantly in the past decade at a national level. The Labour Force survey of 1988–90 showed that Pakistanis comprise 22% of the population of the male unemployed, of which 8% are 'whites'[25]. There is considerable local variation, and in some localities Pakistani male unemployment is higher still[26]. In Oxford, Pakistani male unemployment is higher than it was ten years ago, but lower than the national average.

Official figures may obscure migrants' strategies in adapting to changes in the job market. In Oxford, the closure of the Cowley plant of Rover Group car factory, which had been the largest single employer of Pakistani men, had a number of far-reaching effects on patterns of male employment as well as on rates of unemployment. In anticipation of the prospect of unemployment, some men took redundancy payments and retired, after years of manual or semi-skilled service, deciding to leave the task of wage-earning to their sons; others took voluntary redundancy payments with which they established businesses, becoming entrepreneurs or self-employed taxi-drivers. Zabar used his voluntary redundancy payments towards purchasing a grocery from two Pakistani brothers and a brother-in-law who had found the shop too much work in addition to their other jobs; Zabar, his wife and his eldest son now run the shop. Yacoub used his voluntary redundancy payments towards establishing a vehicle repair business in partnership with a fellow Pakistani ex-factory worker. In the past decade, the number of Pakistani taxi drivers in the city has gradually increased; more Pakistani men now drive taxis than drive buses. The bus company in 1984 was the second largest single employer of Pakistani men but changed its management structure in 1996 and all but six of its Pakistani employees left, many becoming taxi drivers. Myhrban, who had been employed there for twenty-one years, explained why:

> The new management did not give any time in lieu. It was inflexible. You could not work at night or at the weekend and have a day off in the week any more. You had to work the same hours as everyone else. With the taxi, you buy the car and get a licence from the city council, and after that how many hours you work is up to you. If there's a problem or a visitor at home my wife can phone me and I go straight back. You can go home for a few hours. It is important for our people to be flexible, because of our customs, as you know. Some friends said I should stay with the Bus Company because I had been there 21 years. But they are not going to give you a medal for that.

The number of Pakistani-owned businesses has increased and some shops have changed ownership, usually by being sold to other Pakistanis or South Asians. The business run by Gafoor and his brothers collapsed; the brothers sold the shop to an Indian family. Gafoor now drives a taxi, but his wife and daughters continue to cook *samosās*, which Gafoor delivers to other South Asian small businesses in the city. His brother-in-law bought a shop in the outskirts of the city, and that business thrives.

Business enterprise generally is characteristic of South Asians in Oxford; South Asians constitute only 4.6% of the city's population but own 12% of the small shops and restaurants[27]. A few long-standing Oxford Pakistani entrepreneurs are considered locally to be very successful; in two cases, sons now run the shops in Britain while the fathers manage businesses in Pakistan. Even for the less successful shopkeepers, entrepreneurial initiatives constitute an active response to economic hardship, racial exclusion and the limited opportunities of the labour market, through which families deploy the socio-economic and cultural resources at their disposal.

While a majority of first generation wives still do not work, a finding that is in keeping with national figures which show fewer Pakistani and Bangladeshi women in the U.K. labour force than any other group[28], there have been some significant changes in attitudes towards and experiences of women working. In the past decade, some of the women who were at home with children during the 1980s but whose children are now adults or in upper schools have taken up semi-skilled or unskilled mostly part-time paid work outside the home.

Azra and her sister-in-law, for instance, both now clean for an Oxford college. Azra, an out-going woman with six children all now in work, further education or school, heard of cleaning vacancies at the college where an English neighbour was working. She and her husband agreed that she should apply, because her husband's earnings as a hospital porter were barely supporting the family. Her sister-in-law Jabeen took up another vacancy in the same college a few months later, because her husband's long-term ill health has left him unable to work. Both husbands are pleased that their wives bring in a much-needed extra income, even though they say that in Pakistan such work would be shameful, particularly for women of *ashraf* (respectable) families such as theirs. 'Here it's alright', Azra says, 'because we are not working for men from our own community; our husbands would have forbidden that'.

Sometimes husbands have objected strongly to the prospect of their wives working. Yacoub was furious when he learnt that Yasmin and her friend Shagufta had found work in a city-centre department store, and forbade her to start the job. 'I would have felt so ashamed if my wife was doing work like that, hoovering and hanging up clothes', he said. Shagufta started work anyway, and was delighted to earn £75 a week for working for four hours each day, but because Yacoub had forbidden Yasmin to work, Shagufta's husband felt compelled to do the same. Both men say they have since changed their minds, since their financial situations are desperate — Yacoub is heavily in debt with a failing business, and Shagufta's husband is unemployed. Yasmin wants another job, though has lost confidence at her husband's initial reaction to the idea. For the time being, she assembles plastic fishhooks at home for one penny per piece. She hopes that she might find 'better' work than hanging clothes and hoovering, and now regularly attends an English class, enjoying the contact with the other students there — women from many different parts of the world. She commented:

> Many Pakistani women in Oxford nowadays are working, and in any case women have always worked in Pakistan. In our village, as you know, some women work for other families in the village, doing sewing and cleaning, though in our family we like women to be teachers. I want my daughter to get enough education to find respectable work. Why don't you get full-time work, and someone to look after the children? You have enough education.

The increase in numbers of Pakistani women in at least part-time work may be linked with the rising male unemployment of the past decade. However, it is not simply as a response to their husbands' unemployment, redundancy or sickness that some of the wives of 'pioneer' migrants have entered the labour force, usually by taking part-time, poorly paid work. The wives of pioneer migrants were not 'working' in the 1980s but were occupied instead with the care of young children, obligations to kin and other domestic responsibilities, while their husbands were often absent, working long and anti-social hours, including night-shifts. That some of them now 'work' is in part a function of the fact that they are freer of domestic responsibilities

now that their children are, or are almost, adults; their participation in the U.K. labour force is thus to some extent 'life-
course related'[29]. They are also more confident with English
and about living in Britain.

There is therefore no simple correlation between cultural attitudes and experiences of paid work; pragmatic considerations,
family structure, the extent of a woman's childcare commitments and local work opportunities all play a part in shaping
'what happens'. These changes are in turn linked with changes
in attitude, and my impression is that there is considerably less
shame attached to women working outside the home for a
wage than there was ten years ago. Most first generation
women, regardless of whether they themselves worked or not,
are strongly in favour of their daughters securing sufficient education for them to obtain 'respectable' work should they need
to. A high value is still placed on female modesty and
respectability; while education is increasingly valued, it does
not necessarily follow that an educated wife is one who will or
'should' work. But a daughter's education and qualifications
undoubtedly increase her parents' bargaining power in negotiating a good marriage. And to conform to current immigration
rules, a woman bringing a spouse to Britain may have to show
that she has an income. Her education and employment is thus
of socio-economic value not simply, or even necessarily to her,
but to a wider group of kin — father, mother, brothers and
other relatives, including those in Pakistan. Women may also
gain status, influence and a degree of autonomy which has
economic implications in other ways, through their informal
social networks and formal ritual activities (see chapter 8).

East Oxford remains the focus of economic and cultural activities. The mosques, the South Asian shops and businesses and
the Asian Cultural Centre are located in east Oxford, where
planning permission has been granted for the construction of
the first purpose-built mosque. It is also where, concentrated in
a few adjacent residential streets, Pakistani families have their
closest informal social networks. In the past decade, however,
there has also been a gradual residential shift towards Cowley
and the suburbs of Headington and Marston, while some new
families have moved into east Oxford from elsewhere in Britain.
Sometimes an entire east Oxford household has moved to the
suburbs, renting the east Oxford property to university students

and saying they wanted a larger house, more room for a car, and freedom from the noise, congestion and parking restrictions in east Oxford. As Ahmad, a former shopkeeper, put it:

> Each time you leave your car on a yellow line you get a £25 fine. One night a week and it stings you. But four or five times a week, if you go out in the evening and come back late, that's £100 or £125, more than you earn. Here, there's a garage, and a driveway, and if your car breaks down, all you have to do is pull it in.

Others who have moved are young couples setting up homes in the suburbs away from parents or in-laws, often initially in a council-owned property. Traditional cultural and socio-economic pressures deter a young couple from moving out of a husband's parents' house too soon after marriage. In east Oxford, the desire not to move away from relatives and friends and the fear of racist attacks may also inhibit household division. In fact, however, some young couples have turned down east Oxford council houses near their parents or in-laws in favour of improved or new houses in Headington, Marston or beyond the Blackbird Leys estate, and these moves, I suggest in chapter 4, may be entirely in keeping with migrants' instrumental attitudes towards property. Those who were the first to move to the suburbs have since been joined, in nearby houses, by married sisters or sisters-in-law with young families, in effect re-creating in the suburbs the informal and formal networks of friendship and mutual support characteristic of east Oxford[30].

Conclusion

Migrants' initial dependence on each other for work, accommodation and welfare had the generally conservative effect of ensuring that migrants acted according to the expectations of kin in Pakistan. As the settlement developed, several factors in effect weakened it close-knit structure. The range of jobs available to Pakistani men gradually increased, more men became home-owners and, as men's competence in English language, law and customs increased, the need for mutual assistance lessened. Consequently, there were some grounds for the fears of relatives in Pakistan that men in Britain would succumb to the temptations and corrupting influences of the West. At the same time, immigration controls increasingly restricted the entry of new migrants.

These changes, on the whole, did not pose a fundamental threat to migrants' families because the kin- and village-based social structure established during the early years of settlement enabled fellow migrants and migrants' families in Pakistan to take control of men's activities, primarily by arranging a man's marriage or arranging for him to be joined by his wife and children. The arrival of women and children can be viewed therefore not so much as a passive response to the constraints of immigration control, but as a means of maintaining *birādarī* integrity and ensuring that a man continued to recognize obligations to his kin, and this was indeed the immediate effect of the presence of women and children.

As their socio-economic circumstances have changed, families have continued to adapt aspects of their cultural ideals and family organization in order to maintain their commitment to social advancement. Against a backdrop of rising male unemployment, some women of the pioneer generation, free from some of their domestic responsibilities now that their children have reached or are approaching adulthood, have taken up part-time paid work outside the home. Increasingly, young women are working and their families speak of the advantages for daughters of securing academic and vocational qualifications, and some young couples have moved away from east Oxford to the suburbs. Likewise, migrants' proclivity for business enterprise, particularly shopkeeping and property dealing, represents a creative strategy which takes advantage of limited local opportunities in the face of unemployment and structural exclusion. These strategies draw upon a family's social and cultural resources including the increasingly diverse skills or opportunities offered by women, particularly daughters raised in Britain.

NOTES

1. Ballard (ed.) 1994:16.
2. Jeffery, 1976:65–6.
3. Deakin, 1970:54. Similarly, Rex and Moore see the arrival of wives and children in Britain in terms of the increased public discussion of immigration controls (1967:116). For a comprehensive account of immigration legislation, see The Runnymede Trust and the Radical Statistics Race Group (1980:30–54).

4. On Indian immigrants' door-to-door peddling, see Desai, 1963:66. Peddling was still a characteristic Asian occupation in Newcastle in the 1970s (Taylor, 1976:49–50).

5. Griffith and Henderson, 1960: p. 42. On the whole no effort was made to match employment vacancies with the supply of immigrant labour until the introduction of a voucher system in the 1960s. A few employers did recruit directly from the West Indies during the 1960s: London Transport had a recruiting office in Barbados (D. Brooks, 1975:257) and London Transport (from 1956), the National Health Service and the British Hotels and Restaurant Association made direct arrangements with the Barbados government for recruiting skilled labour. These employers were exceptional in taking the initial responsibility for the accommodation and welfare of their West Indian recruits (Rose et al., 1969, pp. 67–8 and p. 78) but this was not the case for most Pakistanis.

6. In April 1958, almost half of the estimated 4,500 Bradford Pakistanis were out of work, comprising 44% of the total Bradford unemployed, according to the Yorkshire Evening Post of 12 April 1958 (Griffith and Henderson, 1960).

7. Griffith and Henderson, 1960:33.

8. These figures probably include a number of Bangladeshis for it is not possible to distinguish Bangladeshi and Pakistani Muslims by name. At that time, Bangladeshis were of course East Pakistanis.

9. Aurora, 1967, p. 36; also p. 52.

10. Halāl means 'lawful'; halāl meat is that of an animal slaughtered according to Islamic law, and the consumption of meat that is not halāl is forbidden in Islam. Halāl meat was first available in Oxford from the mid-sixties.

11. The conditions within these 'multi-occupation bachelor houses' were very much the same elsewhere, for Pakistanis in Bradford and Birmingham (Dahya, 1974), for Indians in London (Aurora, 1967) and for Indians in the Midlands (Desai 1963).

12. See also Aurora, 1967:37.

13. Aurora, 1967:38.

14. Rose et al., 1969:391.

15. Oxford City Council, 1975:19.

16. On the principles of rotating credit associations, see S. Ardener, 1984. This form of credit is still used in east Oxford where kametīs are now mainly organized by women. Typically, twenty women might each pay £20 per week, so that each woman, when it is her turn, will receive £400, which may provide a useful sum for the down payment on a house or a shop.

17. In London, prostitutes who came to know certain all-male Panjabi Sikh lodging houses would pay weekly visits on the men's pay day (Aurora, 1967:73–4).

18. Almost 70 percent of the Pakistani females enumerated on the 1971 Census came to Britain after 1967 (Lomas, 1973:32 and table 1.5).

19. Jeffery, 1976, p. 49 and p. 67.

20. A survey conducted at London Airport in January and February 1967 showed boys commonly joining their fathers, leaving sisters and mothers in Pakistan. Of 387 unaccompanied children under the age of 16 arriving from Pakistan and India (countries which accounted for 80% and 20% of

children respectively), only four children were girls. (International Social Services, 1967).

21. Jeffery, 1976:49–50.
22. These women seemed less inhibited about remarking upon doubts about their husbands' morality than the Pakistani women in Bristol in Patricia Jeffery's study (1976:66).
23. Shaw, 1988:67.
24. Saifullah-Khan, 1976 (b).
25. Trevor Jones, 1993, Britain's Ethnic Minorities: an analysis of the labour force survey, London, Policy studies Institute, p. 20, cited in Baumann, 1996:25.
26. In Southall, for instance, Pakistanis comprise 7% of the population and Indians 50%, but Pakistani men comprised almost one third of all unemployed Southall males in the 1988–9 survey (Baumann, 1996:50–1). In Bristol, an ethnic minority survey showed one third of Pakistani husbands to be out of work (West and Pilgrim, 1995:367).
27. Srinivasan, 1995:200.
28. West and Pilgrim, 1995:358.
29. See also Werbner 1988. In a Bristol study, Pakistani women's labour-force participation increased markedly among those aged fifty and over (West and Pilgrim, 1995:374). In Oxford, figures for Pakistani women over 16 in paid employment are higher than the national averages for Pakistani female employment (Ceri Peach, personal communication). This figure includes young women, the daughters and in some cases granddaughters of women of the pioneer generation, of whom many are now working (see chapter 7).
30. On the face of it, this is reminiscent of the process described by Louis Wirth for Jews in Chicago: those who move out of a ghetto 'are followed by fellow deserters, only to find that a new ghetto has risen up around them' (Werbner 1990:49).

3 HOUSEHOLDS AND FAMILY RELATIONSHIPS

The village we arrived at — after a long bumpy journey over a dirt track, in a crowded Ford transit van still displaying a U.K. tax disc — was visible as a collection of sandy-brown walls, with the occasional painted roof. There was no village name-board, no street signs. A narrow lane with open drains on both sides and high brick walls seemed to be the way into the village. Children appeared as if from no-where to stare at us. We were escorted along a maze of winding lanes to a doorway and then shown into a small room, which appeared to open onto an expanse of mud where a buffalo was standing…It took a while to work out whose house we had come to, for there were in fact two houses in this courtyard, which, it emerged, belonged to two brothers; or rather, one brother and his family lived in one house, and the other brother's widow and her children lived in the other. The families shared a small separate guest room — the room into which we were first shown — and a water pump, but they used different sides of the courtyard and had their own buffaloes (adapted from my diary, 1980).

I was at first surprised that in all the villages I visited in Pakistan, relatives generally lived in adjacent houses and that people would describe their village in terms of areas belonging to different kinship groups, called *birādarī*s. Villagers drew me maps of their villages which illustrated this (see Figures 3.1 and 3.2); one such map (Figure 3.1) shows an area where Rajput families live, another where Jat families live, another where Mochi families live, and so on. These *birādarī* and family names generally identify a caste (*zāt* or *qaum*) or subcaste[1].

While the boundaries between houses of people from the same caste or *birādarī* sometimes seemed blurred, there was a sharper sense of boundary if a neighbouring house belonged to someone from a different *birādarī* or caste. This caste consciousness seemed more pronounced in the layout of villages in the southern canal colony districts than in the long-settled rain-

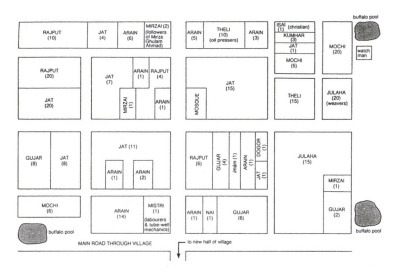

Figure 3.1   A village in Faisalabad district. Names refer to caste groups. The occupation denoted by the caste name is shown only for castes not described in table 4.1. These castes (Theli, Mistri and Julaha) belong to the artisan category. Numbers refer to approximate numbers of houses in each caste group. The outer blocks contain smaller houses than the inner blocks.

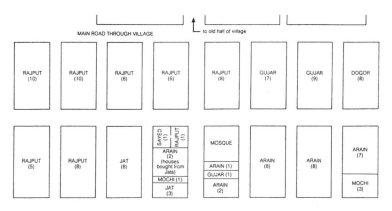

Figure 3.2   New half of the village shown in Figure 3.1. This half of the village was built after Partition. Names refer to castes; numbers refer to approximate numbers of houses in each caste group. Caste names are explained in table 4.1.

fall-dependent areas in the north and there may be historical reasons for this. Many of the southern canal-colony villages, built under the authority of the British at the end of the nineteenth century, were laid out in squares (Figure 3.1) and the Muslim, Hindu and Sikh colonizers were encouraged to settle in blocks according to their caste groupings. At Partition in 1947 when the Hindus and Sikhs fled or were killed, the Muslim refugees who entered the villages also grouped themselves according to their caste, either within the old village houses or in new adjacent settlements. (Figures 3.1 and 3.2 show, respectively, the 'pre'- and 'post-'Partition sections of a village in Faisalabad, still referred to by the villagers as the 'old' or the 'new' settlement). Today, the houses of people from different castes are less clearly grouped according to caste than they were in the past, because people have bought houses in each other's caste blocks, but village layout is still described in caste terms.

Caste was not the only differentiating principle reflected in people's social maps of their village. In some villages, families who had been refugees in 1947 were still known as *muhājir*s (refugees) and their houses were separated from those of families who had been living in the village since before Partition. In other villages, there were distinct settlements of people known locally as *dammī*s (people from the Dam); these people had been displaced from villages in Mirpur when the Mangla Dam was built in the 1960s and had opted for land and re-settlement. Caste, however, was the most common social distinction attached to particular areas of the villages in this region.

In the long-settled rainfall-dependent north, which was a Muslim majority area before Partition, the villages are much older; some, according to local accounts, date back several hundred years to when Mughal invaders set up camps in the area. Here, there were no distinct 'blocks' of houses belonging to particular castes, and the houses were arranged in an apparently higgledy-piggledy manner, divided by winding lanes. Yet, despite the seeming randomness of the layout, the villagers knew exactly which houses belonged to which caste groups and believed the different groups to be the descendants of the troops and servants who had accompanied the Mughal conquerors of this region.

Land and Property

Whereas in Britain a house is most people's major investment, in Pakistan ownership of land is more important than ownership of a house. Nearly all the major disputes that have occurred in the villages have been over land, often over field boundaries. Land is a scarce resource, sold only when a family faces real hardship. People with savings generally consider extending landholdings a first priority and those no longer dependent on their land for a livelihood prefer to have sharecroppers work it, receiving from them a proportion of the produce in place of rent, rather than to sell.

Various animals are usually also important in village life. Householders who can afford them keep one or two buffaloes, on which they may depend for milk. Villagers may also make their own yogurt, butter and *ghī* from the milk. Families usually also keep chickens and goats, for eggs and meat, even if they are not entirely dependent on their own produce for their subsistence.

Providing one has land, houses are relatively easy to build or extend because planning permission is not required, but the building materials used are an important indication of status and wealth. The traditional houses of the relatively poor are described as *kachchā* (literally 'raw'), for they are built of mud bricks. *Pakkā* (literally 'cooked') houses usually belong to wealthier people (such as those with relatives abroad) and are built of kiln-baked bricks and mortar, usually covered in a layer of concrete and often brightly painted. Most houses are *pakkā* in the villages from which there has been substantial emigration. These new *pakkā* houses, quite different from the *kachchā* houses in poorer parts of the village, are also quite easily distinguished from the older-style *pakkā* houses belonging to the traditional village elite, usually comprising families of traditionally higher caste status than the migrants.

Another indication of the new wealth and status of migrants and their kin is the plethora of goods from abroad, particularly electrical goods, such as televisions, cassette players, videos, electric sewing machines, fans and refrigerators. In one village these items, brought to the village by truck along the bumpy unpaved (*kachchā*) track from the city, had been stored unused not for months but for years in the *pakkā* houses newly-built by people with relatives abroad; the village had no electricity. The villagers joked that they had all these *valāyatī* ('from abroad') goods but could not use them. I am told that electricity has now been introduced to the village and a paved road built from the nearest town.

Migrants' accounts suggest that some quite profound changes in living standards have taken place in many of their villages, to a large extent as a result of foreign-earned remittances. In Habiba's village in Faisalabad there was no electricity and no paved road when I visited in 1980. When I met Habiba's father again sixteen years later (while he was staying in Oxford with Habiba before attending a son's wedding in the Midlands and then returning to Pakistan) he told me:

> My house was *kachchā*, you remember. Now it is *pakkā*. All the *kachchā* houses have been pulled down and people have built new *pakkā* ones, with latrines and running water. Hot water, too. Now I have a television. Many people have sold off plots of land as building plots, and with the money they have moved out of the village altogether and bought land elsewhere, where it is cheaper. The value of land around our villages has risen sky-high. And the village has many shops. And many more people. People from outside have built new houses on the plots of land they have bought. The village is now a much busier place.

Remittances from England have enabled other Faisalabadis to extend landholdings and buy tractors, to start brick factories, ice factories, buffalo-milk businesses and chicken farms, sometimes in the villages, but also by moving to the city. In Mirpur, too, remittances have had their impact, for migrants or their kin have built new *pakkā* houses, started businesses or travel agencies. However, these enterprises are aimed mainly at meeting the needs of returning or visiting migrants and there is less evidence of large-scale investment in the area[2].

Purdah and the *Baithak*

English terrace houses generally have a defined number of rooms, each with a specific function, but in rural Pakistan

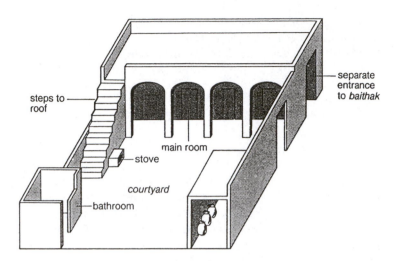

Figure 3.3   Main areas of a house in rural Pakistan. The precise layout varies from house to house; the *baithak* and main room may be on different sides of the courtyard or the *baithak* may be outside the house altogether. Buffaloes, goats and grain may be housed in other rooms of the courtyard.

houses did not have separate rooms for separate activities to the same extent. Houses had three main areas (Figure 3.3): the courtyard, perhaps with an outside staircase leading up to the roof; the main room; and the *baithak* which is a sitting room for men. This layout reflects the influence of the principles of purdah, a word that means literally 'curtain' or 'screen' and also denotes a system of segregation by sex[3].

The ideals of purdah, at least as most Panjabi Muslims interpret them, require that a woman avoids contact with unrelated men: the only men a woman should meet are her husband and immediate male kin, her father, brothers, sons, uncles and nephews — that is, all men who are forbidden as marriage partners. She must be a virgin when she marries and her parents arrange her marriage. From puberty onwards, she should always dress modestly, wearing loose garments such as the *shalwār-qamīs* (loose trousers and a long blouse covering the hips) worn with a *chādar* (shawl) or *dupattā* (headscarf) over her head and concealing the shape of her breasts. Her place is at home, where she has responsibility for the household, cooking and children, and she should only leave the house when absolutely necessary and should then behave with proper modesty.

In practice, observance of purdah varies tremendously according to region, wealth, religious tradition and caste status. Purdah is reputedly stricter among the Pathans and in the north-west of Panjab and more relaxed in the canal colony districts. Within any village, strict observance of purdah is generally associated with families wealthy enough to allow their women not to work. In poorer families, women have to work in the fields alongside men and usually their contribution to the household economy, by harvesting corn, sugar cane, or cotton, or husking rice, is essential to the household's survival. Even so, religiously orthodox or high caste families may be stricter about purdah than wealthier but less orthodox families. Purdah may be more relaxed within the areas of a village where households of the same *birādarī* adjoin, since there may be close links of kinship between household members.

Despite these variations, and despite recent changes in living standard, the principles of purdah continue to affect all household layouts in important ways. A 'typical' village house is surrounded by a high wall, outside which is a narrow lane with open drains and the high walls of neighbouring houses on each side. You enter a house through a door in the wall; beyond this is a large open courtyard, and beyond that is the main room or rooms, but usually a purdah curtain hanging behind the door or a second wall screens the courtyard from immediate view.

If a male visitor comes to the house when no man is at home, the women inside can discover who he is or take a message by speaking from behind the purdah curtain, but men avoid visiting during the day when they know only women are at home. If a man visits when men are at home, he is received in the *baithak*, if the family has one. This is a sitting room, which has a separate entrance from the lane, so that male visitors do not need to enter the courtyard. It usually has a second entrance from the courtyard for household members to use. Male visitors are welcomed, entertained and may even stay overnight in the *baithak* without ever meeting the women of the household. Not all families can afford a *baithak*; it also indicates status and wealth and is often carefully decorated, with pictures or wall-hangings depicting scenes of Mecca, and with shelves of crockery, photographs and ornaments.

When the *baithak* is not in use for guests, the men of the household spend time in it in the company of male friends, when they have returned from work, or when there is no work to do in the fields. Otherwise men meet friends in the mosque or the local shops or a tearoom. Men from poorer families may entertain male visitors in the public men's meeting place in the village, teashops, or in someone else's *baithak*. A large *baithak* continues to be a feature of houses recently built with foreign-earned remittances, sometimes appointed more elaborately and in more 'western' styles than the main house.

Use of the Courtyard

The open and usually sunny courtyard is really the centre of a typical village house because the women of the household do most of their work here, protected from the gaze of outsiders. Sometimes steps lead from the courtyard to the roof, where in summer women dry spices, grain and cotton, or make *seviān* (slender strands of flour-and-water dough, sometimes called vermicelli). Adjacent houses belonging to the same *birādarī* in one village in Jhelum district had steps from the courtyard up to the roof and then down into the courtyard of the next house. This enabled women to walk into each other's courtyards without having to go out into the lanes.

Different areas of the courtyard are used for cooking, bathing, washing clothes and keeping animals. On one side of the courtyard, there is usually a mud fireplace (*chulhā*) where cooking is done in metal or clay pots by women squatting over an open fire. The fuel for the fire is wood or cakes of dried buffalo dung which women make from a mixture of dung, earth, straw and water and leave on walls to dry in the sun. Often a second mud fireplace is almost permanently in use keeping milk hot to prevent it from going sour, which would otherwise happen very quickly without a refrigerator. From the milk, women would make yogurt and churn this to produce butter and *ghī*. Some courtyards have an earth oven called a *tandūr* for baking *chapātīs*. Women from several houses usually share it a *tandūr* oven when it is lit. Sometimes a separate small and usually rather dark chimney-less room serves as a kitchen in winter when it is too cold or wet to cook in the courtyard. Some wealthier families, in 1980–1, had purpose-built kitchens with built-in concrete shelves, steel bins for storing flour and *ghī*, and steel utensils, and they used the more costly paraffin or gas stove in preference to the mud hearth. More village homes, today, have 'modern' kitchens of this type, but I am told that nearly everyone retains the mud hearth as well, for its reliability and economy, even though visitors from England have mixed feelings about it. Saeeda complained that 'getting used to using a *chulhā* again is not easy once you have become used to cooking on an upright stove. You have to squat and it hurts your back, and you have to get the fire alight. Some of the girls brought up in England just cannot do it!'

In 1980–1, most of the villages I visited had electricity but it was not used for cookers or refrigerators. It was used for electric light, though the supply was often unreliable. Saeed's mother used to switch the lights on and off with a stick, because some people had received electric shocks from the switches. Electricity was also used for ceiling or standard fans in the summer and sometimes also for television sets and other electrical goods, usually obtained from abroad. Some wealthier families had private electricity generators, as standby systems for when the irregular village supply failed, which it did periodically. Electricity supplies are apparently more reliable now and some England-returnees have refrigerators and electric cookers in the new homes they have built for themselves in neighbouring towns.

In areas where the water table was not too deep some homes had their own handpumps in the courtyard. Women would wash clothes and dishes by hand at the handpump using a caustic, locally produced soap. In other areas, the water table is too deep to permit the installation of handpumps. In these villages, women at dusk (because of the constraints of purdah) or men during the day men fetched water from a central village well. A man known as the water-carrier also delivered water daily, in huge leather sacks hung over a donkey, to some houses. The water was then stored in clay pots in a shady part of the courtyard and used abstemiously, as required, for drinking, cooking, or washing dishes. To minimize their use of the precious domestic water supply, women would sometimes leave their homes to wash dirty clothes at the village well or in a nearby stream or river outside the village, usually in the company of other women. Water was an everyday concern. Women often asked me about the water supply in England, about whether water really ran from taps in every home. Even after I had lived for two months in Zahida's village, some villagers remained convinced that I had been sent by the water and power development authority to investigate the possibility of installing a water tank.

In all the villages I visited, the water supply is apparently now more reliable, stored in tanks and piped directly to people's homes. In Zahida's village, which is set into a hillside, water used to be delivered by the water-carrier or carried to the house in clay pots from the well below the village. All the houses now have water pumped from the main well via a huge tank erected on the hill behind the village. Water runs in the taps for just two or three hours a day, according to a centralized system, apparently installed by a government authority, which ensures that every house receives water. Some families have also installed private water pumps, with variable success, given the depth of the water table.

A more regular water supply has also permitted some changes to bathroom facilities. The bathroom or *ghusal-khānā* (literally 'wash-place') is generally a small enclosure of three shoulder-high walls against an outside wall, with an outlet in the base of the outside wall through which water runs into an open ditch in the lane. The bather pours water from a filled bucket over the head and body using a steel or plastic *lotā*, which is a vessel shaped like a coffeepot without a lid. In winter, the water is usually heated first, over the mud fireplace. Some bathrooms now have steel tanks with taps providing running water. Habiba's father told me, 'Now I have running water and a motor driven heater for my water tank which turns off when the tank is full of hot water. Now you can have a stand-up bath with hot water.' Some householders have installed showers, but not western-style bathtubs, because Muslims consider that sitting in bath water cannot clean you: to be clean you must wash in running water. One Oxford landlord installed a western-style bathtub and shower not in his new village house but in the guest-quarters of a house he has built in the nearby town; 'English guests', he says, 'can bathe as they please; Muslim guests may sit in the tub of water and shower afterwards'.

The other main change is the installation of latrines. In a village house in 1980–81 there was no toilet and people went to the fields to defecate. Propriety required that women went out at dawn and dusk, when they could not be seen clearly. Usually women would go to the fields in small groups rather than alone, taking with them a *lotā* of water for washing themselves afterwards. In one household, the morning signal for the women's trip to the fields was when the daughter had swept the dust, dirt and dung from the courtyard into a basket and placed the basket on her head in order to carry the rubbish to the fields. On route, if you passed a man, you had to step to the left and look away; only when all men were out of sight could the purpose of the trip be achieved!

Some houses had a latrine built in the courtyard, located as far away from the main rooms as possible. It was usually a small room containing two parallel raised steps to squat upon. Householders sometimes cleaned the latrine themselves, but generally this was the task of sweepers, who, in the villages I visited were Christians. (This is probably because the Christians, called Isai, were originally Hindu untouchables who converted to Christianity but have continued to be regarded as untouchables; latrine sweeping is an occupation associated with untouchability.) A few village households had European-style porcelain latrines, beneath which there was a pit into which waste-disposing chemicals were poured from time to time. One man who had lived in England had installed a flush system. Many more houses belonging to migrants or their kin now have latrines and some have flush systems, and many British Pakistanis now regard these facilities as necessities. Saeeda says she will now contemplate returning to Pakistan for longer next time, now that their house has a flush system and running water.

Another area of the courtyard is used at night for tethering the buffalo, which provides milk for the household, goats, and, if the family has one, an ox. During the day, the men usually take these animals out to the fields to graze, while women tend the chickens or goats that remain in the courtyard. Returning migrants and particularly their children sometimes find this proximity to animals very strange; it is another indication of how rapidly living conditions and the expectations associated with them can change.

The Main Room

Typically, a village house contains one main room, plus one or two storerooms containing grains, pulses, other foodstuffs and clothes (see Figure 3.3). Wealthier people may have several rooms in addition to the main room and a veranda between the rooms and the courtyard. During the day the main room is not much used, unless it is raining, because most activities take place in the courtyard which, being open and large, is light and sunny. The main room is rather dark, with small windows, which often have iron bars across and wooden shutters over them. In older houses the wooden window shutters and doorframes may be engraved in traditional styles. In newer houses, the doors are plain or painted and some houses have decorated concrete doorframes and grilles resembling engraved stonework over the windows and forming a mantelpiece inside the room.

The main room is a sitting room, which doubles as a bedroom for the whole family; it is not divided into separate bedrooms. Usually it contains relatively simple furniture: a number of *chārpāi*s (wooden-framed string beds) set against the walls, a table, and a wooden cupboard or, as has become more common, a metal trunk containing bedding, clothes and jewellery. The trunk usually contains the clothes and other goods that were brought as part of a bride's dowry and it continues to be used to store these items after the marriage celebrations are over. There may also be a high shelf or mantelpiece displaying china teacups, plates, glasses and shiny metal cups. Stacked on a string bed in one corner of the room there may be a pile of brightly coloured quilts for use at night in winter.

These features of a village house show that it is designed for sharing. There is no 'western' concept of privacy: generally, no individual or couple regards a room as their own; each room is everyone's room. Usually all family members sleep in one room, although sometimes the men of the household sleep separately in the *baithak*. This arrangement is not an indication of poverty, for in many cases separate rooms could have been built if the family had considered it necessary, and often there were additional unused rooms. Rather, the whole family expects and usually prefers to sleep in one room. Generally, each person sleeps on a separate *chārpāi*, unless two children or a mother and child share one. In summer, string beds are brought out into the courtyard or onto the roof where people sleep under mosquito nets. There are rarely double beds in the villages, though a more modern single bed called a *palang* frequently features among the goods given in a dowry by more well-to-do people. When a couple are first married, two string beds may be pushed together in a separate room for the wedding night. In one village, two *palang*s were pushed together in the main room for the display of the dowry during the day and the couple slept there at night while the rest of the family slept in the courtyard. After the first few nights, the couple slept in the same room as the rest of the family.

British Houses

Houses in Britain occupied by Pakistanis are quite strikingly different from houses in Pakistan in both layout and amenities. East Oxford houses are generally small, and, whether detached or semi-detached, have clear boundaries between them. No stairs outside allow access to the roof or the neighbour's roof, and one's neighbours are unlikely to be one's relatives. Internal household layout makes no allowances for purdah: there is no 'women's area' corresponding to the courtyard, and no 'men's area' corresponding to the *baithak*. Instead, domestic space is divided into separate rooms, two or three on each floor, and there are usually at least two floors. The amenities available reflect a striking contrast in the general standard of living. British houses have running hot and cold water, a reliable electricity supply, gas or electric cookers, refrigerators and flush toilets. Washing machines, dishwashers, kitchen units and other gadgets are, potentially at least, fairly easily available. Does this mean that attitudes to purdah as reflected in the 'men's' and 'women's' areas of houses in Pakistan have changed over the past twenty or so years since 'united' Pakistani families have been in Britain? Have attitudes to women's roles changed with the availability of modern amenities? And have attitudes to privacy changed, with the availability of separate rooms?

Purdah and the Front Room

Despite the very different physical layout, it is striking how considerations of purdah continue to be very important in almost all east Oxford Pakistani homes, as the arrival of visitors illustrates. If male visitors arrive and a male family member is at home, the visitors may first be detained at the door while the women of the household, modestly adjusting their *dupattā*s over their heads, leave the front room and retreat to the backroom or kitchen. As long as unrelated men are present, the women of the household will not usually enter the front room; instead, the men of the household will go or send children to the backroom or kitchen with requests for food and tea for the guests. Often the men of a family entertaining visitors carry the food or drinks from the kitchen to the front room; when, on occasion, the women do this, they do so without speaking to the male visitors. Men also use the front room to sit in with their friends, to discuss business matters or mosque affairs.

The front room also indicates status and wealth, like the *baithak* in Pakistan, for it is the room to which visitors are shown and which is shown to visitors. A typical front room is furnished with bright fitted carpets, wall-paper in a bold design, easy chairs or a sofa-set covered with vinyl or other shiny upholstery and decorated with hand embroidered cushions. It generally also contains a low coffee table and a large colour television set, which is, it seems, always switched on. Having a television used to be a local status symbol among friends and neighbours; nowadays, it is over having the latest video equipment that friends and neighbours compete. The television is likely to be showing one of the popular Indian or Pakistani films shown on the Asian movie channels or hired from one of several local video-hire shops or the city library. Framed pictures depicting the name or sayings of the Prophet Mohammed, embroidered, perhaps by the daughter of the household, in silver or gold sequins against a background of dark cloth, might decorate the walls. There may also pictures of pilgrims at the Ka'ba, the major shrine at Mecca, and brightly decorated calendars presented by local Pakistani shopkeepers as New Year publicity gifts. The mantelpiece usually displays a cluster of ornaments: a clock, vases of plastic flowers and other bric-a-brac, photographs of relatives in Pakistan, and children's school photographs. In a more lavishly furnished room, there might be expensive ornaments and lamps, a new living room suite, a display cabinet, a large colour television set plus video, and a carpet bought from Mecca hanging on the wall. The extent of elaboration reflects a family's income and their current priorities, but I have only met one family who did not have a front room for guests. They were living in one of the small cottages belonging to the paper mill at Sandford and let to paper mill employees. They apologized profusely for the fact that previous occupants had removed the central partition from their one downstairs room. The wife added that the house they had just bought in east Oxford had a front room, which she would decorate properly and keep locked for visitors, so that the children would not spoil it.

In Britain, the front room is called not the *baithak* but the 'front room'; given the constraints of British houses, it often has to double up as a family sitting room. It is only when male visitors come to the house and the women move from the front room to the backroom or kitchen that the front room temporarily becomes a *baithak*. Families who lived in small Victorian terraces in the 1980s but have moved to larger houses in the suburbs tend now to have a front room for visitors and a separate family sitting room, which is sometimes in a built-on extension or situated on the second floor, where an English visitor might expect a bedroom.

When a couple visit, the woman usually joins the women of the household in the backroom or kitchen, while her husband sits with the men in the front room. If the woman in the couple is English, or considered very 'westernized', she may be treated as an 'honorary male' and seated in the front room where she will meet the men of the household. Women arriving alone are entertained in the backroom or the kitchen, though an English woman might be seated in the front room where she may meet the men of the household.

As in Pakistan, people vary in how strict they are about purdah. The Pathan families and some Panjabi families whose family traditions, caste or religious status is associated with strict purdah remain quite rigorous about it for all but close relatives. But while most people adhere to the rules for occasional visitors who are relative strangers, they tend to regard close friends and neighbours who visit frequently as if they are brothers, sisters, uncles or aunts, addressing them with the words used for these relatives. Someone of approximately the same age is addressed as *bahin* (sister) or *bhaī* (brother) and someone older is addressed as *khālā* (mother's sister) or *chachā* (father's brother). This gives a degree of flexibility to social contacts between friends and neighbours who are not real kin, which extends to the ways in which domestic space is used. A woman who is separated from kin in Pakistan but who regards a Pakistani neighbour as her sister, and consequently all the members of her household as 'fictive kin', expands both the social and physical space in which she moves.

The Backroom and the Women's Area

Within the house too, physical space is used and adapted so as to maximize and extend the downstairs living and working area available to women. While the front room serves as a *baithak*, the 'backroom', as it is called, is the main family living area. Women sew, iron, supervise children reading the *Qur'ān*, entertain female visitors or watch television here, and children generally play, eat or watch television in this room. A typical backroom is furnished similarly to the front sitting room but less meticulously maintained, containing sofas or chairs, and a clock, ornaments, calendars, photographs and other bric-a-brac on the mantelpiece. There may also be an electric sewing machine, an electric iron and a sometimes a table for ironing or sewing.

Generally the backroom is a lower ground floor room, behind the front sitting room but apart from the kitchen. If the house is an old Victorian terrace with no separate backroom but a 'parlour', the latter becomes the backroom with an open doorway providing direct access to the kitchen. In a very large kitchen, the furnishings may be arranged so that the cooking facilities are at one end and a sofa, television, easy chairs and a table for all other daily activities, are the other. Many families have built a kitchen extension mainly for this purpose, an arrangement that often leaves an additional ground floor room free for use as a bedroom. If the kitchen is very small, but the family cannot afford an extension, a separate room at the back of the house may become the backroom during the day and serve as a bedroom, often for the wife and any young children, at night. If no such room is available, an additional ground floor room adjacent to the kitchen may be constructed as a temporary measure or primarily for use in the summer, by covering with a corrugated plastic roof part of the garden adjacent to the kitchen. The emphasis in all these arrangements is on extending and opening out the working space. In short, despite the different layout of British houses, purdah continues to be observed by using the front room as a *baithak*, and extending the backroom area as the main part of the house for the use of the women. These principles have continued to be important among those who lived in Victorian terraces in the 1980s but who have recently moved to larger houses in the suburbs.

Use of Amenities

The basic amenities in British houses such as running hot and cold water, a reliable electricity supply, cookers and refrigerators represent a considerable improvement over living standards in Pakistan, particularly in the early years of settlement. Most east Oxford Pakistani homes now also have such additional items as a television, telephone, electric sewing machine, and, since the 1980s, a video. Ten years ago, clothes washing machines, freezers and fitted kitchen units, which were considered not luxuries but necessities in many 'English' households, were usually absent in Pakistani homes, where kitchens and bathrooms were very simply equipped. Kitchen furniture usually comprised a sink unit, cooker, fridge, wooden table for chopping vegetables and one or two chests of drawers. Utensils included a plastic bowl for *chapātī* flour, a *chapātī* pan and metal saucepans for cooking. Only such foods as flour, pulses, *ghī*, onions, garlic, sugar, tea and some dried spices were stored in quantity. Just a few kitchens, belonging to wealthier or city-origin families, had modern kitchen units, clothes and dish washing machines, food mixers, freezers, microwaves and electric coffee grinders for grinding spices. One woman, from the city of Lahore in Pakistan, used an electric griddle based on the principle of a Canadian waffle pan for making *chapātī*s.

Such gadgets and 'luxury' items were generally given low priority because attitudes towards women's roles had not changed very much. Women pointed out that since they were not expected to take paid employment outside the home, it was only proper that they should manage the household as cheaply as possible and not waste money on electrical gadgets. Women's work was labour-intensive and time consuming. Most women prepared a fresh curry for each meal, rarely making large amounts to last for more than one day. They preferred to crush fresh spices for cooking using a pestle and mortar, rather than use powdered spices, saying that food prepared fresh for each meal by traditional methods and with fresh spices tastes better. Similarly, many women said that clothes washed by hand are cleaner than machine-washed clothes, which always smell dirty. Women would use the bath to wash clothes in. One woman took bedsheets, curtains and cushion covers to the launderette, but washed everything again by hand afterwards, because she felt the machine had not cleaned her laundry properly. Another woman's husband had bought her a second-hand washing machine, but it sat unused because she felt it did not clean the clothes well enough.

By 1988, however, the number of households with clothes washing machines had increased dramatically. In 1985, Sabiha, who had been in Oxford for eleven years and by then had six children, persuaded her husband to buy a machine for washing and drying clothes, which she has used almost daily since. Soon afterwards, her neighbour Fiaz bought one, and a few months after that one of Fiaz's friends bought one. Other women began planning to buy a washing machine when they could afford one, complaining of years of washing clothes by hand and the problems of drying them in Britain's cold, damp climate. Owning a washing machine was becoming an indication of status, like owning a television or video equipment. Today, most households have and use clothes washing machines, and may also have fitted kitchens, microwave ovens and freezers. Some have dishwashing machines and women nowadays debate not whether clothes washing machines clean clothes properly, but whether dishwashers clean dishes properly.

Likewise, bathrooms sport more fitted items, like shower units and bidets, than in the early 1980s when bathrooms, like kitchens, were equipped simply. Usually, in addition to a wash basin, flush toilet and bathtub, there was, and still is — to the puzzlement of English visitors — a bucket and a *lotā* or jug, or sometimes a shower hose in the bath. There is soap but not always towels, and toilet paper and bath plugs may be absent.

These provisions are related to the ablutions necessary before prayer, to pollution beliefs and to the customary practices that embody them. *Vūzū*, the minor ablution, has to be done before each of the five daily prayers (*namāz*) which are 'read' (this is the Urdu idiom; the prayers are usually recited from memory) at sunrise, noon, before sunset, after sunset and at night. *Vūzū* requires washing the hands, inside the mouth, the forehead and face, the arms (to the elbows) and the feet (to the ankles), in that order. If, between one *namāz* and the next, *vūzū* is not broken by a major or minor pollution, then the next *namāz* can be read without doing *vūzū* again, but it is generally considered better to do *vūzū* again before the next *namāz*.

Defaecation and urination are considered to be minor pollutions after which people use their left hand, pouring water from a *lotā* or jug, to clean themselves; they may use toilet paper for drying the area but not for cleaning. Sexual intercourse, menstruation and childbirth are major pollutions, which require a complete bath, called *ghusal*. *Ghusal* should be performed, before eating or praying, after intercourse has taken place, when the menstrual period stops and on the fortieth day after childbirth. First the genitals and anus should be washed and then the hands, with soap. Then *vūzū* is performed and then the *ghusal*, in which the whole body and all the hair should be washed in running water. People generally bathe by showering or standing or squatting in the bathtub using a jug or *lotā* to pour water over the body while the dirty water runs out. Muslims consider that the English habit of sitting in a tub of water does not clean the bather. If you do sit in a tub of water, then afterwards you must pour running water from a bucket or shower over your body to clean it.

Sleeping Arrangements

Just as in rural Pakistan where the whole family may sleep in one room, so too in many east Oxford homes family members may choose not have their own rooms but to all sleep in one bedroom. A bedroom may contain several beds, one or two of which might be double. Typically, a mother sleeps with a daughter or a young son, an elder sister sleeps with a younger one, brothers sleep together, and a father sleeps alone or perhaps with a son. Children of ten years of age or more have sometimes told me that they would be terrified to sleep alone in a room, like 'white' children.

At the same time, the constraints of the layout of the Victorian terrace, in which there is not one large room but two or three small bedrooms, have necessitated some adaptations to sleeping arrangements. Unlike in Pakistan, young couples living with the husband's parents and siblings usually have their own room and a double bed. In wealthier extended households they might also have their own bathroom. In these homes, a senior couple may have a separate room, or else a father sleeps in the same room as his unmarried sons and a mother sleeps in another room with her unmarried daughters. Yet these arrangements do not necessarily mean that the privacy of a married couple is now more highly valued. A couple may have a double bed, but may not sleep in it together; instead, a wife may sleep there with her children while the husband sleeps separately, and this arrangement may persist even when a couple and their children move to their own house.

Outsiders have occasionally remarked with shock that, 'Pakistani families are sometimes so hard up that the whole family has to sleep in one room'. There is some truth in this, but it is also the case that Pakistani parents and children often prefer to sleep in one room. Some women now see this as a distinct advantage, saying, 'our babies do not die from cot deaths because we do not put them in cots in separate rooms like the English. We sleep with our children'. Another advantage of these sleeping arrangements is that they free up rooms that can be let out to lodgers and this has been a source of extra income for many households. By the 1980s, three brothers, Farook, Gafoor, and Habib, and their brother-in-law, Ijaz, who had initially shared accommodation, were living in four separate houses with their wives and children and all let rooms to lodgers. Farook, who had five children, including a married daughter living locally, slept with two teenage sons in one room, his wife and two daughters slept in another room, and the family had one or two lodgers in the third bedroom. Gafoor and his wife slept in the ground-floor backroom, their three sons slept in the back bedroom, and the second bedroom was let to lodgers. Ijaz and his wife slept in one bedroom, his three boys in the second bedroom, his daughter in the backroom downstairs, and the third bedroom upstairs was let. Habib's whole family slept in the front bedroom, mother with daughter in one bed, two sons on a double bed, and father separately. This left two rooms free to let to lodgers. These sleeping arrangements were not made solely in order to let rooms to lodgers; rather, having rooms available to let coincided with the cultural preference for sharing rooms.

The lack of privacy typical of sleeping arrangements in the average household in rural Pakistan seemingly makes impossible any sexual intimacy without the whole household, or indeed most of the village, knowing of its occurrence. However, lack of privacy is certainly no excuse for childlessness. During my stay in Pakistan much concern was expressed that I had not become pregnant and it was kindly assumed that this was due to my husband's ignorance (we were but recently married at the time). When and where in Pakistan were couples supposed to procreate?

Women rarely discussed such matters openly. Several people told me that sexual encounters would either take place surreptitiously in the fields beyond the village or else furtively in the house while the rest of the household was thought to be sleeping or to be out, since it was unlikely that a married couple would have their own room for longer than the first few nights of marriage. In east Oxford, there have been some changes in attitudes towards sexuality with the influence of the western environment and the greater privacy made possible by the structure of British houses.

Houses and Property

The majority of east Oxford Pakistanis are house owners and many families own more than one property, for in Britain a new emphasis has been given to house ownership. Pakistani migrants were quick to realize that in Britain houses rather than land are most people's major investment, and, since the 1960s, property has for many Pakistanis become the main source of capital. Pakistanis use houses to generate income, by letting them to lodgers or by modernizing and then selling them, and property not used in these ways is kept as an investment and insurance for the future, sold only under force of circumstance. During the 1960s and 1970s, owning one house gave a man landlord status and a source of easily capitalized funds. Today, it is not having one or even two properties but having three or four that brings respect and recognition. The impetus towards investment in property is powerful indeed; property ownership is one of the few avenues to becoming wealthy open to Pakistani migrants. As Mahir said, 'We don't have families with money to fall back on; we've got to get established by our own efforts, and buying houses is the best way'. Property ownership has become perhaps the single most important dimension of the local socio-economic hierarchy; the most prosperous local landlord is reputed to own sixteen houses. Men do not have their own house or more than one house feel the sting of failure. Saeed, who bought his council house long after his friends had become property owners, lamented:

> I thought when I bought my house at least I had caught up with people, but now I realize that having one house is nothing. People keep saying to me 'why don't you buy another house; have one for the family and another for commercial use, or buy one on your son's name'. I don't really want to, it's such a lot of work and it's bad enough having one or two lodgers in your own house. But with one house, you're nothing. My mistake was not buying my own house earlier when they were cheap. I shouldn't have waited until my wife and children came to this country.

When Saeed first came to Britain he did not have brothers or sons with whom he could have pooled his income to buy a house; this is why he lags behind many of his contemporaries in the house-ownership stakes. Other men pooled resources — father with son, brother with cousin, and so on — to purchase a house, usually in the senior brother or father's name, and subsequent houses would be bought in the names of younger brothers or sons. Groups of kin with many houses purchased in the names of various family members usually began their investments early on, in the 1960s and early 1970s.

Families expanded their property investments, as sons born or brought up in Britain became wage earners. Zafar's household in 1986 owned two properties. The first was the three bedroomed house Zafar had bought in 1974 and in which he was living with his wife, his married son, daughter-in-law and their four children, his unmarried son and his two unmarried daughters. They purchased the second house in 1978, in Zafar's eldest son Arshad's name, soon after Arshad started full-time work at British Leyland. This second house, a few streets away from the first, stood empty for some years until Arshad's younger brother repaired and decorated it and let it to students. In 1987, Arshad paid off the mortgage on this house and secured a loan to buy another house into which the whole family moved, enabling the original house to be let. Meanwhile, his younger brother secured a full-time job and a mortgage on another house, which was let to students. These relatives continue to live in one house, but between them own four properties.

In another household, Riaz, the younger of two married brothers, bought a small terrace that he let to students when he first started full-time work. Later, he bought a house in Birmingham, when he moved there for work, and let this house to lodgers when he returned to Oxford to live with his parents. A year after this, Riaz's elder brother moved out, with his wife and family, to a house that his father had bought earlier to rent out and had transferred to his elder son. Riaz then moved out with his wife and children to the first house he had bought, renting to students the original parental house, which was held in Riaz's name. This move made Riaz's parents officially homeless and they are now housed in a council property. Other Pakistanis have criticized Riaz and his parents behind their backs, saying that since the parents and sons own four properties between them, the parents could be living in one of the houses rented to students. They see the move into council accommodation as a means of gaining another property. 'They're just after another house', said one critic, 'you will see, in a few years' time they will have bought it'. In this view, in recognition of what parents do for children, adult sons should accommodate and care for elderly parents, and many elderly parents do in fact 'rotate' their residence between the homes of two or more married sons. The fact that Riaz has 'turned his parents over to the council', shows that 'something else is going on', another critic said. Here, the value placed upon caring for parents is at odds with the desire to accumulate property. The council, however, views applicants for council housing individually, not as part of a collectivity; from this perspective the homeless parents, with no property to their name, are perfectly entitled to council accommodation, with the rights to eventual purchase that go with it.

Viewed from the outside, the case of Riaz's family suggests that obligations towards parents, which are part of the ideology of the joint family, have been replaced by individualistic motives on the part of the sons, and that elderly parents are the casualties of this process. On the other hand, as the critics' comments suggest, Pakistanis may also view these moves as strategies that further their interest in property, strategies in which the council's housing department is an unknowing accomplice. Such moves can therefore still be interpreted within the framework of migrants' original intentions.

In recent years, Oxford Pakistanis have told me stories of Pakistani neighbours who have applied for council accommodation, despite the fact that they have sons who could accommodate them. They describe these strategies as tricks, to obtain and eventually purchase a council house. Here is one such account:

> Sharif's family jointly owns three properties. They let two of them and live in one. Then suddenly they are moved to a council house, all except Hanif. The story is that Hanif (the married son) had 'become too violent'. But they made it up. First, Hanif's wife goes to the social services, showing her bruises. Then a few months later, she goes again, with another story of beating. Then it happens again, and this time she says Hanif has kicked them out, and they are given homeless family accommodation. By now there is a record of abuse. So when she claims for a council house she is given priority, so that she can escape her battering husband. Then several months later, Hanif is seen at the council house and there is a big reconciliation. By now, the family house is let, and they will eventually buy the council house.

Extra income from rented property allows further investment in property or in business. This, locally, is the principal route to socio-economic success, competitively followed. Malik, a widower living with his two married sons and their wives and children, bought a second house in the younger son's name and let it to students. Both sons were in full-time employment, and the family was not dependent on the income from this second house, so they used it towards buying a restaurant which one son now manages. Since then they have bought two more houses, both of which are let to students. Property-ownership also allows a house to be purchased or registered in a daughter's name so that she can demonstrate to the Home Office her ability to support a spouse from Pakistan without state assistance; later, the property may revert to the formal control of the girl's father or brothers. Strategies such as these, facilitated by the fact that in Oxford there is a large student population and a continual demand for rented accommodation, have made several Pakistani landlords reputedly very wealthy.

Family Relationships

To a large extent, these property-management strategies and business ventures are dependent upon the co-operation of relatives. The ideals governing relationships between family members, generally expressed by all, but sometimes challenged by younger generations, include a formal hierarchy within which each person has a clearly defined role, determined by age and sex, in relation to other family members. Women are formally subordinate to men but male and female worlds are largely separate and have their own hierarchical structures. Among men, authority lies with the eldest male and each junior male defers to his elder brother and his father. Communication between men is formal and men are not supposed to smoke, talk freely or joke in the presence of their older brothers or father; they should always be respectful and deferential.

Usually, in Pakistan, the male head of the household — the father or the eldest brother — decides where a son or younger brother will live and work. A man who is sent abroad or to the city is expected to remit money home and feels bound by this obligation; the family may be depending on it. The household head also makes the formal decision about when and to whom a man should be married and after the marriage decides whether the wife of a man who is working in the city or abroad should remain at her in-laws or join her husband. Often the bride stays at her in-laws with periodic visits to her own parents, joining her husband only if the family so decides.

Relationships between women are less formal than between men, but among women too there is a hierarchy of age and status. Older women have authority over younger women. A younger sister must treat an elder sister with deference; a new bride in a household must defer to the authority of her mother-in-law and, if her husband has elder brothers, to her husband's elder brothers' wives. Women sometimes say that the personality of the mother-in-law is more important in marriage than what the husband is like, for she will influence her son's attitude to his wife. A daughter-in-law must also defer to her husband, his elder brothers and her father-in-law. It is only with her husband's younger brother that she has a freer relationship, because they have a more equal status.

Since male and female worlds are separate, a husband and wife do not generally spend much time in each other's company. Their relationship is not expected to be one of close companionship, at least not in the early years, and even other family members will not see public displays of affection. In contrast to the ideals of the western system, marriage is not regarded as, or expected to be, a person's primary emotional investment; often an individual's ties with parents, brothers, sisters and children are more important. In a conflict with her mother-in-law, a woman may be more likely to turn to her mother or siblings for moral support than to her husband, and he may be more likely to side with his mother than with his wife.

The fact that within the family each member has a clearly defined role according to age and sex means that there is relatively limited scope for following individual inclinations and initiatives. A woman does not have a choice in her roles as daughter, wife, mother and later, mother-in-law; similarly a man must act within the definitions of his role as son, husband and father. Sometimes unavoidable obligations are deeply resented, but the sense of purpose and identity that these ideals provide, the value given to respecting one parents and elders and pressure not to 'lose face' within the *birādarī* in most cases prevents individuals from rejecting their roles entirely. Individuals can become very successful at their allocated careers within the family, gaining authority, respect and influence over the years. A woman who begins her married life under her mother-in-law's authority can gradually acquire a major role in managing the household, influencing the men around her and making decisions about her own children's marriages.

There are, inevitably, tensions within these constraints. Individual desires and inclinations may conflict with family obligations, and youngsters schooled in Britain may deeply and acutely resent these obligations to kin. For 'westerners', the resentments and frustrations within Pakistani households are generally easier to understand, perhaps because they are expected, that the forces which hold families together. Some of the tensions within British Pakistani families are of course not always or simply a response to the influences of the individual-istic western environment, but are inherent within the joint family structure, while others are a feature of the changing dynamics of family structure in Pakistan. Some aspects of the British environment do present a stark contrast between the ideas of a 'western' and an 'eastern' family system. The flexibil-ity of and the continuities in family structure and relationships in the British environment are, however, equally striking. A young man with professional qualifications may be potentially independent of his parents, but will usually make the decision about where to apply for work in negotiation with his parents and seek their approval.

Another feature of the collective nature of the domestic unit is the fact that within the family biological relationships are often played down. A mother-in-law may have more influence over how her grandchildren are brought up than their mother may have. Children may refer to both their biological mother and their father's mother as 'mother' (*ammī*), sometimes saying 'I have two mothers'. In large households, it may be difficult to tell exactly whose child is which, or whether siblings are 'real' brothers and sisters or first cousins. Cousins will generally refer to each other as brother (*bhaī*) or sister (*bahin*). In Urdu and Panjabi your cousin is your 'aunt (or uncle)-born sister (or brother)' and separate terms denote which aunt or uncle; for example, mother's brother, or father's older brother, etc.; there are no single words for 'aunt', 'uncle' or 'cousin'. In England, adapting the English word cousin to Urdu usage, children sometimes say 'he's my cousin-brother'.

Household Composition in Pakistan

Most people in the villages I visited had other close relatives —
brothers, sisters, cousins, aunts and uncles — living nearby,
with whom they had almost daily contact, as well as close kin
living abroad. Nazir and Noori were a middle-aged married
couple living in a village in Attock district in north-west
Panjab. Although their sons were in the Middle East and a
daughter was in Oxford, Noori's two sisters and their husbands
(Nazir's father's brother's sons) and their married and unmarried children, as well as many other first and second cousins
and more distant relatives, were living nearby in the village. In
fact, Nazir and Noori could (in theory) show that all the
members of their particular caste in the village were related to
them, because they were the descendants of an ancestor who
settled in the village eight generations ago. In total, their
relatives numbered about one thousand people, one third of the
village's population.

Similarly, Bashira, an elderly widow in a village in Jhelum
district, whose daughter was living in Oxford, had close and
distant relatives living nearby. These kin together comprised
approximately one fifth of the population of the village in
which Bashira's relatives had lived for generations. Of these
kin, Bashira had most contact with her cousins and her eldest
brother and his sons and daughters. She also had an only
sister in an adjacent village and they visited each other from
time to time.

Families whose senior members were refugees from India at
Partition in 1947 often had many *birādarī* members living locally,
despite losing many relatives at Partition. Gulshan, an elderly
widow with three sons in Oxford, told me that she had far fewer
relatives in her village in Faisalabad district than she had in her
village in Jullunder before Partition: her relatives had been
separated from one another and many died in the move to
Pakistan in 1947. Yet she regarded all the other Arain families in
her village in Faisalabad as *birādarī*, because they were of the
same caste. She also had daily contact with close and more distant
relatives, with whom she had known genealogical links. She lives
with one married son, who farms the family land, her now
widowed brother lives in the house opposite, and her deceased
husband's brother lives in the house next to that.

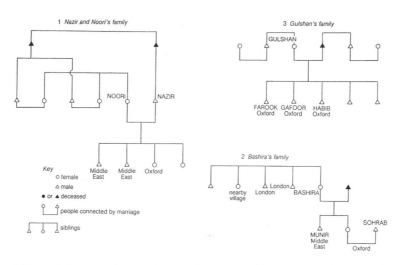

Figure 3.4   Partial genealogies of Nazir and Noori's, Bashira's and Gulshan's families.

While proximity to kin is a feature of village life, at the same time migration abroad or to the cities has been so prevalent in rural Panjab that in some areas it would be hard to find an extended family all living in one place. All three of the families mentioned above (Figure 3.4) had relatives abroad when I visited them, and this is still the case although some of the details of the personnel have changed. Nazir and Noori had two married sons who were living with their wives and children in the Middle East and a married daughter in Oxford. Bashira's only son was in the Middle East and her married daughter was in Oxford. Gulshan's three elder sons were living with their wives and children in Oxford, and a fifth son was in Karachi. Divided households like these are quite typical of the areas of the Panjab from which people have migrated for work; nor is this a recent phenomenon, as there is a long history of migration from these areas.

Even when a family is widely dispersed, family obligations ensure that the remaining unit very often functions rather as if all of its members were within the neighbourhood. Absent members of Nazir and Noori's, Bashira's and Gulshan's households maintained strong links with their family in the village. Those who remained in the village, usually wives or parents, were to some extent dependent on remittances from wage-earning sons and husbands in the cities or abroad. Remittances might meet wedding expenses, or send an elderly parent on *hajj* (the pilgrimage to Mecca), or enable the family to build a *pakkā* house or start a business. Migrants in the cities or abroad visited home when they could, especially for a wedding or if a close relative was seriously ill or dying. Sometimes, the wife of a man living in the city or abroad would return for quite lengthy periods with her children to live in her in-law's house or to her own parents' home. Relatives who remained in the village, such as parents or a widowed mother, would also sometimes visit their sons or daughters living in the cities or abroad, perhaps staying for several months at a time, and living in each of their married sons' households in turn.

Nazir had lived in the Middle East with his wife Noori and their children for twelve years. On retirement, he returned to the village where he built a large *pakkā* house with a separate *baithak*, while his sons, by then both married, remained in the Middle East and continued to send money to him. The sons' remittances enabled their younger sister to complete her education at a girls' college in the city, and recently the elder son sent money for Nazir to buy a tractor to be used on the family land and hired out to people in the village and surrounding villages. In 1981, the elder brother's wife returned with two of her children to stay for several months with her in-laws and attend her brother's wedding. Nazir and Noori's elder daughter spent six months with her brothers and their wives in the Middle East, before marrying and coming to Oxford in 1979. By 1988, she had returned to her parents in the village for two three-month visits. Since then, she has returned four more times, once for a wedding.

Bashira, whose son was in the Middle East, had two brothers in London and a married daughter in Oxford. Her son and her brothers had all sent money for her to build a new *pakkā* house adjacent to her former *kachchā* (mud) one. Her son-in-law in England, Sohrab, also assisted her when her son Munir got married in 1969; Sohrab sent her £2,000 for the bride's wedding expenses. He did this considering himself to be the bride's brother, although she was in fact his mother's sister's daughter, because she was an only child whose parents had died. The wedding was performed with such pomp and expense that in 1981 people still related past events in the village to the year of this wedding. Afterwards, Munir went to the Middle East, but his wife has remained living with Bashira. Sohrab has also kept links with Bashira. His wife and daughters joined him in England in the 1970s, but within a year he had sent his two eldest daughters back to Pakistan for their maternal grandmother to give them a 'proper Muslim upbringing', so that 'they would not be influenced by how English women behave'. The girls stayed there for five years, during which Sohrab sent money for their maintenance. Since their return to England, they have not been back to Pakistan, though they were married to first cousins from Pakistan who came to England in the early 1980s. In 1986, Bashira came to England to visit her relatives. She spent six months divided between her brothers in London and her daughter and son-in-law in Oxford before going to Mecca on *hajj*, and her relatives in England financed her trip.

Gulshan and her eldest son Farook decided that the three elder sons, Farook, Gafoor and Habib, should go to England. The money they sent home was used to build a large *pakkā* house, to purchase fifty acres of land which the fourth son farms, and to establish the youngest, the fifth son, in a taxi business in Karachi. Gulshan keeps close links with her absent sons. When, in 1981, news reached her that her youngest son was squandering money in Karachi, she set off alone for the city. She returned several months later with the errant son, who then joined his brother in farming the land. Farook, Gafoor and Habib jointly paid for their mother to visit them in England, where she stayed with each son and his family for about two months, and then to go on *hajj*. By 1988, all three wives of the brothers in England had returned twice to the village, taking some of their children with them, to visit both their mother-in-law and their own parents. Habiba returned again in 1993 when her mother was dying. Since his wife's death, Habiba's now elderly father has made two lengthy visits to England, to Oxford to visit Habiba and to Lancashire to visit his son, and has gone on *hajj*.

Household Composition in Britain

Families in Oxford are therefore best seen as outposts of families in Pakistan whose members have been dispersed by labour migration. Since the arrival of women and children in Britain, the extent of remittances to and investment in Pakistan has become increasingly variable, with many families sending proportionately less money home than in the early years of settlement. Yet, even thirty years on, links with 'home' remain strong. Many people still support at least some relatives in Pakistan, and most people make return trips if a close relative is ill or dying, or for the wedding of relatives or close friends. They may also finance elderly relatives to visit Britain and go on *hajj*.

Continuing links with relatives in Pakistan are strikingly demonstrated in the custom of burying the dead in Pakistani village cemeteries. To date, very few Pakistanis have been buried in the Muslim cemetery in Oxford and these are mostly children or mothers with children in Britain. Usually the body of a deceased person is flown back to Pakistan. It can cost more than £800 to repatriate a corpse, because the body must be transported to the airport, flown to Pakistan and then taken to the village. Initially, donations from relatives and friends were used to cover these costs, which in 1980 these were formalized as subscriptions to the Oxford Muslim funeral committee. Today, a £10 subscription collected from all members provides a form of insurance for funeral and repatriation expenses. The expenses include the costs of the funeral rites — of washing the corpse, buying a coffin, and bringing the corpse to be viewed by bereaved kin in Oxford — before taking it to the airport. Why should Pakistanis go to this trouble and expense for the dead?

Pakistanis say it is important for the deceased's closest relatives to see the body. They also say that the deceased will gain more *sawāb* (religious merit) from a village burial than from being buried in Oxford, because *sawāb* accrues when relatives visiting the cemetery pray for the deceased; few Pakistanis visit the Oxford cemetery because few Pakistanis have been buried there. The custom also provides a concrete symbol of the importance of kinship. In many Panjabi as well as Mirpuri villages, 'each *birādarī* has its own carefully tended graveyard, in which everyone gradually reassembles after death...the graveyard itself not only provides a strong physical expression of the *birādarī*'s corporate character, but gives it a very strong sense of rootedness'[4].

Household composition and patterns of household organization in Oxford reflect both the history of migration and settlement in the city and these continuing connections with kin in Pakistan. The spacing of children's births often reflects the migration pattern, with a few children born in Pakistan prior to a man's migration, a gap of several years while the father was in Britain, and a 'second' family started once the wife arrived in Britain. In the early 1980s, my survey of 130 east Oxford households showed there were only a few households in which men were still waiting to be joined by wives and children. Eighty seven households (67%) were 'nuclear', comprising a man, his wife and their children, and 22 households (14.8%) were 'joint', containing two or more married couples, usually parents and married son or sons, and sometimes two brothers and their wives[5]. Since then, wives and children have joined 'single' men, some nuclear households have expanded to become joint ones, in a process which has accelerated over the past decade as sons and in some cases daughters have been married and been joined by spouses, (usually close kin from Pakistan; see chapter 5), and some joint households have divided as the families of married sons have grown and dispersed. As a result, a distinctive pattern of living near close kin has emerged, echoing that of earlier migrations within the Indian subcontinent.

A majority of Oxford Pakistanis now have a number of close relatives living nearby. To some extent, this pattern reflects divisions that are expected over the life cycle of a joint family. A large parental household may divide following the parents' deaths or after a second son gets married and household space becomes limited. In several cases where two married sons and their families were living with their parents, one son and his wife and children have now moved out into a separate house, and the mother-in-law divides her time between the two houses, staying with each daughter-in-law in turn.

Division of a household in this way is, however, unlikely when a junior couple is newly married and their children are very young. A family who feels that it is becoming too large for a Victorian terrace may consider dividing into separate households, but there are pressures against this happening. It is generally considered shameful for a man and his wife to move out of his parents' household soon after marriage. The implication is the son, by leaving his parents to manage on their own, does not care for or respect his parents; this, in turn, reflects on the family's *izzat* in the eyes of others. Moreover, even when the junior couple has been married for some years and their children are growing up and household space is limited, many families prefer to remain living together.

Rather than splitting up, such families will try to buy a larger house or extend existing household space to accommodate everyone. One household of ten people tried to buy a plot of land next to their own house, intending to demolish the wall between the properties and extend the original house, so that they would have more space when the younger son marries. They were unsuccessful, but several other families have bought the house next door and by occupying both houses continue to live jointly. Manzoor bought the house next door for his daughters when they were married in 1979 to two cousins, who are brothers, from Pakistan. For more than ten years, the daughters and their husbands lived next door to their parents and two married brothers, their wives, children and several unmarried siblings. As pressure on domestic space in the parental household increased, the married daughters eventually each moved out, with their husbands and children, into council accommodation. One married brother with his wife and children moved into the vacated house while the other brother and his family remained in the parental household. Despite living separately, the married daughters return to their parents' house almost daily, usually eating the midday meal there together. In another case, a divorced woman lives next door to her parents; her unmarried sisters divide their time between the two houses and that of a married sister who lives a few doors away. Another household, consisting of parents, two married sons and their wives and the unmarried children of all three couples, in 1986 bought the house next door. Since then, two daughters have married and eventually moved out to their own homes while the parents and their married sons have remained as a commensal unit, though occupying two separate houses.

Kin may also live near one another not because a parental household has divided but because brother or cousins who initially lived together subsequently moved into their own houses when their wives and children joined them. For example, Farook, Gafoor and Habib, Gulshan's sons in Oxford, who now head three separate households, had lived jointly, together with their brother-in-law Ijaz, during the 1960s, but gradually established separate households:

Farook, Ijaz and Gafoor bought a house in south Oxford in 1963, were joined by Habib in 1964 and then by their wives. Farook's wife arrived first with her two children; then Ijaz's and Habib's wives, both then childless, and Gafoor's wife, with her one daughter, joined them in 1970. At this time Gafoor was employed at a cement factory but the other three men were working at British Leyland. One year later, however, the household began to split, with Gafoor and his family moving out to their own home in 1971. This was because the house was becoming too small for four couples whose families were increasing and also because of disagreements over money that had arisen during the year. At first each brother had handed his wage packet to Farook, who gave his wife, as the most senior woman in the house, an allowance for household expenses and saved the rest in a joint account. However, Gafoor wanted to save separately towards his own house, so each man agreed to contribute a share towards household expenses and make his own savings. Gafoor's wife and Habib's wife both felt that Farook's wife was appropriating housekeeping money and favouring her own children and Ijaz's (her brother's) daughter. After several arguments, they began cooking separately and their husbands started handing housekeeping money to their own wives rather than to Farook's wife. Then an accident occurred just before Gafoor's wife's second child was born which triggered the break-up of the household. Gafoor's daughter wandered out to the river Thames where she drowned, and Farook's wife was accused of leaving the front garden gate open knowing that the child would wander out. Soon after this, Gafoor and his wife bought and moved out to their own house. Then in 1972 Farook decided to sell the house and start a cloth business with Ijaz. They bought a shop and moved with their families into the flat above it, while Habib took his share of the house proceeds and bought his own house.

Both competition and co-operation have continued to characterize relationships within this kinship group. In the 1970s, Farook and Ijaz continued to run the cloth shop, expanding into groceries, but Habib joined them on a part-time basis in 1981 while continuing to work at British Leyland on night shifts. A year later he took voluntary redundancy to work in the shop full-time. In 1983 Farook and Ijaz each took their own shares of the business and set up shops elsewhere, while Habib was joined by Gafoor, who had left his job at the cement factory, in managing the first shop.

By the early 1980s, when the eldest of the children, Farook's daughter, was married, these relatives comprised five separate households — the households of three brothers, a brother-in-law and a married daughter (Figure 3.5). Fifteen years later, they all have moved to larger houses: Gafoor, Habib, and Farook's daughter to the Cowley suburb, Ijaz and Farook to a town nearby. The five 'original' households have all become larger, as married children have had their own children, and household

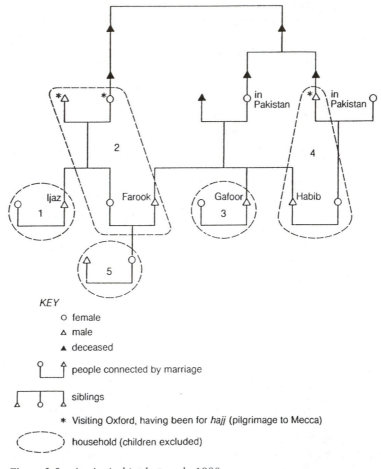

KEY

○ female

△ male

▲ deceased

people connected by marriage

siblings

* Visiting Oxford, having been for *hajj* (pilgrimage to Mecca)

household (children excluded)

Figure 3.5   An Arain *birādarī*, early 1980s.

space has been adapted accordingly: Farook's joint household includes two married sons and their wives, one of whom is Ijaz's daughter. A third married son lives separately, in London. Ijaz's joint household includes three daughters-in-law. Two of Farook's daughters are married locally: his eldest daughter, Zarina, lives in a separate household which now includes Zarina's married son and his wife, who is his father's sister's daughter (Zarina's husband's sister's daughter). Farook's other daughter, married to her Zarina's husband's brother, also lives locally. Gafoor's joint household includes two married sons, one with his wife, the other awaiting his wife's arrival from Pakistan; a third son and his wife live separately. Gafoor's daughter married Habib's elder son and moved to Habib's household, until the household divided. Habib's household contains two 'junior' married couples: Habib's younger son and his wife, and Habib's daughter and her husband, who is Gafoor's second wife's brother, from Pakistan. Some of these relationships, and eight of the nine households in this *birādarī*, are shown in Figure 5.4. There are other local *birādarī*s more extensive than Farook's — *birādarī*s which a decade ago comprised more than ten households (in one case the households of five brothers, one sister, and three married sons and one married daughter); these, too, have all expanded over the years.

Living in a joint household confers a number of socio-economic advantages. In the early 1980s, Zafar's pension and his son's factory wage, supplemented by income from rented property, supported twelve people — two couples with eight children between them — and enabled Zafar and his wife to go on *hajj* and the elder son and his wife to make return trips to Pakistan. Joint living also provides additional social and economic security for a man who is unemployed. Hussain, for instance, and his wife and children lived rent-free in his employed brother's house until he found work and eventually set up his own household. When Gafoor and Habib's business eventually failed, Habib became a taxi driver, Gafoor retired, his son found a job in a hardware store, but Habib's son, who has remained unemployed, helps his wife and sister with their *samosā* business. Joint living may also facilitate business enterprise. Habib's daughter and daughter-in-law, cousins brought up in Oxford, manage the *samosā* business, delivering *samosā*s to local shops and restaurants, while their sisters-in-law, who have come from Pakistan for marriage, have poor English and do not drive, cook the *samosā*s. Habib's new house has been extended and contains a purpose-built *samosā* kitchen, separate bedrooms bathrooms for the married couples, two large sitting rooms downstairs and a more private family sitting room upstairs, though the kitchen and cooking is shared. Like other families, they have kept their first east Oxford house, letting it to students to earn extra income. Like many families, they still send some savings to Pakistan, mainly to support elderly relatives or send them on *hajj*, or else use savings to invest in business or property in Britain and in Pakistan, or to pay for wedding expenses or trips to Pakistan.

The fear of racist attacks has also discouraged some families from dividing. Several racist incidents have occurred over the years, some in east Oxford, but more in the council estates beyond the area in east Oxford where most Pakistanis live. When Saeed's wife and children first joined him from Pakistan they were homeless and housed by the council in a property with a leaking roof in Oxford. Eventually they were moved to a better house on a council estate, but a few months later Saeed applied to be moved back into the east Oxford area because neighbours had broken several windows and hurled racist abuse which had terrified his wife. In another incident in the early 1980s, a shop owner moved back to the east Oxford area after experiencing attacks on his home in Headington; news of the attacks reached his close kin in Pakistan who phoned regularly to try to persuade him to return there.

Such incidents may discourage large households from dividing, because moving house often means moving out of the east Oxford area. Zafar's son Yacoub and his wife Yasmin discussed the possibility of moving out to the family's second property, a house let to students just outside the central east Oxford area, on and off for nine years. In the early 1980s, after being strongly advised to move out by a health visitor anxious about there being eleven people in the house, Yasmin, who had then but recently arrived from Pakistan, said:

> I could not leave my mother-in-law, not now that her health is bad and I would miss Yacoub's sisters. And I need their help with my children, especially now that there is the baby as well. I don't speak enough English to

manage alone, and Yacoub often isn't at home and works on night shifts every two weeks. And there are only three houses of our own people on that street. I would be frightened; you know what can happen if you move away from your Pakistani neighbours.

Yasmin's views also reflect this household's stage in the life-cycle of a joint family. Yasmin's mother-in-law was opposed to her daughter-in-law and eldest son moving out. She spoke of her fears of being left in the house with her retired husband and her unmarried daughters without her eldest son to turn to, her daughter-in-law to help with the housework, and the grandchildren to brighten her days. Yacoub, Yasmin's husband, was also unwilling to move; he did not want the responsibility of running a separate household and said it would be unfair to leave his parents on their own.

In fact, rather than dividing, the family bought a third, larger property in the mid-1980s and all moved into it, letting the previous house. They expected then that the household might divide once Yacoub's younger brother was married, but even then the ideal arrangement would be to buy the house next door and continue to live jointly, as several other families have done. When Yacoub's younger son was married, the three couples continued to live in one household for a few years, but conflict between the younger son and the elder son's wife and between the two daughters-in-law eventually resulted in both sons establishing separate households and the parents moving into council accommodation. That at least one son eventually establishes a separate household is a usual development in the life cycle of the joint family. However, when parents have moved into council accommodation, other Pakistanis have been critical, saying that the sons should have continued to look after their parents by living jointly, and that the move into council accommodation is but another strategy for acquiring property. In this case, Yacoub and his wife also had to confront their anxieties about racist attacks because they were initially housed by the council outside the 'Pakistani area' of east Oxford, though have since been re-housed within it.

Divisions of a large household into smaller household units have coincided in recent years with the residential shift towards the suburbs, for in some cases, young married couples have moved to the suburbs. Sometimes a daughter's parents have encouraged her to apply for a council house, even when she may be unwilling to move from east Oxford, so that she can demonstrate to the Home Office that she can support and accommodate a spouse from Pakistan. Some well-established joint families have moved to larger, better properties, adapting the interior or building extensions to accommodate several couples and their children, while renting their east Oxford houses to students.

Conclusion

Viewed from the perspective of migrants' villages of origin, there are some striking continuities between life in Pakistan and the ways in which Pakistanis have adapted and used domestic space in Britain. Investment in property and other businesses and a gradual upgrading of lifestyles over the past twenty years suggests a greater commitment to remaining in Britain and a loosening of ties with Pakistan. Yet socio-economic and emotional ties with kin in Pakistan remain. Most migrants have invested in their villages of origin in various ways, while some have also invested in new houses in the cities, building in many of the comforts of modern living. Most families maintain close social ties with relatives in Pakistan, usually returning periodically for a few months and sometimes staying for up to several years at a time.

Changes in domestic roles and living standards in Britain have also brought modifications to relationships between family members and to domestic roles. Some women go out to work, on a full- or part-time basis and many women now use domestic appliances such as clothes washing machines and freezers to store prepared food, amenities that were absent in the early 1980s. Young married couples may live separately from the boy or girl's parents and enjoy more independence and privacy than they would have had within their parental household. These changes could easily be interpreted as evidence of increasing individualism and indeed gossip, criticism and censure often follow where values of joint living and co-operation appear to have been violated. But these changes can also be viewed as creative socio-economic strategies that take advantage of local socio-economic opportunities, utilizing the diverse social and cultural resources of all members of the

family. As such, they represent adaptations to, and accommo-
dations from, the new environment, rather than a fundamental
weakening of local kinship ties. As the next two chapters show,
birādarī interests continue to cross not only local but also
national boundaries.

During the early years of Pakistani settlement in Oxford,
migrants were primarily concerned with sending money to
Pakistan. Now that most families have been united in Britain and
have relatives and fellow villagers living locally, they are also
concerned with socio-economic success and status in relation to
the local South Asian socio-economic hierarchy. In this context,
the criteria of success include the extent of property and business
ownership, the size of one's house and the decoration of its front
room. The most successful families in this respect are those with
several wage-earning sons or brothers who have pooled resources
and made strategic property investments. However, achievement
of socio-economic status in Britain and in Pakistan is of course
not mutually exclusive; the most successful Oxford property
dealers also have business investments in Pakistan, or have built a
new house in the city there. Status in Oxford is thus a complex
interplay of factors from both status arenas, expressed and
explored in marriage strategies and in the distinctive forms of
social activity that are discussed in the following chapters.

NOTES

1. I discuss the much-debated issue of caste among Muslims in the Indian
    sub-continent in chapter 5.
2. Ballard, 1990. Imran and Smith (1997) give a vivid photographic and oral
    history of Mirpur.
3. There is an extensive literature on purdah in the Indian subcontinent. See,
    for instance, Jeffery, 1979 and Vreede de Stuers, 1968.
4. Ballard, 1990.
5. Shaw, 1988:181–183.

4 THE IDIOM OF CASTE

Oxford Pakistanis may identify themselves and others in relation to their village or region of origin in Pakistan. This regional classification is also in effect a map of social distance, in that friends and acquaintances tend to be drawn, initially at least, from the same village or region of origin. Cutting across this social map, however, is another classification based on categories called *zāt*s or *qaum*s. Sometimes these terms are used interchangeably. My impression, though, is that people from the North West Frontier are more likely to use the word *qaum*, whereas Panjabis, particularly the Faisalabadis who were or whose parents were refugees in 1947 from Jullundhur which is now in India, are more likely to use the word *zāt* or *jat*. What exactly *qaum* refers to in the Pakistani context is much debated; it may be translated as tribe, race, family, people or nation[1]. Other groups, such as those of the Faisalabadis who were refugees in 1947 from Jullundhur, which is now in India, use the term *zāt* (or *jati*). *Zāt* is very often translated as caste and has more specifically Hindu connotations, yet it meaning in Pakistani usage is far from clear.

Oxford Pakistanis may deny that 'caste' is important, or shrug it off as an irrelevancy, a hangover from the past, asserting instead the Islamic ideology of equality. However, beyond the *ghar* (household), which may comprise two or three generations divided between more than one house, they do see themselves as belonging to distinctive kinship groups, variously referred to as *khāndān*, family (in the wide sense of the English term), or the *birādarī* (extended kinship group). The *khāndān* and the *birādarī* are thought of as being part of larger categories, those of the *qaum* or *zāt*, and these categories have names that denote castes in Pakistan and northern India. A *zāt* or *qaum* name is not always easily identified, as it is not necessarily a 'family' name or a 'surname'. In fact, traditionally, there is no system of surnames in Pakistani Muslim society (or indeed in other South Asian groups in the Indian subcontinent). A woman does not take her husband's second name on marriage and become Mrs X, but retains the name she was given at birth and a father's second name is not automatically passed on to his children. Sometimes a son receives his father's second name, but this is a matter of personal choice rather than of family policy. However, to avoid the confusion in, for instance, medical records that sometimes arises from members of the same Pakistani (or other south Asian) family having different names, British Pakistanis do increasingly use a 'family name' as a surname. This family name may be that of the wider *birādarī*, *zāt* or *qaum* and therefore reveal a 'caste' identity that suggests a particular family heritage.

Whether it is appropriate to talk about Pakistani *zāt*s, *qaum*s or 'families' as castes is indeed problematic. Sometimes Oxford Pakistanis use the English word castes when speaking in English. For example, when discussing her identity, one young woman told me, 'I am an Arain; that is my castes. Others feel that the English word castes carries the wrong connotations, for caste is generally associated with Hindus. There are, I am told, some Oxford Pakistanis who read the previous edition of this book and objected to the fact that I mentioned castes at all. I found the question of caste among Pakistani Muslims extremely confusing. What, if anything, does this contested idea of caste mean in practice? In what situations does membership of a named *khāndān*, *birādarī*, *qaum* or *zāt* matter? Or is castes merely an atavistic trait?

I had hoped the academic literature on caste among Muslims in the Indian subcontinent would help me, but here too the question of Muslim castes has generated considerable debate. Hamza Alavi, in paper on kinship in a village in Sahiwal district in Pakistan, asserts that 'there is no hierarchy of castes' and that kinship rather than considerations of caste status influence choice of spouse in marriage[2]. In a similar vein, Saghir Ahmad argues that class, not caste, is the significant principle of social stratification in the Panjab in Pakistan[3]. On the other hand, Imtiaz Ahmad asserts that there are social categories very similar to Hindu castes in Muslim villages in India. Caste status is inherited, ideally marriage takes place endogamously (within the caste), caste is traditionally associated with a hereditary occupation and lifestyle and caste categories are hierarchically ranked[4]. In more recent work on Pakistanis, Michael Fischer notes the importance of *zāt*, 'a hereditary non-corporate category often translated as caste' in marriages contracted in a new urban community in Lahore, and Pnina Werbner tabulates 'The Pakistani Caste (*zāt*) Hierarchy in Manchester'[5].

While there is no consensus concerning the significance of caste in Hindu society, one characteristic of caste is that it implies ranking, and the issue then is what justifies this ranking. In Dumont's comprehensive analysis what characterizes the Hindu caste system is the way in which religious belief sanctions hierarchy, for priority is given to status over power, to sacred over secular, and purity over impurity: the ritually pure are at the top of the system[6]. There is no such justification for caste in Islam. Nor, as I show below, is there any single overarching principle, such as purity or occupation, which governs a hierarchy of Muslim castes. Caste distinctions are trivial in most aspects of the lives of Oxford Pakistanis, for they do not much affect participation in domestic rituals, eating together, sharing religious worship or economic transactions, and most Oxford Pakistanis do not, or do no longer, follow the occupations traditionally associated with particular caste statuses.

At the same time, however, castes identities did seem to have some importance, for Oxford Pakistanis sometimes spontaneously told me the names of their *khāndān*, *birādarī*, *zāt* or *qaum*, and sometimes gave this information when I asked directly about family names. Occasionally, people did not wish to reveal their castes identity, while others would state it with pride. I also found that almost everyone knows the castes identity of his or her friends and acquaintances. Friendship networks include people from different families and tend also to extend to Pakistan, to the relatives and acquaintances of Oxford friends, and so information about family status or *birādarī* or *zāt* membership is difficult to conceal. What *zāt* identity means in Oxford is closely connected to what it means in Pakistan, for migrants maintain close connections there. I found that these *zāt* categories are not neutral or equivalent, but in certain contexts at least, perceived hierarchically: some *zāt* identities are a matter of pride; others a matter of shame or concealment.

Perceptions of *zāt* status in Oxford are reconstructions of understandings drawn from migrants' villages of origin. In the villages I visited, *zāt* identity was an important aspect of village organization, most strikingly in the layout of the Faisalabadi villages. For some categories at least, it was also traditionally associated with a hereditary occupation. Caste identity is of course no longer directly or simply linked to occupation or to ownership or non-ownership of land. There remain some broad correlations between caste status, education, occupation and wealth in Pakistan, but in many villages middle-ranking landowners with wage-earning kin abroad are wealthier than the traditional village caste elite, or at least fast becoming so. Such processes have, ironically perhaps, heightened the local consciousness of caste, in Oxford as well as in migrants' villages of origin. The first Pakistani settlers in Oxford, who shared the same type of menial work but regarded their stay as transient, paid scant regard to their caste status differences. Since the arrival of wives and children, awareness of *zāt* differences has in some respects increased rather than diminished. Property ownership and business enterprise has enabled some men of low caste or middle-ranking landowning backgrounds to become wealthier than those of traditionally 'high' caste backgrounds. In this process of social mobility, caste status has not been shrugged off as irrelevant. While most social mobility occurs within the *birādarī* at an individual level or at the level of a small group of close kin (as the next chapter shows), a few migrants make marriages across *zāt* boundaries and in doing so they are quite explicitly making claims about their new status.

What is my evidence for saying that Muslims *zāt*s or *qaum*s are perceived hierarchically, in some situations at least? There is no single principle against which *zāt*s are ranked. Yet most Pakistanis broadly accept some grouping of caste categories according to their historical status. Usually this is described in terms of *ashraf* (noble), *zamīndār* (landowning) and *kammī* (artisan) families. Pakistanis attribute Arab or Afghan origins to *ashraf* categories, as the putative descendants of Arab or Afghan invaders and rulers; by contrast, they say, the landowning and artisan castes are of Indian origin[7]. Ranking is implicit in these categorizations and in the ways they are contested. Some *zamīndār* families consider that the main status distinction is between *zamīndār* and *kammī* categories, while some *ashraf* families stress their distinctiveness in relation to both *zamīndār* and *kammī* families. Yet sometimes people of all three backgrounds assert that these distinctions merely reflect a caste or tribal heritage in different parts of Pakistan, and that today no one category should be thought of as any 'better' than any other.

There is also disagreement about which groups fit into each broad category. Pakistanis consider that each caste has a distinct historical and socio-economic status in rural Pakistan, and some of these connotations of caste persist in how members of these different groups view themselves and are viewed by others in east Oxford. At the same time, while caste groups can, with qualification, be ranked in this way (Table 4.1), the caste hierarchy is not rigidly pre-determined but subject to local reinterpretation and definition. A particular status is not merely an inherent attribute of each caste but varies according to the caste's own and others' conception of it's 'worth'. This in turn is influenced by local variables such as numerical strength and economic and political power. While a few people would argue over the broad distinctions between noble, landowning and artisan castes, there is more disagreement over exactly which castes fit each broad category. A ranking from one area may not necessarily apply elsewhere. It is with these qualifications, then, that I outline some of the ideas, perceptions and connotations of different caste categories, for it is particularly in the context of marriage outside the family that the distinctive qualities of different castes are emphasized.

Ashraf Castes

Within the *ashraf* group, the Sayyeds and Sheikhs consider themselves distinct and are sometimes regarded as having a special religious status or particular spiritual powers, by virtue of being the putative descendants of the Prophet and of the Prophet's clan. The reasons for this date back to the beginnings of Islam and in particular to the establishment of the traditions of Sufism (Islamic mysticism) in the twelfth and thirteenth centuries. The founders of the major Sufi orders were generally mystics or *pīr*s (saints) who claimed both spiritual and genealogical descent from the Prophet or his tribe and thus tended to be Sayyeds, or at least Sheikhs.

To this day, the *pīr*s or saints to whom Sunni Muslims of the Barelwi sect (the dominant sect in east Oxford) turn for guidance tend to be Sayyeds or Sheikhs in origin. Their spiritual closeness to the Prophet Muhammad, which enables them to act as intermediaries for 'ordinary' Muslims, is closely linked to their putative genealogical closeness[8]. The *pīr*s I met in Pakistan claimed Sayyed or Sheikh status; one claimed to be a Qureshi

CASTES REPRESENTED IN EAST OXFORD. Note: This list of *zat* or *quam* names is not exhaustive, but indicates the range of 'castes' and the historical connotations of each, which may matter in status negotiations. Yet there is no fixed, composite hierarchy, for people may challenge the connotations and implied ranking of 'caste' through socio-economic success or failure and through marriage strategies.

Caste Name	Number of adults	Historical status of caste	Subdivisions of caste
ASHRAF (Noble)			
SAYYED	8	Highest rank because of their lineage as putative descendants of the Prophet via his daughter Fatima and cousin Ali. Arab origin.	Shah
SHEIKH	14	Putative descendants of the Quraish, the tribe to which the Prophet belonged. Arab origin	Awan Jafari Zaidi Qureshi
MUGHAL	9	Descendants of the Muslim dynasty that ruled India between 1525–1707.	Abbasi Siddiqi Faruqi Mughal Awan
PATHAN	14	Descendants of earlier Afghan invaders and rulers from the north-west.	Mughal Kashmiri Mughal Mirza Khan is a common title for Pathan (though not all Khans are Pathan)

Caste Name	Number of adults	Historical status of caste	Subdivisions of caste
ZAMINDAR (Landowning)			
RAJPUT	30	High caste Hindu converts, dominant in parts of the Panjab.	Bhatti Rajput Khoker Rajput Chohan Rajput
JAT	24	Farming caste, dominant in rural Panjab.	Bajewa
GUJAR	11	Cattle herders.	Dedar Chavan Chech Char Katana
DOGOR	12	Cattle herders.	
ARAIN	26	Vegetable growers and market gardeners (referred to as Maliar bysome but do not use this term themselves)	
KASHMIRI	8	Origin in Kashmir.	Butt
KAMMI (Artisan)			
TARKAN	9	Carpenters and labourers.	
KUMHAR	4	Potters.	
MOCHI	8	Shoemakers.	
NAI	4	Barbers.	
QASAI	2	Butchers.	

Table 4.1   *(Continued)*

and a direct descendant of Hazrat Fariduddin (Baba Farid) whose shrine is at Pakpattan in Sahiwal district.

Zafar's family is Qureshi, of Sheikh origin. When I first met them, they told me of their high status, ranking second only to the Sayyeds on the Muslim caste hierarchy. Zafar's son said, 'our family is very great, it is the family of our Prophet Muhammad'. Later, in Pakistan, the significance of this became clear to me, because in their village all Qureshis are the descendants of a *pīr* to whom Zafar's close kin can trace their genealogical connection over eight generations. The *pīr*'s closest descendants are believed to have inherited the *pīr*'s spiritual and healing powers. In return for ministering to the needs of pilgrims who visit the shrine on Thursdays or Fridays, these being days of particular religious significance, the *pīr*s receive gifts of food and clothing. Today most young Qureshi men are employed in other villages and cities, but the *pīr*'s closest descendants still operate a rota system enabling them to maintain the shrine and attend to visiting pilgrims.

Primarily, perhaps, because the shrine is an object of pilgrimage, the Qureshi women in this village observed purdah strictly and would not be seen in village shops or fetching water: these errands were performed by village or household servants or else by the men of the household. Wealthier Qureshi households had a separate room (*baithak*) for the use of unrelated male visitors so that the women of the house need not meet them, but even the poorest Qureshi households were distinguishable from others by the piece of sacking over their door acting as a purdah curtain. I came across the same thing in another village much further south, in which the only Sayyed family was considered to have special religious status. The women rarely left their house, and when they did were fully veiled in the *burqā*; no other woman wore a *burqā* within the village. Such strict purdah, however, was essential only within the village or when travelling to or from it. Beyond the village, in a large town or city, the very same women who would in the village be carefully veiled, in *burqā*s or in long *chādar*s made by sewing together two normal *chādar* lengths, would abandon their veils and use only a *dupattā* to cover their hair. A *dupattā*, in the city, signals modernity, especially when it is worn not carefully over the hair but casually over the shoulders. The women said that they could easily abandon purdah in a city where no one knew them, but in their own village they had to protect the status of the family.

In Oxford, away from the status arena of the village of origin, such concerns with status may be less rigorously maintained. Even so, Sayyed or Sheikh families may express their status through religious activities or a distinctively religious lifestyle. For men, this involves regular mosque attendance, becoming close friends of the *imām*, or holding prominent positions on the mosque committee. For women, this may involve observing purdah more strictly than women of other castes — with the exception of the Pathans and some Rajputs — but this does not generally mean being confined to the home. Women of these castes say there is not the same necessity for strict purdah where there are only a few other families from the same village. Even so, they are reluctant to take paid work outside the home. In the 1980s, no Sayyed or Sheikh women would contemplate such work: when I gave the example of Arain women who work unpaid alongside their male kin in family-owned shops, Qureshi and Sayyed women exclaimed, 'they are different from us; their customs are different; we would not do that!' By the late 1990s, although some other 'first generation' women had indeed taken paid work outside the home, none, as far as I know, are from Sayyed or Sheikh families. Yasmin obtained a job in a department store, but her husband, Yacoub, forbade her to take it up; the couple needed the money, but Yacoub though the work was not respectable for a family of their status. Such families favour education for their daughters, but are less enthusiastic about the prospect of paid employment or a career for women unless it is in a 'respectable' occupation such as teaching.

Mughal families regard themselves as distinctive partly but less exclusively because of their religious identity as descendants of Muslim conquerors and also because, unlike the Sayyeds and Sheikhs, they were rulers in India. I was also told that the Mughals were among the castes favoured by the British in the armed services: the head of one Mughal *birādarī* in Oxford was in the British army. The Mughal women whose husbands jointly ran a business in the 1980s said that like the Sayyeds and Sheikhs and unlike the Arain they would not serve in family shops. However, by the late 1990s, several first-generation Mughal women did have part-time work outside the home, in order to supplement the household income. They were also strongly in favour of their daughters obtaining further educational and professional qualifications.

There are two groups who call themselves Pathans. Most South Asians identify Pathans as Pashtoo speakers of tribal background from the North West Frontier province, but in Oxford some Panjabis from Attock district, bordering the North West Frontier, as well as from other provinces also call themselves Pathans. The title is a respectable one, denoting descendants of Afghan Muslims. Pathans emphasize their religious identity; in Oxford, Pathan men have played a dominant role in the running of the mosque and the women reputedly observe strict purdah although in practice there is much variation. In the 1980s, some Pathan women worked in family shops and today some young Pathan women work in English shops or businesses. However, a few North West Frontier Pathan women still wear *burqā*s when they go out, which they tend to do only at night.

Zamīndār Castes

Traditionally, the Rajputs, a dominant caste in rural Panjab, comprise the largest caste in the *zamīndār* group and in some areas they are considered *ashraf*[9]. As high caste Hindu converts, considered 'royal' by some east Oxford Rajputs, most east Oxford Pakistanis would rank them at the top of the *zamīndār* category. In one Faisalabadi village there were only a few *ashraf* households and Rajputs were both numerically dominant and considered socially superior. Rajput women were the only women in that village to observe strict purdah. One Arain farmer told me how a Rajput woman had preferred to burn to death rather than 'break' purdah by leaving her home, which had caught fire.

Other *zamīndār* categories include the Jats, Gujars, Dogors and Arain. The Jats are perhaps best known as Sikh landowners, probably comprising a majority of the Sikhs of Indian Panjab and of Jullundri Sikhs in parts of Britain[10]. Most of Oxford's Muslim Jats are from Faisalabad district, with earlier pre-1947 origins in Jullundur, while some are also from Gujranwala district, the location of one village study which notes the predominance of Jat farmers renowned for their shrewdness and political power[11]. The Gujars, traditionally a tribe of semi-sedentary cultivators and cattle herders who converted to Islam, are apparently the people after whom the districts Gujranwala and Gujrat in Pakistan and Gujarat in India are named[12]. The Dogors, like the Gujars, are traditionally herdsmen and are believed to originate from the Dogor tribe in India, with its distinct language Dogri. In Oxford, Dogors comprise one major kinship group.

The Arain constitute one of the largest caste categories in Oxford. They regard themselves as a *zamīndār* caste, as successful as the Rajputs, and with a reputation for being shrewd and industrious. They do not consider it improper for their women to work in their family shops alongside their male kin, or to earn money by sewing *shalwār-qamīs* for other women or cooking *samosās* for sale locally. Oxford Arain are relatively successful retailers and wholesalers, who tell me that many Pakistani businesses in Glasgow, Huddersfield and Manchester are also owned and run by Arain, many of whom are from several adjacent villages in Faisalabad district. Arain do not see themselves as defined by attachment to one place, in contrast, say, to the Pathans, or as divided into sub-castes, but as part of an extensive and potentially infinitely large *zāt* of fellow Arains. One Arain man commented on their ubiquity by quoting a Panjabi saying meaning 'pick up a stone and you will find an Arain'[13].

The academic literature and the opinions of some other Oxford Pakistanis suggest that there is some ambiguity surrounding the status of the Arain. In the context of a 'traditional' occupational hierarchy, two reports state that Arain are vegetable growers and market gardeners, ranking below the *zamīndārs*[14]. In Oxford, Jats and Rajputs from Jhelum consider that the Arain are a service caste, ranked 'lower' than the *zamīndār*s and refer to the Arain by the term Maliar, which is apparently used in Jhelum to refer to people who traditionally grow vegetables around wells. Oxford Arain, however, are Faisalabadis who originate from Jullundur district in Indian Panjab where, before Partition, the Arain caste apparently constituted one third of the Muslim population of the district[15]. It may be, therefore, that their status as *zamīndār*s, in their own eyes and in the eyes of fellow Faisalabadis or Jullundris, reflects at least in part their dominance and numerical strength in Jullundur before Partition. Or else it may be that the Arain in Faisalabad district have successfully raised their status in relation to other castes as a result of their agricultural prosperity. Pnina Werbner suggests that in Manchester the ranking of the Arain may have shifted, for 'Arain are clearly accepted by all Pakistanis, including those from West Panjab [where Arain are reportedly ranked below the *zamīndārs*], to be a landowning *zāt*, and may rank as high as the Rajput *zāt*'[16]. Werbner notes the competitive relationship between Rajputs in ranking order and suggests the marriage of an Arain man to a Rajput girl establishes at least 'a measure of equality between the Rajputs and the Arain *zāt*s which did not exist beforehand'[17]. In Oxford, I have no evidence of such marriages, but neither Arain themselves nor fellow Faisalabadis rank the Arain below the *zamīndār*s and Arain regard themselves as equivalent to the Rajputs and speak of their caste identity with pride.

One other *zamīndār* category represented in Oxford comprises a small group of Kashmiris who fit somewhat uncomfortably into the Panjabi Muslim caste hierarchy. One study of a village in Pakistan mentions Kashmiris among the village artisan castes[18]. Some non-Kashmiris said people wishing to disguise their *kammī* status call themselves Kashmiris, while others said they were neither *zamīndār* nor *kammī* but simply Kashmiri. However, Oxford Kashmiris regard themselves as *zamīndār*.

The *Zamīndār* /*Kammī* Divide

The third group of castes are the artisan castes, which, in the villages I visited in Pakistan, included Tarkan (carpenter), Kumhar (potter), Mochi (shoemaker), Nai (barber), Qasai (butcher), Mirasi (bard), Lohar (blacksmith), Julaha (weaver), Darzi (tailor) and Teli (oil presser). In Oxford, as far as I know, only the first five are represented.

Some writers note a fourth group at the bottom of the Muslim caste hierarchy, that of Muslim untouchables[19]. In three of the villages I visited where there were Christians, restrictions similar to those associated with untouchables in the Hindu caste system surrounded Muslims' contact with the Isai (Christians). The Christian houses were situated at the edge of the villages and Muslims would neither eat nor drink in the presence of Isai nor visit their homes. A Muslim woman giving food to an Isai in payment for his or her services as a sweeper or latrine cleaner would not use her own utensils and would avoid touching the recipient by holding the bread between the tips of two fingers, touching as little of it as possible. Several villagers thought the Isai were Hindus who had chosen to remain in their villages at Partition and become Christians. It appears that despite their conversion to Christianity, this group has continued to be treated as untouchable. In Pakistan, certain occupations such as cleaning are considered fit only for Christians and certain districts within the cities are regarded as Christian areas, to be avoided. This background accounts for the very different expectations Muslim and Christian Pakistanis have of life in Britain and their contrasting responses to racial exclusion[20]. In Oxford, there is a significant number of Indian Panjabi Christians, but as far as I know there are no Pakistani Christians.

East Oxford Pakistanis from *zamīndār* families would often make a general distinction not between the *ashraf* and those ranking below them, but between the artisan or service castes, collectively called *kammī* (menial), and those ranking above them[21]. The main criterion here is traditional occupation; in rural Pakistan the artisan castes are reportedly described as *kammī*[22]. However, the distinction also carries moral connotations. Thus, while Oxford Pakistanis use the term *kammī* to denote families of artisan and service backgrounds, they also use the terms *kamīna* or *kamīni* to describe someone of low status or as an insult. The following quotation indicates some of the connotations of these terms. The speaker, Manzoor, is a Jat:

> You can always tell a *kammī* from the way he acts. A Mochi from our village got into the army by pretending to be a Jat. The village did not split on him, but the army intelligence soon realized he was a *kammī* because he was cowardly in fighting. *Kammī*s are always cowardly. They act low and subservient because they have been kept down. You can always tell. It is the same here. A man who keeps quiet when Jats are in the room is a *kammī*. He feels himself to be lower than the others. And you can always tell a *kammī* from the way they show off, telling you stories about their background. When we were children and used to show off, our parents would scold us by saying 'you *kamīna*, you *kamīni*', meaning 'you behave like a little *kammī*'.

Oxford Pakistanis are curious to find out whether or not someone they have met is a *kammī* and this is often the main purpose of questions about caste status. *Kammī* status is something to be ashamed of and to keep hidden. I was told of a number of cases in which people of *kammī* status had attempted to conceal their caste identity in Britain and pass for a member of a higher caste, a frequent phenomenon in India when Hindus move to towns, or away from their region of origin. Saleem, an Arain, spoke of how he had brought with him to England one of his father's servants in the village in Faisalabad. This man was a Kumhar (potter) by descent who settled in Rochdale, while Saleem found work in Oxford. During his first leave, Saleem decided to visit his friend in Rochdale, but on enquiry at his friend's lodgings, was told that there was no one living there by the name he gave. Persisting, he gave details of his friend's appearance and village of origin, and was told that there was someone of that description but whose family name was Mughal, living in an adjacent street. Saleem told me 'I didn't tell them that this man was my father's servant; that's his business'. Saleem visited him briefly, but did not stay, and did not say what he had heard.

My information on which *kammī* castes are represented was gleaned mainly from stories such as this and from gossip and innuendo. If I asked directly about caste, I would get a variety of responses. People of *zamīndār* or *ashraf* caste status would proudly reveal their caste name, while only one man openly admitted his low caste status. He had gained a reputation for introducing himself to other Pakistanis as 'Muhammad Sharif, Mochi, from Silanwali'. Others of *kammī* status were much more reticent. For example, when I asked one household head whose family, I had heard, were Mochis, about his caste, he evaded the question and instead spoke at length on brotherhood in Islam. Slightly altering my question, I asked about the *birādarī* and was told it as Mulk Khatana, a sub-caste of the Gujars. However, a friend of this family, a Mughal woman, told me that she had discovered they were Mochi not because they had said so, but because when visiting Pakistan her husband had taken gifts to his friend's parents and seen for himself that his friend's relatives were shoemakers. Later, at a wedding, a man of Gujar caste from a village near the Mochi family's referred to members of the Mochi's household as 'those Mochis in X street'. On a later occasion his wife said she had stopped attending an English class is which 'those dirty Mochi women' were also present.

It is difficult to disguise one's caste status successfully in Oxford not only because of the presence of fellow villagers, but also because friendships formed in Oxford extend to Pakistan too. As Manzoor said:

> You can't hide your caste, because there is always someone from your area, and even if there is not, people make new friends. When they go to Pakistan, they visit their friends' homes and find out there. My uncle became a friend of Bashir who calls himself and his family Rajput, and says he is from Lahore. My uncle was staying in Jhelum when Bashir and his children were staying in Wazirabad. At that time there were terrible floods and in Wazirabad the streets were like canals and the houses were collapsing. My uncle was worried about Bashir's family and went to Wazirabad intending to bring them back to his village. He found that the flood hadn't affected them. He also discovered that they were *kammī*: they were Ilharis, a caste of labourers, not Rajputs.

On several occasions I was told about people who were 'in fact' *kammī*s but called themselves by a different title here, and usually these comments were followed by 'but don't tell them I told you'. To call someone a *kammī* amounts to an insult. In a discussion of the two parties in a dispute at the mosque one member of an *ashraf* family supporting the *imām* referred with disgust to an Awan from the other party as a Mochi, and was then severely reprimanded by his father for doing so. On another occasion, a Gujar said 'she's a Tarkan, a bloody *kammī*' when the activities of a woman prominent in local 'community' politics.

Caste Status and Marriage

These, then, are some of the connotations of caste, but what is the significance of caste identity in marriage? In most marriages, caste is important only as a consequence of the fact that most marriages are endogamous, that is, they take place within the family and thus, in effect within the caste. Pakistanis say they don't like to marry outside the family or outside the *birādarī*, and

they may add that this is because other people are not of the
same caste. Since, however, Pakistani *birādarī*s and castes are
ranked, it follows that marriage across a caste boundary may
raise questions about caste status. Whether such marriages are
justified or condemned depends on the relative status of the
castes involved as well as on their socio-economic status.
Marriage across the caste boundary is one way in which
improved socio-economic status may be legitimized. Caste mobility is, in principle, one aspect of social mobility, clinched 'when
marriages formerly not contemplated take place. *Zāt* ranking, is,
in other words, tested and proved though inter-*zāt* marriage'[23].

For Hindus, caste mobility most commonly involves 'sanskriti-
zation': the adoption of the lifestyles of the high castes, through
increased religious activity and vegetarianism, usually accompanying an improvement in socio-economic status[24]. Among
Hindus, the marriage of a daughter into a family of higher caste
(a hypergamous marriage) may raise family standing. For
Hindus, this process may be facilitated by rules of exogamy,
which require marriages to take place with non-kin, with partners sometimes being sought from far afield[25]. Similar though
not exactly parallel processes have been identified among
Muslims in the Indian subcontinent. 'Ashrafization' is the adoption of the lifestyle of the *ashraf* castes, through increasing religious activity among both men and women and the adoption of
strict purdah[26]. A low caste group may adopt an *ashraf*
lifestyle, adopt a new subcaste name, and, by taking advantage
of the preference for marrying close kin that is associated with
Muslims in the Indian subcontinent, marry endogamously and
over a couple of generations transform its caste identity. This
process may be facilitated by migration. Alternatively, a newly
wealthy man may claim his new status by marrying his daughter into a family of higher caste status. This in itself is not caste
mobility, but it may begin the process. Equality with the
higher-status in-laws could only be claimed if the in-laws then
give a bride to a son, or other close kinsman, of the man who
has married his daughter 'up', as well as by the adoption of
their caste or sub-caste name.

There is always the danger of over-interpreting one's data, in
order to satisfy an academic audience, or to elucidate for outsiders the 'rules' of another social system, or to demonstrate
intellectual neatness. Thus I am wary of selecting examples in

order to demonstrate 'ashrafization' or to show that claims to *ashraf* status may be made through particular marriage choices. Such processes occur slowly, over at least one or two generations and are not of course described as 'ashrafization' by the actors themselves. Moreover, both in Britain and in south Asia, social mobility is also achieved and expressed in terms of socio-economic class and it is difficult to disentangle the two processes. Nevertheless, the number of marriages (within my relatively small sample of Oxford families) has increased in recent years as the sons and daughters of first-generation migrants have reached marriageable age. With this, there is some evidence that inter-caste marriage provides one way of claiming or expressing social mobility, which would be entirely in keeping with migrants' original intentions concerning migration to Britain. The process, however, varies, I suggest, according to the initial caste identity of the people involved. For instance, for Sayyed families, already at the top of the caste hierarchy, marriage of a daughter with a non-Sayyed family would involve considerable loss of status. My impression is that for Sayyed families caste endogamy is of far more importance than it is for middle-ranking *zamīndār* families. I offer two examples as illustration.

The first is of marriages between unrelated Sayyed families, arranged, it seems, because of the importance of caste endogamy. The first such marriage concerns Sayyed families A and B, (Figure 4.1). The groom's parents, Sayyed family B, are well-to-do business people from a city in northern Panjab who went to great lengths to find a Sayyed girl for their son as they had no unmarried girls of suitable age among their own close kin. Their family doctor acted as an intermediary in the marriage that was finally arranged with the doctor's sister's daughter, from a poor but respectable Sayyed household in a village in southern Panjab. The groom's family said that marriage with a non-Sayyed girl would have been unacceptable, even if she were from a very wealthy family, for the family's caste purity had never been spoilt. After this marriage, two of the bride's sisters were also married into family B (Figure 4.1), but because of the discrepancy in economic status, girls from family B have not been married into family A. Family B married their daughter to a cousin; they said they would not send an educated girl to live in a village. Family A did not even ask family B for a bride for their son but instead traced distant relatives.

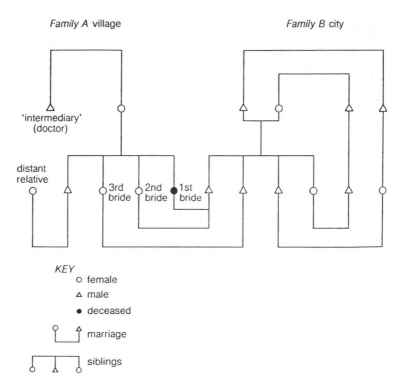

Figure 4.1   Sayyed marriages.

In the next generation, caste status has continued to be an important consideration in this family's marriages. Ruxana, from family A, was the third bride married into family B and she later joined her husband in Oxford (Figure 4.1). One of her sons and one of her daughters are now married. Before the daughter's marriage, Ruxana's in-laws, family B in Pakistan, received several proposals for their granddaughter and discussed these with their son and Ruxana in Oxford. Ruxana's husband finally accepted a proposal from a respectable, unrelated Sayyed family, family C, from the same city in Pakistan whose son, university-educated and known to be a 'good' boy, was keen to come to Britain to study. Ruxana's son, however, was married within the family to his father's brother's daughter, a girl who came from Pakistan to Oxford three years ago and told me that ever since her birth her father had expected her to marry his brother's son and come to England.

The second example is the marriage of a couple from two previously unrelated families of different castes, Mughal and Pathan (Figure 4.2). In this case, maintaining caste purity was not the prime consideration in the marriage arrangements. The marriage was of Azra, a Mughal woman, to Khan, a Pathan man, arranged by Azra's eldest brother Riaz primarily to strengthen the tie which had developed between Riaz and Khan. When Riaz and one of his brothers first came to England they lodged in a house in which Khan, who was then married to a relative in Pakistan, was living. Riaz developed a close friendship with Khan, who helped Riaz obtain work as a hospital porter. Later the two men took a joint mortgage on a house. The fact that both men were originally from Jhelum provided further grounds for developing the relationship. Then when Khan's young wife in Pakistan died, Riaz wanted Khan to marry Azra. Riaz's parents visited Khan's parents in Pakistan, both sides were satisfied, and the marriage took place, with all three men returning to Pakistan for it. Shortly after their wives had joined her brothers, Azra came to England. In 1980, the three men decided to enter shopkeeping jointly: Riaz and Khan left their jobs at the hospital to work in the shop full-time, while Riaz's brother worked there on a part-time basis.

The Mughal family said it is better to receive in marriage a girl from a different caste than for a girl to be given in marriage outside it, because the latter involves loss of status for the wife-givers. Moreover, the children of a Mughal man married to a woman of a different caste will be Mughal, whereas the children of a Mughal woman married outside the caste will not be. In fact (as Figure 4.2 shows), three previous marriages in this family had been of Mughal men to non-Mughal women, in two cases to Rajput women and in one case to a Kashmiri woman, and such marriages were considered acceptable because caste status is transferred in the male line. We would therefore expect the marriage of a Mughal woman to a Pathan to involve loss of status for the Mughals as wife-givers, and thus be disapproved of. However, they justified this inter-caste marriage by denying any difference in status between Mughals and Pathans: they said both were *ashraf* castes whose ancestors were Muslim invaders and rulers. The Mughals also emphasized their equality with the Pathans by pointing out that a second marriage had taken place across the caste boundary, strengthening the affinal link: Riaz's cousin was subsequently married to Khan's brother.

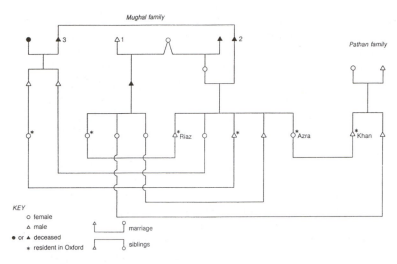

Figure 4.2 Mughal marriages. Unmarried siblings and children are not shown. Previous marriages to non-Mughal women: (1) To Rajput widow; (2) To brother's step-daughter, the daughter from a previous marriage of the widow in marriage 1; (3) To Kashmiri woman.

In the Sayyed case, then, caste was important to the extent that the family preferred to search for a Sayyed bride for their son rather than risk the loss of status to their family that might follow from marriage with a non-Sayyed girl. In the next generation too, of the various suitable proposals for the daughter, a spouse was chosen from a well-educated Sayyed family. In the Mughal case, the attitude to caste was less exclusive: acceptable caste status was defined as *ashraf*, especially for the marriage of Mughal girls, while brides can be taken from lower ranking castes. Although in theory they disapprove of caste exogamy, marriage between non-kin of *ashraf* status was acceptable because, they argue, all *ashraf* castes are equal.

I do not wish to suggest that all Sayyeds have an 'exclusive' attitude to caste and all Mughals a less exclusive one, but merely to suggest that the importance given to caste status may vary in this way from one caste category to another. Moreover, where marriages occur across the caste boundary, they tend to be justified within the idiom of the caste hierarchy. In the case of the Mughal and Pathan marriages, the emphasis was on common *ashraf* status. In other cases, marriage across the caste boundary may be a means of expressing or legitimizing social mobility in caste terms. If those at the top of the hierarchy marry more exclusively than middle-ranking landowner castes, marriage of a *zamīndār* girl into a Sayyed family may express social mobility. For some, migration to Britain has provided new opportunities not only for becoming wealthy but for consolidating this new status by marrying a daughter upwards into a Sayyed or Sheikh family. Here is one example of a marriage of this sort.

Khan is a middle-ranking landowner who is now one of the wealthiest of Oxford's Pakistani businessmen. Having spent twenty-five years building up a chain of shops in Britain, he now runs a manufacturing business in a city in Pakistan while his sons manage the U.K. business. He has been far more successful than other men from the same village who have worked abroad, including men from the traditional caste elite, a Sheikh family, in his village. No families of this Sheikh *birādarī* would risk their reputation and pride by asking for Khan's daughter for a bride, regardless of how wealthy he now is. Yet such constraints may not operate outside the village. In this case, new business alliances have enabled Khan to claim a new position in caste terms, by marrying his only daughter, a beautiful university-educated girl, considered by all to be very *sharīf* (respectable), to the son of a wealthy Sayyed business partner. Khan's wife, a very pious woman, had wanted her daughter to marry her maternal cousin (her mother's sister's son) in Pakistan, but Khan's interests dominated in the final decision that was made. After the marriage, both parents emphasized the advantages for their daughter of the comfortable and luxurious international city life she would now lead. This is evidence of individual social mobility, expressed in the idiom of caste by marrying a daughter 'up', but whether Khan's family is considered to be 'equal' to the Sayyed family will depend on whether there are subsequent marriages of Sayyed girls to Khan's sons. This, only time will tell; as yet, Khan's sons are unmarried.

Marriage across the *zamīndār /kammī* boundary is considerably more difficult. The very suggestion of marriage across the *zamīndār /kammī* boundary arouses particularly strong emotions: this boundary, I was told, is one that should never be crossed. When I asked Sohrab, a Gujar, whether it would be acceptable for one of his daughters to marry one of the sons of a friend of his who is a Kumhar, he replied:

I would not marry my daughter to a black man or a man who was ignorant and illiterate, because if she went anywhere she would feel shown up and ashamed. You have to marry with your equals. That is why you don't marry with low caste people; you must marry from your own *birādarī*.

Even if a proposed spouse was, in fact, of equivalent or superior educational or socio-economic status, the match would be strongly disapproved. As far as I know, only five marriages have taken place across the *zamīndār*/*kammī* boundary, all of them without parental consent and with great social condemnation. In one case, the marriage of a Nai girl to a Rajput boy, both families rejected the couple. It was only after several years, by which time the Rajput boy's mother had died, that the Nai girl and her husband were accepted into the Rajput father's house.

As mentioned above, one recognized strategy for claiming or expressing social mobility within the idiom of caste available to *kammī* households is 'ashrafization'. This is the adoption of a religious lifestyle and of the name of a high-ranking caste or subcaste, accompanied either by marrying closely within the family or by marriage with members of a higher-ranking caste or by some combination of the two. In theory, migration to Britain provides new opportunities for this type of social mobility, for instance by marrying close kin in Britain and loosening connections with other close or more distant kin in Pakistan. In practice, though, other considerations may conspire against this happening, as I show in the next chapter. Even so, there is some evidence for such processes.

Pnina Werbner provides two examples from Manchester of caste mobility involving members of lower *zāt*s, Tailors (Darzi) and Bards (Mirasi). By adopting a religious lifestyle, members of the Darzi *zāt* raised their status locally through several marriages with members of higher castes, substantiating their claim 'that Darzi was merely an occupational section of the Rajput *quom* [sic] (*zāt*/nation)'. Through close-kin marriage, a socially mobile Bard family attempted to transform its caste status. Werbner adds that whether a family achieves a new *zāt* identity in the long run, given that friends and neighbours know their original caste status, involves 'an element of collusion...If a family is successful and respectable, no one in the community has any interest in challenging their claims to belong to one *zāt* or another'[27].

In Oxford, I have no evidence of the first strategy, though some tenuous evidence for the second. One family told me eighteen years ago that they were landowners and gave as their caste name a title that I recognized as that of a Gujar subcaste. I did not visit their village, but other migrants who have visited their kin in Pakistan have told me that the family is Tarkan, of the carpenter caste. The family has now added the title Malik to their sub-caste name, and uses this title, which means 'owner', as a family surname. The family are considered very respectable: the senior man in this household, always a regular mosque-goer, took early retirement from the car factory in order to play a major role in the management of mosque affairs. In recent years, his role has involved raising funds for the building of a new purpose-built mosque in east Oxford. His sons are considered very dutiful: one lives at home and supports his parents financially, while the other son lives nearby. Both sons have married their father's sister's daughters from Pakistan. This process of marrying close kin, adopting a religious lifestyle and changing one's family name may be interpreted as 'ashrafization'. I recorded a similar process in a village in Pakistan, where a family who, I was told, were traditionally barbers (Nai) were now called *maulvī*s. They lived near the village mosque and the senior man in the household and his sons were the mosque caretakers. In both cases, the families are respected for their religious lifestyle though are not particularly wealthy; no one has seen fit to challenge their change in family name.

Conclusion

There is, then, a conceptual hierarchy of castes, although different individuals would give different versions of the detail of caste ranking and there is no single criterion that justifies the hierarchy. These 'castes' are in practice largely endogamous. Occasionally marriages occur across caste boundaries and may be condemned or justified with reference to the relative status of the families concerned. Inter-caste marriages also provide a mechanism through which claims to higher socio-economic status may be made or expressed. The marriage of a daughter into a family of higher caste status, in the hope that reciprocal marriages will follow, or the adoption of an *ashraf* lifestyle, usually accompanied by a change of family name and close kin marriage over several generations, would constitute a claim to higher caste status. Usually, however, the question of caste status in marriage does not arise explicitly because most marriages take place with first cousins or other close kin, as the next chapter demonstrates. For many Pakistanis, the practice of marrying within the family is one that represents a fundamental difference between the Muslims and the Hindus of the Indian subcontinent. The *Qur'ān* permits, though does not prescribe, marriage with close kin outside the group prohibited as spouses by incest prohibitions and Islamic law, whereas for most Hindus first-cousin marriage is prohibited and marriage must take place outside the family. Yet despite this fundamental difference in marriage rules, the very practice of close kin marriage is nonetheless compatible with a caste structure and can even serve to protect and maintain it. The effect of the practice of marrying cousins or close kin is to maintain the exclusivity of the *birādarī* or caste. But what precisely is the endogamous group? What is the relationship between caste and *birādarī*? From the point of view of marriage alliances and commitments to social mobility, what is the significant unit of kinship? I turn to these questions in the next chapter.

NOTES

1. See, for instance, Donnan, 1988, especially pp. 47–59.
2. Alavi, 1972.
3. Ahmad, 1971. Both Ahmad (1971) and Alavi (1972) adopt a Marxist perspective.
4. I. Ahmad (ed.) 1973 (a) and I. Ahmad (ed.) 1973 (b).
5. Fischer, 1991:97 and Werbner, 1990:94.
6. Dumont, 1980.
7. This distinction is acknowledged in the literature on Muslims castes. Most works on Muslim castes in India refer to Uttar Pradesh, on which the classic work is Ansari, 1960. See also Z. Ahmad, 1962:1–83, Vreede-De-Stuers, 1968 and Roy, 1979. For details of castes in rural Pakistan, see Ullah, 1958; Eglar, 1960 and Cambridge University Asian Expedition, 1962. General works on Hindu castes which refer to Muslims include Ibbetson, 1883; Blunt, 1931:161–207; Hutton, 1946; Mandelbaum, 1970:544–559 and Dumont, 1980.
8. See for instance, Currie, 1978 and Jeffery, 1979:6.
9. Dumont, 1980:208; Blunt, 1931:35; Roy, 1979:15–16.
10. See Pettigrew, 1975 and on British Sikhs, see Helweg, 1979 and Ballard, 1994:88–116.

11. Ullah, 1958:170–2.
12. Khatana, 1976:85–86.
13. Werbner (1990:98) quotes almost exactly the same saying among Manchèster Arain.
14. Z. Eglar, 1960:32; I. Ullah, 1958:172.
15. The Punjab District Gazeteer, Jullunder District, 1935.
16. Werbner, 1990:99.
17. Werbner, 1990:103
18. Eglar, 1960:32.
19. Blunt, 1931:35–51 and p. 57; Ansari, 1960:50–51, 73 and pp. 77–80; L. Dumont, 1980:208; Mandelbaum, (Vol.1), 1970:549–551; Roy, 1979:15.
20. Jeffery suggests that British Pakistani Christians be regarded as 'refugees' rather than 'migrants': in Pakistan they feel foreign and vulnerable; in Britain they want to assimilate and therefore more keenly feel difficulties in being accepted by English people (1976:40–43).
21. Some writers note among Indian Muslims a major status distinction between the *ashraf* or noble castes and the *ajlaf* or commoners, predominantly Hindu converts to Islam (Ansari, 1960; Vreede-de-Stuers, 1968); others note its absence (I. Ahmad, 1966:269; I. Ahmad, 1973 (c), 1973:159, and Roy, 1979:115). I did not hear the term *ajlaf* used in Britain or in the villages I visited in Pakistan and it is not mentioned in the literature on Muslims in Pakistan or Britain.
22. Eglar, 1960; Cambridge University Asian Expedition 1962; Ullah 1958; Ahmad, 1977. In northern India, the term *kammin* is used to denote the servant or artisan castes whose families are bound to the *zamīndār*s from whom they receive patronage and protection in exchange for services rendered; see Aggarwal, 1976:282; Aggarwal, 1971:71, 74, 94–104, and Vreede-de Stuers, 1968:117. This meaning of *kammin* follows Hindu usage; for example see Parry, 1979:78–81.
23. P. Werbner, 1990:100.
24. Srinivas, M.N. 1968:189–200.
25. Parry, 1979.
26. 1. Ahmad, 1973 (c); Vreede-de Stuers, 1968; P.M. Jeffery, 1976.
27. Werbner, 1990:113–119. The quotations are on pages 110 and 118.

5 *BIRĀDARĪ* SOLIDARITY AND COUSIN MARRIAGE

Most Oxford Pakistanis initially viewed migration as a means of improving their socio-economic status 'at home', and to this end, a father, brother or other close relative often sponsored a man's migration. Thirty or so years on, to what extent have migrants been successful in this respect and how have their ideals changed? Migrants view and assess socio-economic status through wealth, property ownership, type of occupation and an *ashraf* (respectable) lifestyle. Labour migration has enabled most Oxford Pakistanis to build better houses, extend their landholdings and to provide better dowries for their daughters' and sometimes their brothers' daughters' weddings. Some migrants have established businesses and others have also moved to the cities in Pakistan. These changes are often linked with maintaining or adopting an *ashraf* lifestyle, and, in a few cases, this desire for social mobility may be expressed through the marriage of a daughter into a family of *ashraf* caste status. However, as Pakistanis themselves point out, the vast majority of marriages take place within the caste and within the *birādarī*. To what extent do these marriages also represent strategies for social advancement, or are other processes or considerations involved?

Pakistanis say, 'we like to marry our relatives' and 'it is better to marry in the family than outside it', expressing a preference for marrying kin which is typical not only of Pakistan but of parts of the Middle East and North Africa[1]. Moreover, in discussing their marriage preferences they give explicit emphasis to equality between kin rather than to social advancement[2]. Of the various reasons they give for their preference, they especially emphasize the advantages for a daughter who marries a relative. Marrying close kin, they say, means that the living standard and personalities of the groom's immediate family (most importantly, of his mother, as the bride's prospective mother-in-law) are known beforehand. They also say that marrying kin minimizes the trauma of a daughter's separation from her parents at marriage and enables parents more easily to maintain contact with their daughter and offer her support after the marriage has taken place. Many Pakistanis will justify the preference for close kin marriage by referring to Islam, which permits though it does not prescribe marriage with close relatives outside the group of kin prohibited as spouses by incest prohibitions. They may also make reference to the life of the Prophet Muhammad whose daughter Fatima was married to Ali, the Prophet's cousin[3]. They also sometimes say that marriage with relatives maintains the 'purity of the blood', emphasizing the particular qualities of the family or caste.

This stated preference presumably has some bearing on actual marriage choices, because most marriages do indeed take place with relatives, particularly with first cousins and other close kin. My analysis of the marriages which have taken place so far (mostly during the past 15 years) among the sons and daughters of 24 first-generation couples (see table 5.1) shows 76% of these marriages to be with kin: 59% with cousins, 17% with other kin[4]. Yet marriages also take place with more distant relatives from the same *birādarī* and, in certain circumstances, with unrelated people including people of other castes. What, then, is the socio-economic and cultural significance of this high proportion of marriage with relatives, especially first cousins, in the context of migration to Britain? Is the significant unit of kinship, from the point of view of *birādarī* endogamy and social advancement, most often a small group of agnatic kin, such as several brothers? Or are the deliberations involved in marriage negotiations more complex than this?

As Hastings Donnan's perceptive analysis of marriage preferences among the Dhund Abbasi of northeast Pakistan demonstrates, it is quite insufficient to say 'they marry their cousins because this is their cultural preference'; many other factors besides a cultural preference affect marriage outcomes. A stated preference for marriage with kin, itself part of a package of cultural ideas, is but one of a number of deliberations which come into play. Other relevant factors are the family's reputation and socio-economic position, the socio-economic status and reputation of the family of the proposed spouse, the nature of relationships within that family and the personal preferences of the potential bride and groom. Each marriage choice does not simply follow the cultural preference for marriage with kin, 'but is the outcome of balancing or weighing all of these factors in relation to one another'[5]. It follows then that:

MARRIAGES OF 70 YOUNG ADULTS		
	No.	% of total
First cousin (incl. 2 'double' first cousins*)	41	59
Other relative (inc. 3 second cousins & 3 affinal kin)	12	17
Unrelated, same *biradari*	8	11
Unrelated, different *biradari***	6	9
Non-Pakistani ***	3	4
Total	**70**	**100**

Notes: I counted the 'type' of marriage made, mostly in the past 15 years, by 70 young Oxford Pakistanis in 24 east Oxford households. In two cases, marriages were to cousins in the same sample whom I therefore 'counted' twice (so this information pertains to 138, not 140, individuals). I compiled these data from observations and conversations in many different contexts, cross-checked with various different family members in ways that included poring over wedding albums. Some of the spouses of young Oxford Pakistani adults were youngsters whom I had known or met briefly in their villages in Pakistan in 1980/1 and who have since come to Britain for marriages.

*   The term 'double' first cousin refers to being a first cousin in more than one way; thus, if a man's father and his bride's father are brothers, and if his mother and his bride's mother are sisters, his bride is both his father's brother's daughter (his 'fbd') and his mother's sister's daughter (his 'mzd').
**   Of these 6 marriages, only one was arranged entirely by the parents; the others were 'love marriages', that is, marriages formally arranged by the parents after they had consulted or been advised by their sons or daughters. Such marriages may reflect an increasing trend; see chapter 7.
***   These three marriages comprise two marriages to English women and one marriage of a Pakistani woman to a student from the Middle East with whom the woman eloped; fifteen years later, she had not renewed contact with her natal family.
Cautions: These data show little of the processes that have led to this particular statistical outcome. For instance, some of the marriages here are of girls who had previously eloped with or wanted to marry other men, but had returned to their families and subsequently accepted an arranged marriage. This 'typology' of marriage also gives no indication of marital 'success'; some of these marriages involve now separated or divorced couples.
A large proportion of first-cousin marriage is not, in principle, incompatible with some degree of dissent and dissatisfaction, as chapter 7 discusses.

Table 5.1

marriage choice and the negotiations that surround it must be understood in terms of the strategies adopted by the different participants, rather than in terms of any rule or preference. In pursuing their own interests people use the rules and preferences as rhetorical devices to support their case and to judge, bargain, and negotiate with others[6].

Kinship and cultural preference are thus not the only factors involved in marriage choices; 'various considerations having nothing to do with kinship are brought into play'[7].

How do these processes operate among Oxford Pakistanis? Pragmatic considerations of wealth and socio-economic status play a large part in determining, for example, why one cousin is chosen as a spouse and not another, but the respectability of such matches is secured by reference to the preference for close kin marriage. In this context, the flexibility of the notion of *birādarī* is of central importance, and for this reason I begin with a discussion of it.

Just what is a *birādarī*? The answer, of course, depends on context, for the concept has a range of meanings, from that of a kinship group of virtually infinite size — the *qaum* or *zāt*, the equivalent of 'caste' or subcaste — to a small group of inter-marrying close kin between whom spouses are exchanged. Gulshan, Gafoor's wife, first told me her *birādarī* consisted of all her close kin in Oxford (Figure 3.5). She also talked of all her closest kin in Britain and Pakistan as her *birādarī* (Figure 5.1). Later, when contrasting the Arain with the Rajputs, their local business rivals, Gulshan, Gafoor and Habib spoke of all Oxford Arain families as *birādarī*, even those with whom there is no known kinship connection. Oxford Arain also, sometimes, refer to all Arain everywhere as *birādarī*, regardless of whether they know them personally or not. *Birādarī* thus has a range of meanings: at the most restricted, denoting one's closest relatives living locally, more generally, including all other relatives in Britain and Pakistan, and most generally referring to all caste members[8]. The simple definition of *birādarī*, covering all Gulshan's meanings, might therefore be 'the kinship group I belong to', and the sense of kinship widens or narrows its focus depending on context.

Capturing this flexibility in the term's usage, its 'sliding semantic structure', Hamza Alavi has described the *birādarī* as having two constituent principles, descent and ties between contemporaries[9]. In practice the emphasis tends to be on ties between contemporaries rather than on ties of descent; this is what matters most in the context of marriage. For instance, Zahida first described her *birādarī* as comprising herself, her husband and children, her two brothers and their families in Pakistan, her sister and brother-in-

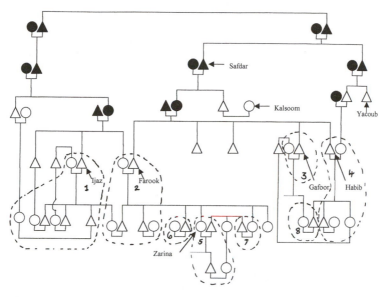

Figure 5.1   An Arain *birādarī* in Britain. Households 1 to 5 are in Oxford, 6 and 7 are in Glasgow, 8 and 9 are in Newcastle and 10 to 12 are in Pakistan. The six marriages with unrelated Arain shown here are those of households 1, 5, 6, 7, 11 and 12. The other six marriages shown here (households 2, 3, 4, 8, 9 and 10) are with relatives, as indicated.

law Rafiq's family in Birmingham, her mother's brother Sadiq's family in Cardiff and her husband's brother and his sisters in Pakistan and their families (Figure 5.2). Zahida perceived these relationships primarily in terms of ties through siblings and parents' siblings, rather than in terms of descent. Zahida and her husband Zafar in fact disagreed on the precise relationship between two ancestors three generations removed: Zahida said her mother's paternal grandfather and her father's paternal grandfather were cousins, while Zafar said they were brothers. They did agree that these relatives were descended from a common ancestor perhaps five generations back. Zahida added that all the Qureshis in her village were in fact the descendants of an ancestor eight generations back, and that tracing relationships between them would show all the Qureshis to be related, thus constituting one *birādarī*. So in Zahida's definition of *birādarī* ties of descent and contemporary ties of kinship were both important, but descent from a common ancestor or membership of the same caste was taken for granted and not necessarily demonstrable; the emphasis, instead, was on contemporary kinship.

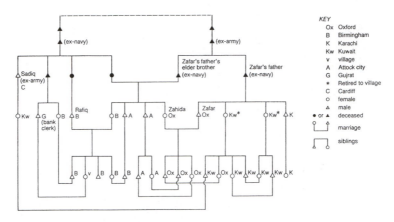

Figure 5.2   Zahida and Zafar's immediate *birādarī*.

Later, I learnt that Zahida's initial description of her *birādarī* did not include certain other close relatives. In Zahida's village, I met another branch of the *birādarī* who were closely related to Zafar's family in Oxford, being the descendants of Zafar's father's younger brother and his paternal grandfather's brother (Figure 5.3). Back in Oxford, I asked Zahida about these relatives and discovered that she had a detailed knowledge of all the marriages which had taken place within this village branch, into which her younger sister and a cousin, her father's sister's daughter, had married. The fact that she had not mentioned this

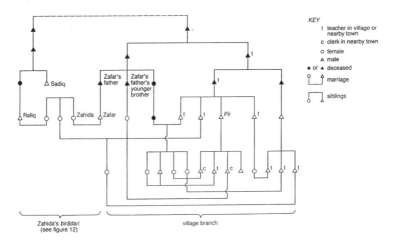

Figure 5.3   Zahida and Zafar's wider *birādarī*.

village branch of close kin when she first described her *birādarī*
in itself suggests that other factors besides descent and kinship
ties may be important in determining which of ones relatives
come to be regarded as one's 'immediate' *birādarī*.

The Direction of *Birādarī* Endogamy

Within Zahida's wider *birādarī* (Figure 5.3), many first cousin
marriages had taken place, but the fact that the particular
choices of spouse had in effect created two separate intermarrying groups suggests that spouses were not randomly selected
from among those available. The last marriage into the village
branch was that of Zahida's sister, in 1952. Why did the
marriage preferences take this direction?

One feature of Zafar's *birādarī* in relation to the village branch
is that the adult married men live abroad or in cities, with their
wives and children. The few exceptions are not really exceptions:
Zafar's sister and her husband have retired from working in
Kuwait to a large *pakkā* (brick and mortar) house in the village;
Zafar's other sister, now widowed, used to live in Kuwait, and
Rafiq's daughter lives with her children in the village but her
husband, Rafiq's brother's son, is a bank clerk in a small town in
Gujrat. This couple had failed to obtain a visa to join Rafiq
in England; they might have been living in Birmingham. In the
village branch, by contrast, no one lives abroad; most men are
teachers in the village or in nearby villages, two men are clerks in
a town nearby and one man is a *pīr*.

Members of Zafar's 'immediate' *birādarī* all explained the
choice of spouse for their daughter by saying that they wanted
their daughters to marry into households where the standard of
living matched that of their own homes. They also said that a
girl brought up in town is unsuited to the harsh life of a village.
They therefore stressed the equivalence of socio-economic status
and the well being of their daughters, in explaining to me (after
the marriages had taken place; I was not present when these
marriages were discussed and negotiated) why they had made
these particular choices. The structural consequence of these
marriages, if not the motive for them, is that Zafar's *birādarī*
have stopped marrying their daughters to poorer village-based
relatives; instead, marriages have taken place between households of kin in Kuwait, Britain and other cities in Pakistan. The

particular choices of spouse that in these cases have led to the formation of two separate intermarrying groups follow from considerations of a family's living standard, a groom's employment prospects and opportunities for male employment offered by labour migration abroad. Within the constraints of caste and in keeping with a preference for marrying close kin, particularly first cousins, marriage choices are made with a number of pragmatic considerations in mind, which may have the effect of maintaining or improving the status of a section of a *birādarī* in relation to other *birādarī* members.

Marriages with Non-kin

Sometimes marriages are arranged with people with whom there is no known kinship relationship and are not condemned for violating the cultural preference for marrying within the family. In the Arain *birādarī* (Figure 5.1), six out of twelve marriages took place with fellow Arain with whom there were no genealogical connections and these marriages were not regarded as violating cultural norms. Four of these marriages, arranged within the village in Faisalabad district, took place, I was told, because there were no close kin with whom marriages might otherwise have been arranged; many relatives had been killed or had disappeared without trace when they left Jullundhur at Partition in 1947. It was apparently not uncommon then for spouses to be drawn from among unrelated Arain who had settled in the same village.

Later, after the migration to Britain, two other marriages took place with unrelated Arain and these marriages were explained to me in terms of the relationships established between the respective families. The first of these marriages took place, I was told, as the result of a friendship between Safdar, who was from Faisalabad and whose descendants are now in Oxford, and Ali, an Arain from Multan. Safdar and Ali had lodged together in the same house in Glasgow in 1957. When Safdar returned to his village in 1959 for a short visit, he took presents from Ali to Ali's relatives in Multan. Then in 1961, Ali returned to Pakistan for several months to arrange for his wife and two elder sons to join him in Glasgow, and made a point of visiting Safdar's relatives in Faisalabad. In the early 1960s while they were both still living in Glasgow, Safdar and Ali, together with Safdar's nephew Yacoub (Figure 5.1), decided to pool their resources and buy a grocery store. At first they made little money, but gradually the business improved and they decided to sell fabrics, mainly of the sort bought by Asian women, in addition to groceries. In 1967, Safdar sold his share of the business to Ali and Yacoub, and set up his own grocery in an adjoining area. Later, in the early 1970s, Yacoub sold his share of the business and moved to Newcastle to set up another business with a relative there. Safdar and Ali remained in Glasgow, and although they were no longer in business together, their friendship persisted and was reinforced by a friendship between the women of the two households. On the basis of this, Safdar negotiated the marriage of his son to Ali's daughter Kalsoom.

Kalsoom justified this marriage outside the family by saying that her mother and her husband's mother (Safdar's wife) regarded each other as sisters. A relationship like a kinship relationship had been established between the two households long before the marriage took place. Later, when talking about Safdar's funeral, Gafoor's wife (Safdar's granddaughter in Oxford) told me how Kalsoom's parents had played a major role in organizing and bearing the cost of the funeral, a role which generally falls to the close kin of the deceased. Kalsoom, Safdar's granddaughter, and various of their other relatives in Oxford said that the strong tie of mutual trust, support and economic cooperation during the years of the business partnership provided a sound basis for the marriage that was subsequently arranged. Both families had also prospered in Britain.

Farook's eldest daughter Zarina's marriage was the second marriage between non-kin to take place in this *birādarī*. Farook's closest agnatic relative with a son the right age was Yacoub, his father's father's brother's son (FFBS — see Figure. 5.1), in Newcastle. In order to consider Yacoub's proposal that Zarina be married to Yacoub's son, Farook went to Newcastle to visit Yacoub and his family. Farook decided, however, that Yacoub's son, who lacked any formal qualifications, would be a poor match for his daughter who had a College of Further Education diploma and that the couple would not suit each other. Later, he discussed the matter with his daughter, who told him briefly about a classmate whom she had liked at the college where she had studied, who was now an electrician. Farook and his wife made discreet enquiries and discovered that the boy's father was a fellow Arain, also from Jullunder before 1947. In fact, Farook had met this man about ten years earlier when he first came to Oxford, but had recently had little contact with him. They also discovered that this family now has extensive landholdings in Multan district and a house in a city there. They renewed contact and the wedding took place a year later. A few years later, while discussing marriage arrangements, Zarina said that the success of her own marriage proved that her father, who was a good judge of character, was wise to discount Yacoub's son. She also said it did not matter that there were no known kinship links with her husband's family, because they were Arain, but marrying someone from another caste would have been a different matter.

Was it primarily because, in both cases, these matches made such good pragmatic sense that Ali had not married his daughter Kalsoom to his brother's son, and Farook had not married his daughter Zarina to his relative Yacoub's son? What of the claims of kin? I visited Kalsoom's father's village in Pakistan briefly quite soon after Kalsoom's wedding. It was clear, from his *pakkā* house built from remittances from Glasgow, his tractors and his landholdings, that Ali had prospered in relation to his close kinsmen who had not gone abroad. It was also clear that Ali's brother in Pakistan had expected his eldest son, who was of the right age, to have married Kalsoom (his FBD) and come to Britain. This young man was working on his father's land in Pakistan and now expected to marry Kalsoom's younger sister, instead. Would this be a futile hope? How easily can the expectations of kin be disregarded? If the claims of kin can be ignored, is the preference for marrying within the family not meaningless?

In fact, the claims of kin cannot be so easily dismissed. Ali's brother's eldest son (Kalsoom's FBS) had been turned down by his uncle Ali in Glasgow as a husband for Kalsoom, but in 1981 expected to marry Kalsoom's younger sister and come to Britain. Farook had not considered any of the sons of his younger brothers — two in Pakistan and two in Oxford — as husbands for Zarina, as they were too young. However, when I visited them in 1981, his two younger brothers in Pakistan clearly expected that at least some of their children would be married into the three Oxford households. Karamat, the fourth brother, and his wife were in effect grooming their second son as a prospective spouse for one of the cousins in Britain, by sending him to school and providing him with good clothes. (They were not investing such hopes in their eldest boy, who had received no schooling beyond the third grade — about age eight — and was working the family land). They also expected that at least two of their seven daughters would be considered as spouses for cousins in Britain. Bashir, the youngest brother, and his wife expected both of their children to be married to cousins in England. In fact, there were considerable tensions and rivalries between the two daughters-in-law in Farook's mother's household because of these expectations for their children.

It seemed clear to me, in the early 1980s, that the relatives in Britain had rather different expectations for their children. While recognizing a responsibility towards these kin in Pakistan, they considered that marriages with them would not necessarily be advantageous. In 1984, Habiba, Farook's brother Habib's wife, returned to Pakistan taking her nine year old son and her fifteen year old niece, Gafoor's daughter Farida, with her. Habiba wanted to visit her mother who was seriously ill and also to see whether Karamat's children would be suitable spouses for her own children. She concluded that they would not, commenting disparagingly on the fact the Karamat and his wife had made no attempt to control their family size (they had nine children, of whom seven were girls) despite the advice of the three elder brothers in England. 'So many children drag a family down', she said, adding that she and Habib did not want to have to contribute towards the dowries of these seven nieces in Pakistan. Her son commented that his female cousins in the village were like 'wild animals'. Habiba thought she would do better for her children by looking for spouses among fellow Arain in Britain. In 1985, Habiba's eldest son was married to his cousin Farida in Oxford, Gafoor's daughter, rather than to a cousin from Pakistan. Farook's son was married the following year to his father's sister's daughter in Oxford, who moved from working in her father Ijaz's shop to working in Farook's business. By 1985, the marriages that had taken place in Farook's *birādarī* included one to an unrelated Arain and two to first cousins, all brought up in Britain[10].

On the basis of this flexible definition of *birādarī*, then, we might reasonably expect, with time, a decline in the proportion of marriages to close kin and an increase in the proportion of marriages with non-kin. This expectation would be in keeping with global trends, because the frequency of close kin marriage is apparently declining in most populations that practice it, as a result of social change and migration[11]. My own observations, however, suggest that there has been no significant increase in the number of marriages with non-kin, nor any necessary decline in the frequency of close-kin marriage. My analysis of the types of marriage made by 70 young Oxford Pakistanis from 24 households over the last 15 years (table 5.1) shows 59% of marriages to be with first cousins (and 17% with other kin, and 11% with non-kin of the same *birādarī*). Whether this represents an increase or decrease in the rate of cousin marriage is difficult to say, because establishing a 'base rate' from which to compare rates of cousin marriage is problematic — it is rarely clear that what is being compared is directly equivalent[12]. However, evidence from West Yorkshire that suggests that the rate of first cousin marriage among British Pakistanis has in fact increased also provides a direct comparison. In their survey of 100 mostly young Pakistani mothers in the postnatal wards of two West Yorkshire hospitals, Darr and Modell asked the young women they interviewed about their mothers' marriages. They found that among the young mothers, 55% of marriages were with first cousins, 28% to other close and more distant kin and 15% to non-kin. By contrast, of women in the grand-mother generation, 33% were married to first cousins, 24% within the *birādarī* and 30% to non-kin[13].

It is also the case that, unlike the marriage of Habiba's elder son to Gafoor's daughter and of Farook's son to Ijaz's daughter, most first cousin marriages are not to cousins raised in Britain, but are to cousins from Pakistan. In my Oxford sample, the vast majority (86.7%) of close-kin marriages are with relatives from Pakistan (table 5.2), rather than with other cousins in Britain. This is so even where the circle of kin in Britain does include potential spouses. Darr and Modell do not give the origin of spouses, but they do suggest, in explanation of the apparent increase in first-cousin marriage, that for many British Pakistanis residence in Britain for more than twenty years means that the circle of close acquaintances in Pakistan 'tends to shrink within the limits of the extended family'. They

ORIGINS OF SPOUSES OF 70 YOUNG ADULTS		
Relationship to spouse	Total No.	No. From Pakistan
First cousin (incl. 2 double first cousins)	41	37
Other relative (inc. 2 second cousins & 3 affinal kin)	12	9
Unrelated, same biradari	8	3
Unrelated, different biradari	6	1
Other	3	0
Total	70	50

Table 5.2

imply, therefore, that marriages take place with close kin in Pakistan because British families have few other people to choose from[14].

This does not seem to be the case for Oxford Pakistanis. For many British Pakistanis the circle of acquaintances expands rather than shrinks, often encompassing people from a wider range of districts than before migration, as the extent of Pakistani social networks, discussed in chapter 9, demonstrates. Occasionally prospective spouses are drawn from these circles of acquaintances. Rubina was married to her father's brother's son, and her sister to a more distant relative, both from Pakistan, but her brother was married to an unrelated girl of the same caste background from Derby, whose mother Rubina's mother had first met at a wedding reception in Oxford. Circles of acquaintance also extend to Pakistan and close contacts there may also result in new marriages being contemplated; this strategy may be more common among the economically successful migrants such as Khan whose daughter's marriage was discussed in the previous chapter.

If the *birādarī* system is flexible enough to tolerate a variety of marriage strategies within these broadly defined limits of 'kinship', if the motive is social advancement, and if marriages are arranged not as a result of blindly following a cultural preference for marriage with close kin but on the basis of many different considerations, how do we explain this apparent increase in the rate of marriages with first cousins from Pakistan? Following Donnan and Holy[15], I suggest we need to look within the broad context of social advancement and cultural preference at the specific advantages of such marriages.

The advantages of marriage with close kin from Pakistan are, on the face of it at least, much greater from the viewpoint of kin in Pakistan than from the point of view of families in Britain. For most Oxford families, maintaining some close contact with kin in Pakistan is important because of shared interests 'at home' in property or business and so that there are people to depend upon for hospitality and practical support during return visits. Even so, for most Oxford families, close kin in Pakistan are not the people on whom they depend in business ventures, for day-to-day support, or for immediate help in family crises. British Pakistanis are more likely to depend on relatives and friends made in Britain in such circumstances, unless a family has prospered in such a way as to have established business and property in Pakistan too and to spend a large proportion of their time there.

For close kin in Pakistan, however, the expectation that a son or daughter will marry a cousin in Britain is also linked to the desire to send another relative to Britain, and thus to the prospect of socio-economic advance. From the point of view of kin in Pakistan, the desire is deep rooted: despite being rejected as a husband for Kalsoom, Kalsoom's father's brother's son in Pakistan still expected to come to Britain to marry Kalsoom's sister. While I was in Pakistan, I was often asked, 'Will you get me a visa for England?' After I returned, a family with whom I had stayed in Pakistan sent their relatives a cassette tape, on which one of them jokingly said, 'You sent us a *gori* (white woman); that was fine, but you sent us one with her husband. What was the benefit of that? If you had sent an unmarried one, we could have sent a man to England with her'. I have, on several occasions, been asked to find a 'good girl' for the male relatives of Pakistanis settled in Oxford and it would not matter, I was told, if she were not Pakistani. It is now the case that for most Pakistanis the only way to get a potential wage earning man into Britain, other than by seeking political asylum, is through marriage to a girl settled in Britain. Having daughters of marriageable age gives parents in Britain considerable bargaining power in relation to both kin and non-kin in Pakistan; equally, some kin in Pakistan may manipulate their

relatives' sense of duty towards them in order to send sons to
Britain (and not all of such marriages have been successful).
The preference for marriage with close kin is one that can be
manipulated to people's advantage, on both sides.

It is of course possible for kin in Britain to ignore their Pakistan
relatives' claims over their sons and daughters as spouses for
their own children. Sometimes none of the children of a couple
in Britain have been married to close kin in Pakistan. All six of
Farook's three sons and three daughters have been married in
Britain, for example (see Figure 5.4). On the basis of the
success of Zarina's marriage outside the family, Farook decided
that his second daughter would be married to Zarina's
husband's brother, rather than to a cousin from Pakistan.
Although this marriage did not take place, as Farook's second
daughter eloped with and married an Arab student in 1986, a
few years later Farook's third daughter married the man to
whom her elder sister was to have been married, strengthening
in this way the affinal tie established by Zarina's marriage.
Farook's eldest son married his mother's brother's daughter
(Ijaz's daughter — Figure 5.4). Born and brought up in Britain,
Ijaz's daughter, who had been working in her father's shop
since leaving school, moved when she married to work in her
father-in-law's shop. Farook's two younger sons married unre-

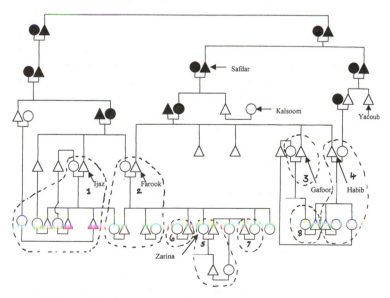

Figure 5.4   An Arain *birādarī*, early 1990s.

lated Arain girls brought up in Britain: one girl was introduced through family contacts; the other marriage was an arranged 'love' marriage which took place some years after the couple had first met as university students.

How typical, though, is Farook? We might begin by considering, for instance, the marriages that have taken place in the other families which constitute Farook's *birādarī* in Britain, the families of his brothers and his brother-in-law (Figure 5.4). In Habib's family, there has been a mixture of types of marriage, though none have been to first cousins from Pakistan. Habib's eldest son was married to his father's brother Gafoor's daughter, brought up in Britain. His second son was married to an unrelated Arain girl from a well-to-do family in the village in Pakistan, rather than to any of his father's brother's daughters, and his daughter married Gafoor's second wife's brother from Pakistan, strengthening the link between Gafoor and Habib's household in Oxford.

Likewise, none of Gafoor's four children have married a cousin from Pakistan. After considering and rejecting the proposal that his daughter be married to one of his brothers' sons from Pakistan, Gafoor married his daughter to Habib's eldest son in Oxford. Gafoor's eldest son married an 'English' Muslim girl, the daughter of a Pakistani father and English mother at a marriage which was 'arranged' after the couple had already met at social gatherings. The next son married an unrelated Arain girl from Cardiff, whose family, introduced through acquaintances, turned out to have lived in the same village in Pakistan, and the third son married a girl from Pakistan who is the more distantly related daughter of his step-mother's sister. Before this youngest son's marriage took place, Gafoor had also carefully considered as a potential wife for his son one of the daughters of his brothers, Karamat and Bashir, in Pakistan. He concluded, however, that there would be many potential problems with such an alliance, one being the fact that between them Karamat and Bashir would still have seven unmarried daughters, all in need of a respectable marriage and dowry. If one of these daughters came to Britain as a bride, the chances were that her allegiances would first and foremost be to her father and brothers, and thus, indirectly, her sisters, and this conflict of interest would be likely to cause rifts between her and her husband and in-laws. Gafoor concluded that it would be more sensible to consolidate the alliance created by his own second marriage and build up his links with his second wife's immediate kin in Pakistan. It was also for this reason, as well as to strengthen the link between Habib and Gafoor's household, that Habiba's daughter was married Gafoor's second wife's brother who came from Pakistan to Britain after the marriage.

Farook's brother-in-law Ijaz has done well in shopkeeping. He was for many years in partnership with his sister's husband, Farook, and the first marriage in Ijaz's family was of Ijaz's eldest daughter to Farook's eldest son. Since his early years in Oxford, Ijaz has sent regular remittances to his brother in Pakistan, enabling his brother to establish a chicken-farming business in the village. Ijaz's eldest son married his father's brother's daughter, who came from Pakistan to Britain and now works in the family shop. Ijaz's second son married a cousin, his mother's brother's daughter, also from Pakistan, who works in the family shop. Ijaz and his wife considered it important to build up their connections with Ijaz's wife's close kin, because they are 'respectable' and quite prosperous residents of Sahiwal city. Through his wife's relatives, Ijaz and his family now have a house there to which they return periodically in preference to returning to the village. Ijaz's third son has married a second cousin, his father's mother's brother's daughter, from Faisalabad city.

What this suggests is that whether families make use of their obligations to consider the sons and daughters of their siblings in Pakistan as spouses for their children is to a large extent a result of quite diverse pragmatic considerations, some of which have been outlined above. Indeed, it may be that those who have prospered in Britain are more able to disregard the claims of close kin, if it suits them to do so, than those who have not. We could therefore conclude that the majority of British Pakistanis have so far married their offspring to close kin from Pakistan (rather than to non-kin or more distant relatives in Britain or Pakistan) as consequence of weighing up the pragmatic advantages and disadvantages of particular marriage choices.

However, this conclusion leaves unexplained the power of the cultural preference for marriage with kin; given the diversity of practical considerations that may be involved, why should people both with this preference at all? Migration to Britain was perceived not solely in terms of individual social mobility, although it provides opportunities for this, but in terms of raising the status of a group of kin in relation to their wider *birādarī* and neighbours in Pakistan. Increasingly, the arena within which status is assessed encompasses fellow-Pakistanis in Britain. Within this arena, status derives not only from wealth, mainly in terms of property and business, but also from respectability (primarily expressed by an *ashraf* lifestyle). One element of being considered a man worthy of respect derives from having a reputation as being someone who honours his obligations to kin. Cousin marriage is one of the most important expressions of this obligation. The majority of east Oxford families have not achieved social mobility and status though massive accumulation of property and business. For them, the marriages of their children to the children of their siblings in Pakistan is an important symbol of honour and respectability, a public statement that even families separated by continents recognize their mutual obligations. Moreover, while it is analytically possible to separate 'pragmatic' and symbolic or 'expressive' aspects of marriage[16], it would be misleading to draw this distinction too sharply, because actions performed to express a particular cultural value may in turn bring pragmatic pay-off, and vice-versa.

A man who has turned his back on his relatives in Pakistan, however prosperous, is liable to be criticized for acting out of self-interest. Farook, a prosperous shopkeeper who also has extended his landholdings in Pakistan, did not marry any of his children to the sons or daughters of his brothers there. He is well aware that in making the best of the opportunities his children's marriages offered, and in rejecting Bashir and Karamat's claims on his children, he has let down his brothers in Pakistan. In this respect, his honour could be questioned. Indirectly, Farook's honour, as the eldest brother especially, is linked with the respectability of his brothers' daughters in Pakistan. Of course, Farook cannot be criticized for having totally disregarded his kin, for his eldest son is married to Ijaz's daughter, and the family themselves justify the daughters' marriages within the terms of the preference for marrying relatives because they took place with fellow-Arain. Yet Farook himself wishes to make amends toward his brothers in Pakistan: now that he has discharged his obligations toward his own children, he is giving his brothers in Pakistan practical and financial support with finding suitable spouses and in providing dowries for their daughters. Farook's eldest daughter told me her father was concerned that he had allowed his relationships with kin in Pakistan to wear thin and was now going to put some effort into repairing the situation. 'A new brick strengthens the wall' she said, virtually paraphrasing a Panjabi proverb 'that "when the fence gets old, it is your duty to put new wood in it" i.e. new marriages with relatives are necessary if the kinship relationship is not to crumble away and disappear'[17]. Links with kin, most explicitly through cousin marriage, but also through for example assisting a brother with the marriages of his daughters, are an important symbol of *birādarī* honour and solidarity.

Another element of these aspects of cousin marriage concerns its relationship to ideas of gender and in particular to the control of female sexuality. The honour of a family is linked to female chastity, and honour threatened by the behaviour of a daughter in Britain may be quickly salvaged by marriage to a first cousin in Pakistan. Parents are extremely fearful of the influences of the western environment, to the extent that some parents take their daughters out of upper school and back to Pakistan for the critical period of fourteen to eighteen years. Many parents are afraid that if their daughters remain unmarried and go on to college or university they will have premarital sexual relationships and in so doing will insult the respectability of the family. Usually a girl suspected of premarital sex or a love affair is taken to Pakistan where she is likely to be married quickly to a first cousin, thus preserving family honour. Rubina was taken to Pakistan after her elopement with Tariq and married a first cousin there. Her sister, about whom there had been no such worries, was married with more careful deliberation to a more distant relative, and her brother was married outside the family, but inside the caste, to a respectable girl brought up in Britain. Within one family, there is thus often a mixture of marriage strategies — some marriages are with close kin, on either the mother's side or the father's side, and some are outside the family. In each case, the particular outcome of marriage deliberations is a function of the nature of the relationships involved and considerations of socio-economic advantage, which include those of honour and respect. As Donnan writes of the Dhund in Northeast Pakistan, 'The preference for marriage with kinsmen is thus only one of several notions Dhund have about marriage and it becomes relevant to activity not by its mere existence, but only by people taking account of it.... as part of a strategy directed towards contracting the most advantageous marriage'[18].

In this context, 'advantage' includes not just pragmatic considerations, such as the cementing of a business partnership or the prospect of migration to Britain, but the 'expressive' aspects of marriage, as a symbol of respectability, honour or fulfilled duty. These are 'subject to the actors' strategic manipulation' just as much as are pragmatic considerations[19]. It often is in people's perceived interests to take notice of the preference for cousin marriage but sometimes it is not; the balance of honour and economic-advantage swings one way in one case, and the other way another time. Migration abroad would appear to have broadened the range of choice to the extent that, for some at least, socio-economic advantage and consanguinity do not necessarily coincide in the most advantageous marriage. In such cases, though, even marriage with non-kin tends to be justified within the idiom of kinship; by invoking a kinship relationship migrants are making a statement about the respectability of the proposed match. In Oxford, kinship may be re-interpreted, or invoked in a looser sense, to incorporate non-kin who have become 'like kin' or share a common caste status, in the justification of particular marriage strategies. For families dispersed through migration, the fact that at least some of their offspring marry close relatives is important as a means of maintaining the reputation and honour of a family in its village of origin and in relation to other Pakistani *birādarī*s in Britain. Such marriage symbolizes its members' commitment to maintaining the *birādarī* structure despite living apart. This in turn may have important practical consequences, especially given migrants' continuing commitment to retain roots in Pakistan.

Conclusion

In the Sayyed, Mughal, Sheikh and Arain families discussed in this and the previous chapter, marriages over several generations have been mainly with cousins but not exclusively so, nor exclusively within the *birādarī* or caste. The preference for close-kin marriage is but one of a number of considerations which may be relevant in any given case. Sometimes, marriages are arranged outside the *birādarī* or caste, primarily on the basis of considerations of socio-economic status and the compatibility of spouses, and are variously justified in relation to perceptions of caste status and *birādarī* membership.

Given this flexibility, it is at first glance surprising that the rate of close-kin marriage, particularly marriage with first cousins from Pakistan, seems to have increased among British Pakistanis in recent years rather than to have declined. The trends in marriage patterns documented here mainly represent the outcome of parental deliberations over the advantages and disadvantages of particular proposals of marriage, both with kin and with non-kin. That most marriages are with first cousins from Pakistan to a large extent reflects the socio-economic position of most British Pakistanis, which remains one of relative insecurity; it may be that those who have integrated most successfully into the U.K. economy may be less concerned with meeting the expectations of kin in Pakistan. Even so, it is unlikely even for the most socio-economically successful migrants that the expectations of and sense of obliga-tion towards relatives in Pakistan will be easily or necessarily shrugged off. Close-kin marriage continues to be important as a demonstration of migrants' continuing commitments to the *birādarī* and to retaining the option of social mobility in terms of Pakistani society. In families in which some marriages have been with non-kin, the continuing symbolic and practical importance of kinship is usually expressed through other marriages with close kin; within one family, different types of marriage may satisfy different criteria. One son may have a marriage 'arranged' with an unrelated Pakistani girl he met at university in Britain; another son may marry a distant relative from Pakistan; a daughter may marry a first cousin from Pakistan; another son may marry an English Muslim girl, and so on. None of these marriages will necessarily be regarded as a violation of cultural norms, and in most cases will be justified, broadly or narrowly, within the idiom of kinship (unless the matter is taken out of parents' hands, if a son or daughter acts or makes a decision that their parents cannot accept, as the next chapter shows).

If the importance of kinship in both its material and symbolic sense were to decrease we might expect to see a decline in close kin marriage, but the evidence to date suggests the contrary. Close-kin marriage remains important, for both relative socio-economic security and for maintaining family honour.

Pakistanis remain committed to both Pakistan and Britain, as the high proportion of marriages to relatives from Pakistan suggests. The most economically successful British Pakistanis may, increasingly, consider unrelated spouses — either from the U.K. or from Pakistan — for their children, arranging their marriages on the basis of socio-economic and class interests. Yet they will probably still justify their choices within the idiom of kinship and with reference to the notions of trust and reciprocity which characterize kinship: kinship is thus likely to remain a central idiom of social interaction.

We have come a long way from migrants' rationalizations for close kin marriage, such as that it is in a daughter's best interests because it reproduces most closely the values of her natal home. Such rationalizations are best regarded as symbols of the values of 'real' or 'fictive' kinship solidarity, values which migrants are likely to uphold where the co-operation of kin, or indeed of non-kin, is an important socio-economic resource. Through this view of kinship it is possible to reconcile the apparent increase in cousin marriage with the fact that there are clearly cases where British Pakistanis resist or ignore the expectations of siblings in Pakistan. Some of the cousin marriages recorded here have proved to be, at a personal level, unsuccessful. Pakistanis themselves may vigorously debate the traditional rationalizations for close kin marriage, because the marriages of first-cousins brought up continents apart have not always been stable or lasted: close-kinship does not necessarily, of itself, ensure the compatibility of spouses. This issue is also related to the question of gender stereotypes, of changing expectations of gender roles and to the issue of female chastity as a symbol of family honour, a component of the symbolic significance of the preference for marriage with close kin. I turn to these issues in the next chapter.

NOTES

1. On Pakistani marriage preferences, see: Donnan, 1985; Alavi, 1972; Das, 1973; Eglar, 1960, and Perhson 1966. On close-kin marriage in the Middle East see Holy, 1989 and Tapper and Tapper, 1992/3.
2. This is, of course, compatible with a strategy of social mobility and may indeed facilitate caste mobility, as discussed in the previous chapter. See also V. Das, 1973.
3. Close–kin marriage is usually associated with Islam, but some Muslim groups disapprove of it and some non-Muslims favour it. Holy

(1989:119–120) discusses the cultural features, not of specifically Islamic origin but 'reinforced by the Islamic tradition', common to the parts of the worlds — from the Middle East to areas of Asia and north Africa — in which people favour close kin marriage.

4. Evidence of a high proportion of first cousin marriage has also raised the sensitive issue of genetic implications. See, for instance, Modell and Kuliev and relevant chapters of Clarke and Parsons (eds.), 1997.
5. Donnan, 1985:195.
6. Donnan, 1985:194.
7. Donnan, 1985:194.
8. Not surprisingly, the *birādarī* has been variously defined; see Blunt, 1931:10; Eglar, 1960:75, 76–7, and Alavi, 1972:2.
9. Alavi, 1972:2.
10. In 1988, I wrote that it was 'still too early to speak of trends in marriage preferences, since most second-generation Pakistanis are still of pre-marriageable age' (Shaw, 1988:107). I thought that 'families may tend to select a spouse from among kin in Britain rather than in Pakistan on the basis of economic interests, equality of status and the compatibility of spouses. For the same reason, there may also be a tendency among some families to consider non-relatives in Britain as spouses' (1988:107). As in the Arain and Mughal marriages discussed above, I suggested that the various justifications for such marriages would be made broadly within the idiom of kinship. They will make reference to common *birādarī* member-ship, as in the case of the Arain where *birādarī* is re-defined as equivalent to 'caste', or to an equivalence of 'caste' status, as in the *ashraf* marriages, or else to a '*birādarī* -like' tie based on the trust and reciprocity associated with kinship, where those involved are not real kin (1988:107).
11. Darr and Modell, 1988: 188–9.
12. Tapper and Tapper 1992/3.
13. Two other studies lend some support to this 'pre-migration' estimate. Werbner calculates rates of endogamy based on reported details of 72 marriages within four extended families, two of rural origins in Jhelum and Gujrat, two from cities, within the generation of 'pioneer' migrants in Manchester, marriage which presumably took place prior to migration. These data show 35% of marriages to be with first cousins, a rate Werbner writes is comparable with rates throughout the Middle East (1990:347). A study of 900 women in hospital in Lahore gives a similar 'base-rate': 36% of marriages were with first cousins and 53% were with unrelated spouses, of which 25% were from the same *birādarī* (Shami, 1982).
14. Darr and Modell, 1988:189.
15. Donnan, 1985; Holy, 1989.
16. Holy, 1989.
17. Werbner, 1990:96.
18. Donnan, 1985:195.
19. Holy, 1989:90.

6 HONOUR AND SHAME: GENDER AND GENERATION

Tariq had been seeing Rubina for about one year without his parents' knowledge before deciding to ask his father for permission to marry her. Tariq's parents were disappointed to hear of their son's intentions because they were already arranging a good match with a relative's daughter but they agreed to speak to Rubina's parents. Rubina's parents, however, rejected the proposal, so Tariq and Rubina decided to elope and get married elsewhere. Her family alerted all contacts in Britain, but failed to trace her. A fortnight later, Rubina returned home of her own accord, to tell her parents of her marriage. Her enraged father took her back to Pakistan, where, several months later, she was married to her father's brother's son.

Some months after Rubina's elopement with Tariq, another Pakistani girl, Jamila, eloped with a Sikh boy. Her outraged brothers and their friends took revenge on the boy's male relatives by assaulting them one evening and threatening their lives if Jamila was not returned to them. A few days later, Pakistani friends in the midlands telephoned Jamila's parents to tell them where their daughter was, and Jamila's brothers fetched her home. Jamila's parents took her to Pakistan for nine months and then brought her back to England for a six-month period of religious instruction under the guidance of a *pīr* (saint). She continued to live with her family for two years until her marriage to a cousin in Pakistan took place.

Elopements like these from time to time provide dramatic news headlines in the local press, and they are not confined to Oxford. A recent television documentary draws attention to the extremes to which dishonoured Pakistani families may go in their attempts to salvage their pride when daughters reject arranged marriages and elope with and marry white men. The film, based upon the stories of six young Pakistani women in Yorkshire, shows that families may keep errant daughters as prisoners in their own homes, or else issue death threats and engage 'bounty hunters' who tap into south Asian networks across the country seeking information about fugitives[1]. The price such couples pay for their love, poignantly described in a book written by one of the couples depicted in the film, is high indeed[2]. In Bradford, the number of girls being sought by bounty hunters has apparently doubled in the past four years, according to a unit established to help young Asian women who refuse to go through with arranged marriages[3]. The recent call for more government support and protection for young women forced into arranged marriages follows the life-sentence upon a mother and son for murdering a daughter (whose husband was in Pakistan, and whose father was dead) for the dishonour of her adulterous pregnancy[4].

None of the Oxford incidents, as far as I know, has involved a Pakistani woman eloping with an English man — the elopements have been of Pakistani girls who have run away with other Pakistani, South Asian or Muslim men. And none of these cases has, as far as I know, involved murder, but there have been violent incidents and there have been death threats. But then, the Pakistani population of Oxford is so much smaller than that of a city like Bradford, so it may simply be statistically less likely that elopements from Oxford will involve English men, or that the wrath of parents at the dishonour inflicted upon them by a daughter's behaviour will result in her death. These cases may indeed represent extremes, but there are also some common principles at work in the less dramatic as well as the more sensational cases.

So what in fact do these incidents reveal about the lives of young Pakistanis in Britain? Are incidents like these the tip of the iceberg, symptoms of widespread and increasing discontent, especially among young British Pakistani women, with the 'chauvinistic' system of arranged marriage? Do they testify to the 'culture clash' which both westerners and many south Asians assume will inevitably follow from being educated in Britain and absorbing western liberal values such as the 'right' to choose one's spouse or lover? How do most young Pakistani adults resolve the conflict that might arise between the interests and opportunities they may wish to pursue outside the family with the obligations they have towards parents and other relatives?

Purdah and *izzat* in Pakistan

It would be wrong to assume that the fact that elopements occur at all is in itself sufficient evidence that young adults must have absorbed liberal 'western' values, because in Pakistan too young adults sometimes reject their parents' marriage plans for them and run away from home. While I was staying in a village in north-west Panjab, a Rajput boy and a Mughal girl disappeared. They had been meeting secretly in the fields behind the village during the previous few months. The girl became pregnant and the couple decided to elope rather than face the family's wrath, which could result in her death. When the girl disappeared, her parents alerted the village and the police and discovered that a boy from the village was also missing. Guessing what had happened, the girls' enraged parents accused the boy's parents of ruining their daughter and insulting the family. Three months later the couple was found in southern Panjab. They had been married there according to Muslim law by an *imām* who did not know them, and the girl was about five months pregnant. They were returned to the north-west and held by the police while the families decided what should be done.

Why should a daughter sometimes feel she has no choice but to elope? And why should her family become so angry? The honour (*izzat*) of a family depends to a large extent on the behaviour of its women, especially its daughters. Respectable female behaviour is linked with the observance of purdah, which literally means 'curtain' and is usually described as a system of segregating unrelated men and women from puberty onwards[5]. Purdah is usually but not exclusively associated with Muslims and there is considerable variation is how it is observed in practice[6]. Among Pakistani Muslims, the strictness with which women observe purdah varies according to 'caste', family status and context. Purdah is more than a system of screening women from men, however, for it is also moral code that governs relationships between the sexes. This moral code operates even where strict observance of purdah is not apparent.

The principles of purdah in Pakistan require boys and girls to be segregated from puberty onwards; men and women should avoid all contact with the opposite sex, apart from their spouses and immediate kin. Pakistanis say that these restrictions are designed to control sexuality, to ensure virginity at marriage and chaste behaviour thereafter. These restrictions are necessary because the sexuality of both men and women is regarded as dangerous. Pakistanis believe if a man and a woman are alone together, their minds inevitably and naturally turn to sex and sexual activity will follow. 'The devil comes into their hearts', one man explained. A common image is of a constant battle within a person between 'animal nature' ruled by the devil and the spiritual self ruled by God. In this view, the purpose of the Islamic purdah system is to control 'nature' and to prevent sexual anarchy. Sometimes, despite these preventative measures, men and women are alone together, and, since their sexual desires are 'natural', it is inevitable that they will succumb to temptation. When this happens, God will punish them both.

Commentators sometimes ignore the fact that purdah affects both men and women, focussing their attention on the restrictions on women in particular[7]. There is no doubt, however, that the constraints of purdah affect men and women unequally. In Pakistan, after puberty, girls tend to be confined to the home and to domestic tasks, while boys and young men play and socialize around and beyond the village. Likewise, the part of the male body that must be kept covered is the area just below the navel to the knees, while women must cover their bodies to the ankles and the wrists, conceal the shape of their breasts and cover their hair.

Why should purdah from puberty onwards affect men and women so differently? In Pakistan, sons are more highly valued than are daughters. As Hastings Donnan shows for the Dhund Abbasi of the Murree hills in northeast Rawalpindi, property is customarily passed on through male heirs and the continued existence of a family depends upon the male line. This is why the birth of a son is more celebrated than the birth of a daughter[8]. A woman's chief value lies in her ability to produce sons, an ability that she acquires at puberty. This resource must not be squandered, but 'must be protected until it is handed over intact, and in the proper manner, to the right person'[9]. It is therefore of critical importance that a girl be *sharīf* (respectable) from puberty until marriage and at her marriage a high premium is placed on her being a virgin.

Not surprisingly then, 'romantic' love or illicit sex, when it does occur, occurs in secret. If parents discover that a daughter is meeting a boy, the consequences for her may be serious. They may take her to stay with far-away relatives so as to preserve their reputation, avoid further, scandal and protect marriage prospects, or quickly arrange her marriage to a close relative. More serious consequences follow if an unmarried girl is pregnant, for the girl's pregnancy usually means that the relationship can no longer be kept secret. Parents may try to procure an abortion, or, in extreme cases, may literally 'throw out' their daughter for she is no longer marriageable and her parents' honour has been severely insulted. Reportedly, a daughter's permanent disappearance or death may be easier for parents to bear than a constant reminder of their dishonour[10]. At this point, or just before this point is reached, a couple may decide that elopement is the only alternative.

The discovery of an illicit relationship, especially if it involves an unmarried girl who becomes pregnant, can therefore endanger not just the honour of the families concerned but their lives. For men,

> the safest way of obtaining illicit sex is therefore adultery with a married woman. This way children will not be born out of marriage; should the woman conceive, the child will be mistaken for her husband's, and none of the problems of what to do with it will arise. On the other hand, sex with an unmarried woman presents a number of problems; for the girl, for the boy, for their respective families and for the future of the child. Sexuality, a girl's behaviour and family honour are thus intricately bound together. The Dhund view is that a daughter is a family's point of weakness and as such she should be protected and shielded by the father and brothers, until such time as they relinquish control of her sexuality to her husband[11].

Purdah and *izzat* in Britain

To what extent do these ideas hold sway among British Pakistanis? Of the many differences between living in Britain and living in Pakistan, the most striking is surely the relative freedom of 'western' women. In the light of this, have at least some young adults, such as women who have been to school and entered further education in Britain, begun to challenge the status of women in rural Pakistan? Has the impact of 'traditional' values declined and the status of women changed as a result of being brought up in Britain?

Traditional ideas about gender, sexuality and marriage do continue to influence the behaviour and attitudes of the majority of young Oxford Pakistanis, despite the experiences of being schooled or employed in Britain. This, however, is not to say that the attitudes and experiences of the pioneer generation and reproduced without challenge among their children and grand-children. On the contrary, patterns of gender relations are in practice constantly under some degree of re-negotiation within most families, especially where women are working, and as other family members adapt to changing opportunities and experiences. Young people sometimes vigorously debate such questions as whether arranged marriage is 'customary' or 'Islamic', whether they should have more 'say' in marriage arrangements, what constitutes appropriate work for women, how purdah should be interpreted and whether it is justified by Islam. Young people adopt a range of different strategies in negotiating their social lives and their experiences of education, work and marriage, with varying degrees of autonomy.

These variations exist within families as well as between them. Parents generally show more flexibility towards their sons than their daughters, but may adopt different strategies for different same-sex children. One daughter may leave school at sixteen and accept an arranged marriage to a relative from Pakistan, while her sister enters further education and a profession, post-poning the question of her marriage. Parental attitudes can also change over time; parents may become more — or less — ready to accommodate change in the light of their own and others' experiences. Yet in all of these situations and in all debates, tra-ditional attitudes are an important yardstick or reference, and for this reason I begin with an outline of these ideas as they expressed locally.

One mosque committee member used this image to explain the ideals of purdah:

> If you have something valuable, you keep it safe. If you
> have a diamond you lock it in a case. You don't leave it

for anyone to take. A woman is like a diamond. She is precious. You should keep her inside the four walls of your house. She should look after the house and children, and you look after her. Inside the house, she is in charge. My place is outside.

For many people across the generations, the experience of living in Britain has reinforced aspects of the traditional view of the relationship between men and women. This is because images of women in the west provide constant reminders of the contrasting Islamic ideal. A corollary of the idea that a woman should be protected is that a woman who is 'outside', among men, unprotected, is 'free for anyone to take'. Western women in particular appear to break all the rules of purdah. They are regarded as sexually promiscuous, moving freely from one man to another, behaving and dressing in order to provoke men. A woman out alone is in effect 'asking' for sexual relations with a man. Rape, young and older men have insisted, is always the woman's fault, because it is the 'natural' result of a woman dressing provocatively and being out alone. In this view, western women are simultaneously exciting and despised for having no sense of shame and being 'used by more than one man; like prostitutes'. As the man quoted above put it:

Women are exploited in English society. They are like toys for men to play with. They are cheap. Women are out on the streets, in shops, on the television. They work like slaves for a pittance in factories, in shops and as cleaners. There's no respect for them.

His wife then showed me what she thought of English women by pulling her *shalwar* tight across her buttocks, loosening her hair and swaying her hips, in imitation of how an English woman attracts a man.

Usually people say that that purdah protects women from men, that women must be protected because they are the dependants of men; sometimes people say that purdah protects men from women. Shabnam, who was eight when she came to Britain and is now in her thirties, said:

Especially before marriage, but also after it, women should not reveal their legs, should tie their hair, should cover their heads and chests with a scarf and should not wear make-up. This stops men from succumbing to temptation.

Shabnam has brought up her daughters, young 'third-generation' women, to dress modestly and avoid the company of unrelated men. Another young married woman, Zarina, gave this account of the divine punishment that will follow for a woman who fails to follow the rules of purdah:

> The Prophet Muhammad was out walking one day when he saw a woman in torture, hanging by her hair, but still alive. A little further on, he saw a woman being hung by her breasts and then he saw a woman being put into a huge fire, screaming. Horrified, he asked Allah, 'Why are these women being tortured like this? Please let them go free!' But Allah replied, 'The first woman used to tantalize men with her hair, the second used to reveal her breasts to strange men and the third slept with a man who was not her husband. That is why I cannot set them free.'

I have not heard any equivalent stories of the divine punishment that would be meted out to men for illicit sex.

Young Men: Socializing and 'Girlfriends'

These ideas, linked as they are to the premium placed on female virginity at marriage in the traditional context, have a number of unequal implications for how young men and women socialize with peers and for their experiences of education and marriage. In general, parents show far greater leniency towards their sons than towards their daughters, especially their unmarried daughters. Boys and young men have fewer domestic responsibilities than their sisters and spend much of their leisure time outside the home. They may help their fathers, in shops or other small businesses, or go to the mosques, or 'hang around' with other young men — with their Pakistani or other South Asian, English or Afro-Caribbean friends — at street corners and in shops, and parents do not closely monitor their activities. At the same time, young men may also be required to keep a close eye on the activities of their sisters, for example by chaperoning sisters to and from school. Among their friends, they often pass judgments about the behaviour and respectability of the sisters, or the wives, of their friends.

In general, responsibility for a daughter or sister's behaviour lies to a large extent with her father and brothers, for the reputation of men and of the family is at risk if doubts circulate about a girl's respectability. Fights sometimes break out if a young man makes insulting remarks about someone else's sister's behaviour. An incident which was portrayed in the local papers as an inter-racial clash between a Pakistani Muslim and an Indian Christian youth gang had in fact occurred because a boy in one group had teased the sister of a boy in the other group. Some years earlier, Amjad's son Asad had died in hospital following a knifing incident in which he had been defending his family's reputation from the attack upon it in the form of another boy's insulting remarks about Asad's sister.

In the logic of the traditional view of sexuality, while a man's own wife, sisters, daughters and other close kin are regarded as and expected to be pure and chaste, protected from unrelated men, all other women are potential sexual partners. Thus, there is often an implicit double standard in attitudes towards relationships with women. Parents do not encourage young men to have girlfriends, nor are they openly tolerant of sexual liaisons. On the contrary, they avoid discussing the subject of pre-marital sex unless to condemn it, and are generally censorious of talk of sex-education in schools. Young people who have 'romantic' or sexual relationships usually strive to keep them hidden from relatives and from other people who know their families. Yet the leniency with which parents regard their sons' activities outside the home also extends to 'going out' with girls. One mother, unusual for her bluntness, admitted that she had encouraged her son to find a girlfriend:

When he first started at university, he kept on asking us to arrange his marriage as soon as possible. I was worried, because I thought it would be better for him to wait about five years, until he was qualified and had got a job. After all, he is only twenty, and when you marry, it's for life. We talked about it, and it seemed that he was worried about sex. All his friends had girlfriends or were married or getting married. So I told him he should enjoy himself first, before he gets married. A boy should have some experience, and there are plenty of English girls around.

Very often, as this quotation suggests, the girls that Pakistani boys go out with are English. Sometimes young men say that because most English women do not share Islamic moral values there is no contradiction between upholding these values on one hand and taking advantage of women who do not share them on the other. Izhar, for instance, is an unmarried twenty-two year old who has recently applied for his father's brother's daughter to come to England as his fiancée. Unknown to his family, he has had a number of English girlfriends:

> The point is, English girls don't mind; there's no restriction for them. In fact, they chase you and laugh at you if you don't go with them. It was like that at school: the girls chasing men. I know I shouldn't have, it's against our religion, but how could I refuse? It's natural for a man to feel like that; you can't really avoid it. I blame the western system. I was in a mixed school and it was too free — all the boys thought about was the girls, and all the girls thought about was the boys.

Many unmarried men, like Izhhar, have had clandestine relationships with English girls, yet do not feel that this contradicts their acceptance of an arranged marriage or the Islamic moral code. Most men and women tacitly accept that men will have girlfriends because 'men are like that' and because English girls are 'outside', free from the constraints of purdah and therefore sexually available.

This logic extends to all women known or suspected to be sexually promiscuous, including other Pakistani girls. Oxford Pakistanis may assume that a South Asian girl who go to college or works, or cuts her hair short or wears western dress is very 'modern' and therefore has boyfriends, 'like English girls'. A common insult for a girl who wears western dress and looks 'modern' is *desī gorī*, which means literally 'home-made white woman'. One young man regarded the South Asian women he had slept with as 'no better' than English women. Others considered some Asian girls as being 'much worse' than

English girls, enjoying the freedom of the contraceptive pill 'just like English women in the 1960s'.

Tariq, who came to Britain as a teenager and spent a few years at the college of further education, had several pre-marital sexual relationships with married Pakistani women. A self-confessed philanderer, he said, 'I've had someone's wife or daughter in every street'. He regarded these affairs as not very serious, saying, 'You have your fun and move on to someone else.' However, his secret courting of Rubina, with whom he eloped, only became more serious, he said, because Rubina had fallen in love with him; he only tried to marry her because she was innocent and his parents were in favour of avoiding a scandal. In another case, Shabbaz, who eloped and married Sakina, had similar views. Sakina was a young woman who had been in England only three months when her neighbour Shabbaz, who had a wife and children in Pakistan, began to pay her a lot of attention and finally seduced her. Eventually they eloped but were pursued by Sakina's father and brothers, who kidnapped Shabbaz for dishonouring them. Shabbaz's relatives contacted the police and subsequently Sakina's father and brothers served a short prison sentence. The couple then married according to Muslim law, though not under British law. Shabbaz viewed Sakina as just another woman with whom he had had an affair. He said 'she's just my girlfriend, like English people have, not my wife; I have her for pleasure.' He said he married her because she had not been 'used' before and so that her family could not say anything. He now intends to bring his first wife and children from Pakistan.

Young Women: Socializing and 'Boyfriends'

From puberty, a young woman's leisure time, outside school or college, is usually spent mainly at home or with female relatives and friends. She does much of the domestic work including childcare and preparing food for the family and for visitors. She participates in her mother's social activities with local friends and neighbours locally but friendships outside the circle of her parents' friends and relatives are not encouraged.

Girls themselves are well aware that, as Zahida's now teenage granddaughter Zena put it, 'people judge a family by the behaviour of its daughters. If a girl has no shame, then the whole family is disgraced'. A girl who 'wanders about outside' or is seen chatting to a man on the street or at the school gates, or is seen wearing make up or in 'immodest' dress will be the subject of speculative talk about her sexual morality. The fear of gossip means that parents may go to great lengths to prevent their daughters being seen in mixed company, or they ensure that daughters are chaperoned by parents or brothers.

Gossip about girls who appear to have violated the appropriate standards in their dress and behaviour is in effect a form of social control, for fear of gossip may curtain social activities, preventing, for example, a young woman from simply walking to meet a girlfriend[12]. A young woman's behaviour is scrutinized especially by other women and girls, who may then make comments that might damage her reputation among her friends, acquaintances, and even people who do not know her. Nadia was once given a lift home from school by her friend's Shamma's brother, in an arrangement made by her parents. Other girls witnessed the event, ignoring the fact that Shamma was there too, and mentioned it at home. Several weeks later, Nadia's mother heard from a neighbour that there was a rumour in the community that Nadia was secretly meeting Shamma's brother[13].

The fear of gossip and the fact that girls' behaviour is scrutinized by just about every other member of the community therefore places severe restrictions on the opportunities young Pakistani men and women have to meet each other. In the context of their peer group, at school and with teachers, Pakistani girls talk about boys, boyfriends, and marriage, and may express the desire for more freedom to meet young men[14]. Pakistani girls' talk of boyfriends is influenced by both media images and the themes of doomed romantic love in the Urdu and Hindi films avidly watched in most homes. It is, however, mostly sexually innocent, for most girls do not have the freedom, opportunities or confidence to develop relationships with boys.

In fact, girls are often vulnerable to the attentions of men. Unused to dealing with boys, Rubina was flattered by Tariq's desire to meet her in secret. She said later 'I didn't know what I was doing, but it seemed so exciting at the time, just like in the films'. Jamila, too, became thoroughly immersed in her love affair, even though it existed more as fantasy than reality since the couple could snatch only a few hours together each week. The affair was conducted in a distinctly Pakistani romantic idiom. Jamila's mother said later that she had been unaware that Jamila had been meeting anyone, because, apart from doing the cooking for her family, Jamila spent every evening on returning from college shut in her room listening to Urdu and Hindi film songs. She did not consider this particularly strange because, she said, many teenage girls do the same. She said she only realized later why Jamila did the cooking everyday — Jamila had obtained from a *pīr* in Pakistan a potion that she put daily into her family's food. This potion was supposed to contain words of the *Qur'ān* that would protect the lovers against discovery[15].

When a relationship is discovered, or when lovers decide that they have no choice but to elope if they are to remain together, the men of the girl's family are outraged. They have to be seen to be upholding the moral code; their own honour is under threat. Jamila's brothers and their friends, who included boys like Izhar who have English girlfriends, were furious when they heard of Jamila's elopement and they retaliated by assaulting Jamila's boyfriend's brothers. One of the assailants said, 'Jamila is like my sister; she could have been my sister — it's my duty to take revenge on him for his insulting us like this.' When I pointed out the English girl he went out with was also someone's sister or daughter, he replied:

> That's different. The difference is, English people don't care. The girls don't mind; you tell them you can't marry them, you're just passing your time, and they don't bother. They're just passing their time too. If their brothers or fathers got angry, we would understand, but they don't bother. Mostly, they are not even living in the same place. How can you respect men like that? They just say it's the girl's choice, it's her life, and that's what the girls say too.

Despite the fact that several affairs with Asian girls have become local public scandals, in most cases the incidents have not, in the long run, involved fundamental changes to parents' original plans and as a result have been 'forgotten'. Rubina returned home to her parents a fortnight after her elopement with Tariq and her parents took her to Pakistan, where several months later she was married to her father's brother's son. Two years passed before she returned to Oxford. Meanwhile, Tariq's family arranged his marriage to a relative, a young woman brought up in London. No public objections were made when Tariq's marriage took place, and Tariq accepted the arranged marriage, resigned to the fact that Rubina was now in Pakistan. When I asked his mother whether the elopement had hampered the subsequent marriage arrangements, she replied:

> Why should it? Most boys do something wrong, it's only natural. People forget quickly; we've had no trouble. He's good looking, has his own house, his own business and good prospects and the girl's family are very happy.'

For Rubina's family, the consequences were not quite so straightforward. When affairs become public, as they do when a couple elopes, the girl's character is inevitably tainted. Rubina's family took care that this would not unduly affect the honour of the family. By preventing a number of telephone calls, they apparently managed to hide the matter from relatives in Pakistan and quickly arranged her marriage there. In fact, even if Rubina's father's brother's family did learn about the elopement, it is likely that Rubina's marriage to her cousin would still have gone ahead. The groom's family was being offered the opportunity to send a son to Britain, in return for sharing the responsibility for ensuring that the honour of the family is protected.

Sometimes girls are taken back to Pakistan against their will, as reports from the Home Office, British airports and south Asian women's groups testify. However, it would be wrong to assume that in every case a girl who has eloped with a boyfriend is necessarily unwilling or is being forced to return to Pakistan for marriage, though undoubtedly there are cases in which this is true. Jamila, who had eloped with a Sikh boy, and had been fetched home by her parents after they were informed of her whereabouts, said later — before she was married — that she had decided on her own accord to phone her parents and ask them to bring her home, and I have no reason to doubt her sincerity. She said her elopement was not as perfect or as romantic as she had imagined, and she was now content to live at home until the marriage her parents were arranging took place. Similarly, when Tariq sent the police in pursuit of Rubina, who was being taken to Pakistan by her parents in order to end the liaison, she apparently told the police at Heathrow that she was leaving of her own free will. When Rubina returned to Oxford a year after marriage to her father's brother's son in Pakistan, she had clearly accepted the inevitability of her marriage. Ten years later, with her husband now in Oxford and working as a taxi driver, several children at school and her parents and siblings living nearby, she is glad that she had an arranged marriage.

To the extent that it poses no fundamental threat to marriage plans, pre-marital romance is tolerated, though more so for boys than for girls, as the perhaps inevitable consequence of tensions within a social structure in which marriages are arranged and relationships between the sexes are constrained. This attitude to romance may even stretch so far as to accommodate elopements, for although elopements do indeed challenge parents' plans for the marriages of their offspring, they may not in every case seriously hamper these plans in the long run.

Young Women: Education, Work and Marriage

Despite this degree of latitude, most marriages are not the 'free' choice of individuals. In Oxford, most of the young married women have had marriages arranged by their parents and their experiences of secondary schooling and of employment have, to varying extents, been shaped by their parents' concerns to protect their daughters' marriageability. Several parents, fearful of sending teenage daughters to even the single-sex secondary school in Oxford have sent daughters to Pakistan, in recent years, for the 'critical' years between the ages of about 14 and 18. These girls have returned after a few years, either married or considered sufficiently mature to continue in further education. Other girls stay at school but leave at sixteen to get married while others leave school at 16 but spend a few years at home, or working in the family business, or in paid employment, before being married. Some stay on into the sixth form or take courses at the College of Further Education and might negotiate the postponement of their marriages so that they can continue in further or higher education.

Contrary to the popular belief that Pakistani girls are forced into early marriages, many girls who leave school at 16 are not in fact married immediately but spend the years between leaving school and marriage working in various ways. They may take on a large proportion of tasks in the home, including looking after younger siblings, or may work in family shops where their competence in English is highly valued, or their mother or parents may take them to Pakistan to visit relatives, often with a view to finalizing marriage plans. Work in family shops often continues after marriage: Shakila left school at 16, worked at the till in her father's shop and dealt with large grocery orders. After she was married at 17, she worked in the shop owned by her father-in-law, who is her mother's brother. Farida left school and was married at 16, when she began to work in the shop owned by her father and her father-in-law (her father's brother), freeing Farida's husband and mother-in-law to manage their second shop, which they had bought when Farida married. Farida and her husband now run this shop themselves.

Daughters sometimes want to obtain qualifications in further or higher education and have the option of a career beyond the household or shop. In some cases, girls who leave school at 16 have continued to study at the College of Further Education before they get married. Shabnam, for instance, studied at the CFE where she met the man to whom her marriage was later 'arranged'; and since her marriage she has successfully run a family business. Other women have obtained qualifications in such professions as nursing, nursery nursing and social work, or have taken up other forms of paid employment, for instance, as shop assistants, secretaries and interpreters. A few have gone on to university, two to study law.

My impression is that there may now be more girls than boys taking A levels and entering higher education. In 1987, most Pakistani girls attended Milham Ford, the all-girls' secondary school in Oxford, where a significant number of pupils (15% in 1983/4) were Asian. Yet only about two Asian girls per year took A levels, the majority leaving at 16 or 17. There are now between 20 and 30 Pakistani pupils in each year at the school and nearly all of those who obtain the necessary grades stay on for A levels and about 90% of the Pakistani A level students try to enter higher education. Moreover, while the daughters of the most 'orthodox' families usually attend Milham Ford, a roughly equivalent number of Pakistani girls attend the local co-educational secondary school.

While parents fear that young women at school, at college or in paid work outside the family will be 'led astray' into liaisons that will jeopardize marriage plans, at the same time education is highly valued. An educated daughter is usually considered an asset in marriage; qualifications may increase her marriage-ability. It may also be important in some circumstances that a daughter is able to obtain 'respectable' work after she leaves school. A young woman who is bringing a spouse from Pakistan may have to demonstrate that she can support him. She may not necessarily continue with paid work once her husband has found work in Britain, or once she has children, but in several cases couples have been dependent on the wife's income while the husbands learn English or until they obtain full-time work. Parents now sometimes also say that a woman needs qualifications so that she can find 'respectable' work if a marriage fails, in recognition of the fact that this might happen, or if a husband becomes unemployed, or if the family falls on hard times or simply to supplement her husband's income.

Young women's experiences of education and work are generally the outcomes of negotiations between girls and parents in relation to marriage plans. Sometimes, young women combine marriage with further education or agree to a marriage that may have been arranged since childhood but negotiate its postponement so that they can study. Alim received very little schooling in Britain because her father, fearful of 'western influences', had sent her back to Pakistan. She returned too old for school, desperate to learn, and studied and memorized all the lessons in the books that her younger siblings brought home from school. Eventually, Alim's father allowed her to take O levels at the College of Further Education and later to take a part-time clerical job, reassured that she would accept a marriage which had been planned for some years and would not be 'led astray'. Alim's married her father's sister's son from Pakistan during the year in which she was at college.

Unmarried girls must take care not to give their parents grounds for mistrusting them while they are attending school or college if they are to continue their studies. Occasionally, a girl at school or college elopes with a boy, and parents' worst fears are justified. Rubina and Jamila had both been attending the College of Further Education when they eloped; neither was allowed to continue studying there afterwards. Other parents became more cautious about letting their daughters attend the college as a result. Some parents still regard the CFE as a 'dangerous place', where 'boys and girls go to meet one another, not to study'.

The negotiations between daughters and parents may differ within the same family, according to the personalities involved. Alim had been desperate to study, after spending her late teens in Pakistan and returning to Britain too old to go to school. Her elder sister Khamida, on the other hand, showed no interest in school and readily adopted a fairly traditional role at home after her marriage. Two of her younger sisters, in contrast, have realized Alim's frustrated ambition and studied at university. Often, for parents, the critical issue in relation to daughters entering higher education is whether they will 'go wrong' or be 'led astray' into relationships with boys that would jeopardize marriage plans. Parents who have agreed that their daughters should enter higher education often remain considerably ambivalent about it. When Zohra did not obtain the expected grades; her angry father responded, 'then you will get married'. In this case, the issue was taken up by Zohra's schoolteachers who negotiated a place for her at Oxford Brookes University, while Zohra agreed meanwhile to be married at the end of her first year there. Parents usually prefer their daughters to remain in Oxford for their higher education if they can, and the girls themselves sometimes say that they lack the confidence to live away from home.

Parents and siblings of may be variously supportive or suspicious about the behaviour of unmarried girls in higher education. Young women at college or university often point out that increasingly in Pakistan too, especially in the cities, young women attend college and have careers, but their male contemporaries may be severely critical. Young women are acutely aware of the double standard this may entail; on many occasions they have pointed out that when a man says Pakistani girls who study have been 'spoiled' by the freedom of the west, he may be implicating his own sister. Often, though, the young women who study or have paid work continue to play important traditional roles within their families and beyond as well: they may take on the community roles previously played by their mothers, such as teaching the *Qur'ān* to Pakistani girls in the Saturday morning community classes, or convening *khatmi Qur'ān*s and attending and convening the other family rituals described in Chapter 8. They may have become educated, and may have paid work outside the home, but they remain socially and morally bound into networks of *birādarī* and friends.

The fact that, increasingly, girls have completed higher education while remaining *sharīf* in the eyes of their *birādarī* and their parents' friends and neighbours has made it easier for other girls to follow. With this, parents' attitudes have sometimes changed. Fifteen years ago, Naseem was offered a university place, but her parents, afraid that she would reject the marriage they had arranged for her, tried to prevent her from taking it up. Naseem contemplated running away from home, but, with advice from her friends and a school teacher, managed to convince her parents that they would simply have to wait a few years to have her married. Naseem went to university and became a practicing lawyer. She is still unmarried and her parents now accept that, for Naseem, marriage will be her own decision. Her younger sisters have been allowed to go to university too, and have been allowed to decide whether they want arranged marriages. One of them, after graduating, asked her parents to go ahead with arrangements for her marriage to a relative. She is currently not 'working' but bringing up young children and living near her parents. The third daughter has so far postponed the question of marriage.

Just as a young woman's experience of higher education and of paid work is usually negotiated in relation to her parents' plans for her marriage, a young woman's experience of paid work after she is married is closely related, often inversely, to the 'success' of her marriage. Parents also now consider it important that a daughter is able to 'stand on her own two feet', to obtain employment if a marriage fails. Over the past decade, a number of marriages have indeed failed, sometimes ending in divorce. The rate of divorce among Pakistani families in Britain is low, much lower than the national average, but parents are increasingly concerned about marital instability. A number of problems may sooner or later arise especially in marriages of girls raised in Britain to boys from Pakistan. Alim was married under British law to a first cousin from Pakistan, but despised him from the moment she saw him. The marriage was never consummated and the groom eventually left, marrying another relative from Pakistan some years later. Husbands of the more assertive of the girls raised in Britain sometimes find it very difficult to manage these relationships. Using a method of asserting male authority over women which, in Pakistan, I saw was quite acceptable, Yacoub hit his wife with a shoe when she answered him back, but she hit him back; Yacoub, stunned, did not know what to say or do. Male status and authority may also be challenged if wives speak better English, are more qualified and more employable than their husbands. Shahnaz's husband became increasingly demoralized by his wife's competence and his own poor English and was led into 'bad company'. Shahnaz tried hard to make the marriage work, but eventually her husband left, and later married a girl from Pakistan; Shahnaz, who had obtained a professional qualification before she was married and has continued to work throughout, now works full-time supporting her three children. Saira would not submit to her husband's authority and insisted on working; eventually her husband also left, to marry another relative from Pakistan.

Parents do not condone these failed marriages. 'They are both stupid', said the father of one woman raised here whose childless five-year marriage to a relative from Pakistan had ended in separation, 'they won't try to get on'. If the couple is related, their failed marriage can cause a major rift within a family, sometimes with serious economic consequences such as the collapse of a business. Yet parents are often quite matter-of-fact about the possibility of divorce. 'It is important for a daughter to get qualifications,' said Saeeda, herself illiterate, 'so that she will be able to find work and support herself if her marriage fails'. For some families at least, divorce seems to be an acceptable price to pay for enabling the migration of, say, a brother's son. The man can re-marry, perhaps bringing over a new wife from Pakistan. The wife remains tainted, and re-marriage for her is far less likely. However, for girls raised in Britain divorce and single-parenthood is not the disaster it often is in rural Pakistan, for the girls can work, can obtain a council flat and state benefits, and in many cases they also have the support of at least their mothers and sisters, if not their fathers and brothers.

For married women, despite the prevalence of traditional ideals and the power of gossip and censure, the experience of further education or paid employment outside the home is therefore to a large extent a function of factors that affect most women in western societies. These include the stage they have reached in their 'careers' as mothers (their children's ages, their childcare options, whether their children are at school, etc.), their husbands' income, the constraints of husbands' working hours and the experience of divorce or widowhood.

Young Men: Education, Work and Marriage

For young unmarried men, experiences of education and employment are not much shaped by concerns to prevent contact with potential sexual partners. Social norms and gossip constrain the activities of both young men and women, but there is less surveillance of young men in their interactions with friends outside the home, and men are more at liberty to pursue clandestine relationships. At the same time, expectations of and obligations towards kin also shape men's activities in important ways.

Young men have taken a variety of different paths since leaving school. Those with no or few qualifications have usually entered the same types of semi-skilled or unskilled work as their fathers, with many of them, in response to the constraints of the labour market, taking up self-employment in recent years. Akbar, who was nine when he came to Britain, and left school at 16 worked first as a hospital porter, as his father had done, and then worked for several years on the production line at the Rover Group factory. His lifestyle echoes his father's: it is centred on the mosque, family social events and work, and, especially now that he is married to a cousin from Pakistan and has young children, his contacts with English people rarely extend into his leisure time. He took voluntary redundancy in anticipation of the closure of the car factory, when his father also retired, and became a self-employed taxi-driver.

Men who enter further or higher education usually aspire towards the professions, and many parents want their sons to become, ideally, doctors or lawyers. Ten years ago, Riaz was taking a Polytechnic degree course; Bashir was taking A levels and re-taking O levels at a College of Further Education; Mahir was re-taking O levels for a third time and beginning an A level course at a CFE, encouraged by his father. Despite the difficulties he experienced in school with English and mathematics because of his late arrival in Britain, Izhar had started a Polytechnic diploma course and hoped to transfer to a degree course.

Only a few of the men who, a decade ago, wanted to become professionals have in fact done so. Most have instead turned to various form of self-employment, mainly by running small businesses, while some have obtained clerical or management jobs. They are all now married, have established their own homes, and usually maintain regular contact with their parents, for instance by sharing with siblings the responsibility of supporting and housing a widowed parent. Those who did obtain professional qualifications, sometimes saying that their chosen careers are ones which would be useful were they to return to Pakistan, have also remained close to their parents and peers, despite acquiring the trappings of western culture in that they are more comfortable socially than their parents and some of their peers in middle-class 'English' company. These men generally retain strong social and sometimes financial links with each other and with their families, contributing, for instance to a joint family budget or to family property investment. Most have had arranged marriages, a few have postponed the question of marriage, while one man married the English girl he met at university — she became a Muslim and the couple lives with his parents in east Oxford.

The professionally qualified young men are respected for their achievement but are not unambiguously considered 'more successful' than factory workers, taxi-drivers or shopkeepers, nor have they necessarily remained in the professions. Some now work in family businesses, in shopkeeping or in property, considering their previous occupations neither sufficiently lucrative nor adequately geared towards family interests. Earning money 'for the family' remains a primary concern and families do not feel any great sense of loss if a young man abandons his professional training or career in order to enter the family business. Khalid, for instance, trained as an electrical engineer and began working with an engineering company in the midlands, but eventually, returned to Oxford to manage a business jointly with his friend Riaz. Faizan, who has a Polytechnic diploma, also in engineering, was managing his father's chain of grocery stores. He said, 'what's the point of studying if it doesn't make you any money? You might as well go into business.' Mohammed Ali had trained as an accountant and worked for several years with a reputable firm, but then took up a role in a family business. He said, it is now time that I took some of the load off my father's shoulders'.

A sense of 'working for the family' tends to combat the jealousies that might arise when one brother is encouraged to go to college or enter a profession and another to become a wage earner. One elder brother, with only a few years of schooling in Britain, worked on the production line at the Rover Group factor. His younger brother, educated in Britain, became a graduate engineer with a reputable firm. Yet the younger brother usually deferred to his elder brother in family matters and both gave their wages to their mother. Two other brothers worked at British Telecom, supporting their younger brother while he was studying. One elder brother is still with BT but the other now runs a shop, and the younger brother now runs a property business. They have established separate households — the two elder brothers married to relatives from Pakistan, the younger brother married to the English girl he met at college, and they share their responsibilities to elderly parents between them.

The relative freedom parents give young men extends not only to girlfriends but also, often, to strategies for making money: as long as sons are contributing to the family budget, parents may not ask for details. As one mother commented, 'as soon as they are out of the door, the boys forget what their parents have told them. And the parents turn a blind eye when they come back with so much money. If I suddenly noticed my son had a big new car, I would want to know why'. In the past decade, a small proportion of young men, mostly those with few qualifications who have failed to obtain or keep regular work, have drifted into various kinds of semi-or illegal trading, including dealing in heroin. Some of them, arrested for the parts they played in drug-dealing — in local so-called 'gangs' that are not exclusively Pakistani — are now serving prison sentences. A few parents have been so concerned that their sons might also 'get into bad company' and be drawn into buying and selling drugs that they have moved their families away from east Oxford. In recent years, east Oxford parents have expressed more concern about the activities of their sons than their daughters — perhaps because these are activities over which they have less control — despite the fact that more popular and academic discussion has been directed towards the attitudes and experiences of young south Asian women.

The general leniency shown to sons in comparison with daughters including the sexual double standard means that in most cases sons have no good reason to object to an arranged marriage. Sometimes young men with girlfriends try to post-pone their arranged marriage, or else they try to break off their relationships with girlfriends when they get married or soon after their Pakistani wife arrives in Oxford. An English girl-friend might discover months or years later that her boyfriend is married; likewise a Pakistani wife generally finds out, sooner or later, if her husband has an English girlfriend, and some-times children by him. In a few cases, young Pakistani men have in fact married their English girlfriends who have become Muslim. My impression is that their families are more likely to accept such marriages if the son has a good income and the family does not want to risk alienating him, if the boy's father's authority is weak, if the father is dead, or if at least one other son has been married within the *birādarī* and obligations towards close kin have therefore been discharged.

For a man, more easily that for a woman, marriage outside the *birādarī* may sooner or later be accepted, for a woman from 'outside' can in principle be incorporated within her husband's *birādarī* without any necessary insult to the family's honour. (There is one very successful polygamous household east Oxford household, in which one wife is English, the other Pakistani — the husband is married to one wife under English law; Islamic law permits more than one wife). Men rather than

women are seen as perpetuating the *birādarī* 'blood' (*khūn*) and
so the children of a union between a man from the *birādarī* and
a woman from 'outside' are regarded as belonging to their
father's *birādarī*, not their mother's. In one case, a Pakistani
wife who discovered from her Pakistani friends, soon after she
arrived in England following her marriage to a cousin, that her
husband has a son with an English woman eventually discovered where the English mother lived and went to see her to ask
if she could adopt the baby. By contrast, if a woman marries a
man from a different *birādarī*, caste or 'race' her children are
regarded as having their father's caste, *birādarī* or racial identity, and as being, therefore, of little or no value to their
mother's *birādarī*. A woman's sexuality, that is, her
reproductive potential, threatens the integrity of the *birādarī*,
whereas male sexuality can extend the boundary of the
birādarī.

Relationships or marriages which involve breaking with the family

Relationships, elopements or marriages against parents' wishes
and in which the couples, despite the odds, stay together, may
therefore, for young women and sometimes also for men, at
least initially, involve totally severing ties with their natal
families. Shabbaz seduced Sakina soon her arrival in Britain
and later eloped with and married her under Muslim law. They
are of different castes, his caste, Sakina said, is 'low'. Sakina
has felt too ashamed and too afraid to contact her parents since
then, particularly since her father and brothers served a short
prison sentence after assaulting Shabbaz. She lives in Oxford,
where no one has openly objected to this marriage, to be far
from the town in which her parents live. Her Pakistani
neighbours sometimes speak in hushed tones of Sakina's 'love
marriage', as Sakina also describes it, but do not object to
Shabbaz being already married because 'in our religion, a man
can have two wives'. They add, now, that Sakina was unlucky,
for Shabbaz has since brought his wife and children from
Pakistan and Sakina is in effect a single-parent, caring for two
young children without the support of her mother or sisters.

A woman marrying against her parents' wishes is in effect
choosing between her family and her lover. Women in this situation may decide that the price is too high and the future too

uncertain to go ahead, for if a marriage to an 'outsider' fails, the woman is likely to lose everything, for she will have no *birādarī* to turn to. Farook's second daughter eloped with a student in the-mid 1980s, on the eve of her arranged marriage to her elder sister Zarina's husband's brother. She knew that by doing so she would be severing her ties, perhaps forever, with her natal family, especially with her father.

She has returned to Oxford a few times since, to visit more distant relatives, and has stood outside her parents shop once or twice but not found the courage to see them. 'What hurt my father most', said her sister Zarina, 'was that she said nothing to us and let us go ahead with the marriage plans. She ran away the night before. If she had spoken to us about it, my father would have listened; he is a reasonable man. As you know, I did not have an arranged marriage'. However, the circumstances of Zarina's marriage were very different. Zarina's husband is from the same caste, his parents' business interests matched Zarina's father's interests, and the marriage that took place was in effect 'arranged' by Zarina's parents after Zarina had told them about her boyfriend. It was one of an increasing number of arranged 'love marriages' between Pakistani Muslims of similar backgrounds who in effect 'become' *birādarī* (as I have discussed in the previous chapter). Zarina's sister's relationship with a non-Pakistani 'outsider' would not have been in the *birādarī* interests in the same way; Zarina's sister was probably quite correct in her assessment of her options.

Girls who elope and marry 'outside', or, as in a few cases, have boyfriends but refuse to marry, are in effect denying their fathers the opportunity to fulfil their duty to marry their daughters respectfully, as virgins. If there is no other way of salvaging reputation, a father and brothers may sever all links with the girl, to avoid being reminded of the shame.

Marriage in defiance of parents' plans and *birādarī* interests may also enrage parents to the extent that a father may disown a son. When Hasan was in his final year at college with a the prospect of a good full-time job ahead of him, his father went to Pakistan, to complete the arrangements for Hasan's marriage to his father's brother's daughter. Hasan's father wrote to his son with the details of the marriage and describing the girl. Hasan wrote back to say that he rejected the marriage and wanted instead to marry

Shamim, a local Pakistani Muslim girl whom he had met at college. To this his father replied that if Hasan defied him then he was no longer his father's son.

The night before his father was due back from Pakistan, Hasan packed his bags and left home. The following morning, his family discovered he was missing and contacted the police. When the police found him, Hasan told them not to reveal his whereabouts to his family. Three months later, while visiting friends in a nearby town, Hasan's father discovered where Hasan was living, and sent one of Hasan's elder brothers to tell him that if the girl he wanted to marry wore traditional Muslim dress the family would accept her. Hasan agreed to this and returned home, where he lived for a year. During this time, his father would not speak to him but occasionally asked the rest of the family whether Hasan was changing his mind about rejecting the arranged marriage. Meanwhile, although the other member of Hasan's family were beginning to accept the idea of Hasan marrying Shamim, for she was at least a Pakistani Muslim and educated, Hasan's father went ahead with an application to bring Hasan's fiancée — his father's brother's daughter — to Britain. This triggered Hasan's second and final departure from home.

This time, Hasan ensured that his father's attempts to trace him were unsuccessful. He finally married Shamim according to both English and Islamic law, at a ceremony which took place in Oxford, eighteen months after his second departure from home. Unlike some other marriages of men to women outside the *birādarī*, it was some years before Hasan's family would acknowledge this marriage. Hasan's father vowed that he would never again consider Hasan his son, for Hasan had shamed him, causing him to lose face within the *birādarī*. This was primarily because one of Hasan's relatives had informed Hasan's father's brother in Pakistan that even though an engagement had already taken place, Hasan's family would in the end reject the fiancée in Pakistan, an action which would be very shameful for Hasan's father's brother's family, because people would think there was something 'wrong' with the girl. As a result, Hasan's father's brother wrote to Hasan's father, slandering him and his family for the insult he was causing them. 'My father lost a lot of respect,' Hasan's brother said, 'the people there don't understand the situation here, that it was not my father's decision to reject the girl but my brother's. Only the more educated people there are likely to understand.' Hasan's mother, too, though less harsh in her attitude, also severed contact with her son out of respect for her husband. One *Id* day, she and her two married daughters went to visit relatives. Approaching the front door, she heard Hasan's voice from within, so, summoning her daughters to follow her, turned back down the path. Hasan's sisters shared their parents' attitude because their husbands, who are brothers, had also been insulted, since Hasan was to have married their sister. It was only with the passage of time, following Hasan's father's illness and with the birth of Shamim and Hasan's sons, that the barriers have gradually come down; Hasan and Shamim now — fifteen years later — have regular social contact with all members of Hasan's family, spanning various households, and including his parents.

Forms of Challenge

The romantic liaisons and elopements described here are in large part a consequence of a social system in which a high premium is placed on female chastity and marriages are arranged to create or strengthen socio-economic links between households. The purdah system serves to prevent the threat to the social order that sexual liaisons or romantic love between individuals potentially represent. Romantic love in such circumstances is by definition illicit: clandestine love affairs and elopements have occurred for generations. Much of Urdu literature — particularly a genre of poetry called the *ghazal* — takes as its theme this type of illicit love. As Ralph Russell explains in his discussion of concepts of love in Urdu poetry, much of the power of the poetic imagery comes from the fact that the love it describes is illicit: 'the key to the understanding of the *ghazal* is the realization that it is the poetry of illicit love'[16]. Love in such circumstances is a threat to the social order: the lovers have few opportunities to meet, no hope of living together permanently, and 'finally, the lovers themselves in the last resort accept the social code that condemns them'[17]. These themes of ill-fated romance and star-crossed love in *ghazal* poetry are also expressed in popular Urdu and Hindi film songs; indeed the song lyrics are often the work of renowned poets. This tradition provides an important part of the cultural idiom in which the clandestine relationships of British Pakistani lovers are often conducted and reflects some of the constraints upon them in contemporary real-life situations. Moreover, as I have suggested, some of the girls involved have readily accepted arranged marriages after their elopements or short-lived romances; to a degree, then, the romantic liaisons I have described here are an accepted consequence of the system of arranged marriage, and are not necessarily, or solely, and indication of the metaphoric 'culture clash' in terms of which they are generally described in the media.

At the same time, it is also the case that for some young adults, particularly those with a college or university education, a rejection of an arranged marriage may indeed represent a conscious stand against parents, a challenge to their authority, and to the authority of the *birādarī* and to the power of 'tradition'. It is important to emphasize, however, that such a stance usually involves not a wholesale rejection of a 'culture' or 'religion' in favour of 'western' values, but is instead an attempt at reform from within. Young adults like Hasan and Shamim, for example, self-consciously challenge the traditional or customary ideals of purdah, which, they say, in effect reduce women to the status of property, a status for which there is no justification in Islam. Hasan also argued that his parents' attempts to impose upon him a marriage he did not want was quite contrary to the spirit of the Muslim marriage; there was nothing in Islam, he said, that would justify his parents' stance:

> I have nothing personally against the girl they had chosen for me — I'm sure she is very nice — but I didn't want to marry a girl who has come straight from Pakistan, who doesn't know English, and knows nothing of my life here. My parents are living in the 1960s. They arrange marriages with relatives not according to our religion but to keep property in the family; they regard women as property. In our religion, it is wrong to force someone to marry. Both the girl and the boy should be asked if they consent. But very often our people don't even ask, they just go ahead because the marriage is in their interests, expecting everybody to agree so that no one loses face. That's all they think about, their face, not whether what they're doing is right or wrong in the religion. Our Muslim *nikāh* (marriage ceremony) is a contract between a man and a woman who have to consent to the marriage in front of witnesses, that's all. You don't have to marry

your cousin, that's just tradition. And it's the couple who
have to give their consent, not the parents.

Hasan also differed from many of his contemporaries and from
many of the older generation in rejecting the hypocrisy he
perceived in their attitude to women, echoing the views of the
college-educated girls who are acutely aware of the double
standard of many of their male contemporaries' attitudes to
women. He said:

> I didn't want to accept a marriage that I didn't want, and
> then have girlfriends on the side like so many men do.
> Why should I ruin the life of a girl from Pakistan who
> could be happily married to someone else? Just because I
> couldn't say no to my parents?

Hasan's consciously reformist stance is one that an increasing
number of college-educated young adults are adopting. It is one
in which the proponents attempt to disentangle aspects of what
they see as 'outdated tradition' from the 'genuine' spirit of
Islam. In this, they may be acutely critical of aspects of their
'culture', while considering themselves committed Muslims,
through, for instance, their regular observance of the prayers
and fasting.

These reformist views were also evident — to a greater and a
lesser extent — among Hasan's friends, some of whom had
been to college, some had not. Some of them opposed Hasan's
marriage before it took place simple because the couple 'had
gone against their parents' wishes'; others felt that the marriage
was acceptable because the couple 'were not going against their
religion', and some were ambivalent, expressing sympathy for
both sides. The following exchange took between some of these
friends a few days Hasan's marriage took place, while they
were debating whether or not to turn up to the marriage
ceremony:

> **Zafar**: I don't think we should go. What would our
> parents say? That couple went against their parents'
> wishes. Hasan's family won't be there, and Shamim's
> father is not there. It is an insult to them. If we go, it's like
> saying we approve. We have to set an example to the
> younger children.

Riaz: But what have they done wrong? They haven't gone against Islam; they are both Muslims and they are having a proper Muslim wedding. They're not just having the English ceremony; they are having the *nikāh* and the reception just like any other Muslim marriage. It's the parents who are wrong. They are throwing away a son because their pride is hurt, not because Hasan has gone against our religion. The parents are living in the past. Why should Hasan marry a girl from Pakistan who doesn't know English or anything about life here?

Zafar: But you've got to respect your parents.

Riaz: Yes, but sometimes the parents are wrong. How can they think that a girl they haven't even seen for years straight from the village is going to be suitable for you? I don't want to marry a girl like that, who doesn't know anything. I'd rather marry a girl from here.

Zafar: But the trouble with girls from here is that they are too modern. They're too clever. They'll be nothing but trouble. Look at Shamim; she's very westernized, she wears jeans and cuts her hair.

Riaz: That's just not true. You've not seen her, or if you have, you've forgotten. All you can see is what your parents tell you, and it's prejudice. Hasan's family has never set eyes on her, and yet they are the ones spreading these lies.

Afzal: And another thing, I think you are saying this, because you're married already. You're stuck. And so you don't want anyone to be different.

Khalid: That's rubbish. He doesn't wish he'd married a girl like that, who's broken up two families. Look at what those two have done. They've really hurt Hasan's parents and shamed them in front of their relatives, and Shamim's family is now broken up. I couldn't do that to my parents.

Riaz: But that's the parents' fault. They didn't have to behave like that. They could have swallowed their pride and accepted it — after all, he's not marrying an English girl. Good luck to them, that's what I say.

As it happened, a few of Hasan's friends did indeed attend the marriage ceremony, considering it important to support a couple who, as they saw it, were marrying according to Islamic tradition and had not 'gone against' their religion. Of the pioneer generation, however, only Shamim's widowed mother[18] and two of her friends attended the marriage ceremony itself; others expressed their support in private but not in public, for fear of angering Hasan's father.

Conclusion

Disputes over love affairs and marriage are therefore not necessarily symptomatic of a wholesale desire to adopt a 'western' or 'individualistic' lifestyle and values, but of stresses inherent in the culture itself — of pressures to fulfil obligations to parents and conform to the demands of family and *birādarī* versus individual needs and desires. Such disputes occur in Pakistan too, and may take place within a 'traditional' idiom as well as one in which western influences are, to a greater or less degree, at work. Men especially may reconcile these two sets of needs without major conflicts through behaviour that is essentially hypocritical; they may publicly uphold 'traditional' moral and religious values and conform to the demands of the *birādarī* and at the same time have clandestine affairs.

The major conflicts arise when people openly challenge this double standard by, for example, marrying according to their own choice. The consequences then are usually more serious for women, sometimes involving a long-term break with their natal family. At the same time, the young adults involved do not, usually, see their actions in terms of a wholesale adoption of a western lifestyle and western values. On the contrary, they explain their actions with reference to interpretations and re-interpretations of Islam, and perceive their challenge to the 'double-standard' as a 'reform from within'. They may refer to Islamic texts to justify their views on the status of women and about marriage, making reference to the equality to be found in modern interpretations of Islam rather than to the arguments of western feminism. Nevertheless, this type of dispute with tradition uses a modern style of argument, one that a Panjabi villager in Pakistan would be very unlikely to use. To argue a case on the basis of interpretation or re-interpretations of Islam is in itself perhaps a particularly modern thing to do, one that reflects to a large extent a style of education in which youngsters are encouraged to challenge rather than accept uncritically the assumptions of their elders. The young people who take this line are not, therefore, necessarily motivated entirely by Islamic values but also by western or at least by modern ones. A person who falls in love with someone and wants to marry them but has to overcome traditional opposition is likely to seek Islamic arguments to attain that end, because these arguments will be the most convincing, to their parents, to others, and indeed to themselves. Yet the very search for Islamic arguments to support their case in this way owes much to a modern style of education. It is also the case that in Britain, in contrast to Pakistan, those who more or less openly challenge their parents' plans for their marriages may seek some outside state support, from teachers, social workers, women's groups or the police, for instance. In the wider socio-economic context of modern British society, the institution of arranged marriage is generally seen as anachronistic. The issue of how far the state can intervene in matters which reflect minority cultural interests arises whenever conflicts between parents and children over arranged marriage result in domestic violence, emotional black-mail, sexual abuse, death threats or indeed murder. I shall return to this issue in the concluding chapter.

NOTES

1. Rachel Coughlan's Inside Story: *Forbidden Love*, BBC1, February 3, 1998.
2. *Jack and Zena*, Gollancz, 1997.
3. 'The fugitives', *The Guardian*, September 25,1997.
4. 'Shame', *The Independent*, May 25, 1999; 'Terror of couple fleeing arranged marriage', *The Guardian,* May 27, 1999.
5. See, for instance, Vreede de Stuers, 1968, Jeffery, 1979.
6. I. Ahmad, 1978 (1973); De Souza (ed.), 1975; Papanek, 1973; Vatuk, 1982.
7. However, see Donnan, 1988:99 (and Vatuk, 1982) for a discussion of the etiquette of male behaviour towards women, which is necessary 'for the system to work properly'.
8. Donnan, 1988:87–111.
9. Donnan, 1988:97.
10. Donnan, 1988:100–1.
11. Donnan, 1988:101–2.
12. See Gillespie (1995:37–9 and pp. 150–8) for a discussion of the role of gossip in restricting individual freedom and threatening family honour among young people of Panjabi backgrounds in Southall.
13. See Gillespie (1995:154) on the distinction between gossip and rumour.
14. Gillespie's Southall ethnography (1995) shows how 16 year old girls in Southall express and explore attitudes to courtship, boyfriends and mar-riage through their discussions of television programmes, particularly the soap-opera Neighbours.
15. See Chapter 7, pp. 207–9, 211, on uses of passages from the *Qur'ān*.
16. Russell, 1969:114.

17. Russell, 1969:114.
18. Widowed, divorced (or otherwise single) mothers are sometimes more flexible in their attitudes to their daughters' education, employment, pre-marital relationships and marriage plans than mothers who must defer to their husband's authority. A married woman who continues to support a daughter who has been disowned by her father generally does so without her husband's knowledge.

7 HEALTH, ILLNESS AND THE REPRODUCTION OF THE *BIRĀDARĪ*

This chapter turns to what is at first sight a very different set of issues — ideas about health and illness, particularly as they relate to sexuality, childbearing and birth control, as these are matters which are of concern to Pakistanis themselves. The production of children is central to the perpetuation of the *birādarī*; this is one reason why the issue of whether or not to control births, for example, is especially sensitive, and again it is possible to distinguish a traditional from a more modernist Islamic position in this respect. But what happens in practice is very often influenced by much more pragmatic concerns.

British Pakistanis draw from a range of ideas and systems of practice in matters of health and illness, reflecting the fact that in Pakistan there is no single all-encompassing traditional 'medical' system but several often-overlapping ones[1]. They may, to varying extents, use western allopathic medicine, Unani (Greek humoral) medicine, traditional 'home' remedies — called *desi ylāj* — and homeopathy. 'Islamic' beliefs and practices also exert an important influence over attitudes to health and illness and health-seeking behaviour.

In drawing from this range of systems, Pakistanis, like most other groups of people, recognize many possible causes of illness, and may take treatments from more than one practitioner, from more than one system, during the same episode of illness. They may also consult different practitioners, from different systems, at different times[2]. The sketch I offer below of each system does not provide any firm guidelines for predicting which system will be used in any given case of illness or set of circumstances. How an individual or a household manages a particular illness is usually the result of pragmatic considerations such as convenience and socioeconomic contingency, their previous experiences of particular illnesses and of particular practitioners, and the suggestions of their friends and neighbours. Moreover, although each system can be described separately, practitioners sometimes themselves draw upon more than one in effecting a remedy. In Pakistan, some *hakīms* — who practice Unani medicine — may also dispense western medicines, and some *pīrs* — who are Islamic healers or saints — may also be *hakīms*[3]. Each category of practitioner may itself be quite diverse (Table 7.1); one *hakīm* may have had a modern professional training, while another might have learnt his trade from his father.

In fact, however, access to the range of practitioners that exists in Pakistan is necessarily more limited in Britain, where, for example, a *hakīm*'s qualifications from Pakistan do not constitute a licence to practice. In Britain, moreover, Western allopathic medicine provides a far more comprehensive system of medical care in Britain that it does in Pakistan, and most British Pakistanis turn first of all to the National Health Service in any episode of illness. Nevertheless, the various systems that exist in Pakistan continue, variously, to influence how British Pakistanis think about health and illness and how they manage ill health. This influence is maintained by the two-way traffic of ideas and information between Pakistan and Britain, especially through marriage and through periodic return visits 'home' to see relatives.

TYPES OF MEDICAL PRACTITIONERS AND THE SYSTEMS THEY USE.	
Practitioner	System
hakim (qualified and unqualified)	Unani medicine (Tibb Unani; Hikmat); sometimes also western medicine
pir (also *fakir*, *amil* [exorcist])	Religious (or ritual) healing; sometimes also Unani medicine
Homeopath	Homeopathic medicine
Doctor (in Pakistan, includes doctors trained abroad; MBBS doctors; doctors without	Western medicines, sometimes also Unani medicine and homopathy
degrees; 'compounders' and dispensers)	

Table 7.1

Western Medicine

Western allopathic medicine has been exported to Pakistan, in that, in the cities, there are hospitals and medical colleges modeled on the western system. However, the infrastructure that supports allopathic medicine in the west is absent and allopathic medical practice seems to have been incorporated within and adapted to Pakistan's socio-economic structure. The result is that access to it is shaped by hierarchical principles, and medical practice is itself highly stratified[4].

Despite the increasing rates of urbanization in Pakistan, Pakistani society remains predominantly rural and in the villages access to western medicine is difficult and expensive. There is no 'free' National Health Service, few social services, and medical facilities are limited. One village I visited had a government health clinic, but the qualified doctor was rarely in attendance; an untrained office clerk dispensed medicines — antibiotics, vitamins, steroids and injections for enhancing labour — to the villagers, in-between the qualified doctor's visits. I was told that an unqualified person can easily practice as a 'compounder' or 'dispenser' of western medicines by re-selling in rural areas medicines bought in the city, and that there is no control over the consequences. For childbirth, women usually rely on the help of the traditional village *daī* (midwife) — and on 'over the counter' medication — rather than travel to a city hospital because of the uncertainty and expense involved.

In the cities, there are government hospitals and private doctors, but many people cannot afford regular health care or the expense of hospital admission, medications and injections; access to western medical services is generally associated with a wealthy, urban lifestyle. Many Pakistanis would like their sons, or indeed daughters, to become doctors, for in Pakistan a western medical training carries high status and is likely to bring a good income. (The signboard advertising the 'very good foreign-trained' private doctor to whom our hosts in Rawalpindi took my husband read: 'MBBS fail'). Western patent medicines can be bought over the counter with neither prescriptions nor warnings that courses of treatment should be completed. (The 'MBBS fail' doctor prescribed for my husband's diarrhoea a list of various tablets to be purchased from a dispensary, which, when we looked them up in a dictionary of medicines, turned out to be several different antibiotics, two vitamins and a drug given to women in labour).

In Britain, most Pakistanis value highly the accessible and 'free' National Health Service and they usually consult their GPs (general practitioners) first in managing most episodes of illness. They use the N.H.S. to treat much the same range of physical conditions as does any other group of people: for dealing with accidents and emergencies, for conditions which require surgery and for the treatment and management of conditions such as heart disease, diabetes and cancers.

The expectations Pakistanis have of the British N.H.S may also reflect the fact that in Pakistan allopathic medicine is but one of various medical systems. They sometimes bring some of the expectations they have of consulting *pīr*s (saints) or *hakīm*s (practitioners of Unani medicine) to their appointment with a GP (general practitioner). A patient may present with pervasive bodily pains, for which a GP cannot find a physical cause, and may nevertheless expect the GP to prescribe a remedy and may be dissatisfied if the GP does not[5]. In Pakistan, a *pīr* 'knows' what may lie behind a particular presentation of a physical problem and will give an appropriate ritual or spiritual cure without eliciting a full history or conducting a detailed physical examination. A *hakīm* diagnoses a patient's humoral status by listening to the patient's account of their problem and by making a brief physical examination, primarily of the pulse, and prescribes a remedy on this basis. Oxford Pakistanis tend to have the highest regard for those GPs who (irrespective of their ethnic background) take their patients' physical symptoms seriously, even when no obvious cause can be found. They tend to prefer GPs who offer sympathy and reassurance and tolerate repeated visits, rather than those who brusquely turn away patients with no obvious symptoms of an organic complaint. Pakistanis are of course like very many other people in this respect!

Unani Medicine

In Pakistan, Unani (Greek) medicine provides a more comprehensive framework than that of western medicine for understanding health and illness and for treating common ailments. This system, also called Tibb Unani or Hikmat, is used throughout the Islamic world. It shares ancient roots with European allopathic medicine in the legacy of the Greek physicians Galen and Hippocrates and was probably brought to northern India with the invasion of Alexander the Great more than two thousand years ago. *Hakīm*s became the established practitioners of Unani medicine in India under the Mughal empire (1523–1857)[6]. Although traditionally associated with Muslims in the Indian subcontinent, there has long been some overlap with and mutual influences and borrowings from the ideas and practices of the Ayurvedic traditions associated with Hindus in the Indian subcontinent[7]. In Pakistan today there are both traditional and professionally qualified *hakīm*s. Traditional *hakīm*s have usually learnt their trade from a relative, whose knowledge may have been passed on within a family for generations. Professionally qualified *hakīm*s have completed a lengthy training, at the end of which they may obtain a government licence to practice. In some large hospitals there are wards offering treatment exclusively by Unani medicine or by both Unani and allopathic remedies[8].

The Unani system is based on the theory of the four humours, which is derived from the Greek idea that all matter is formed from fire, air, earth and water. Each element has hot, cold, wet and dry properties: fire is hot and dry, air is hot and wet, earth is cold and dry and water is cold and wet. Eating and drinking transforms the elements of food into the four humours: yellow bile (*safrā*), blood (*khūn*), black bile (*saudā*) and phlegm (*bhalgam*), each associated respectively with fire, air, earth and water. Every individual has a natural humoral balance; this idea is rather like the medieval physicians' view of temperaments as choleric (anxious; a predominance of yellow bile), sanguine, melancholic or phlegmatic. Illness occurs if an individual's humoral balance is upset; for example, if phlegm predominates over blood in a sanguine, jovial individual, then the person becomes ill[9].

To ascertain the state of the humours, a *hakīm* examines a patient's pulse, assesses the patient's appearance of health and listens to their account of their symptoms and their family situation. Treatments involve following dietary advice and taking mineral or herbal remedies which are designed to redress the humoral balance through their particular combinations of hot, cold, wet and dry, properties.

As far as I know, there are no practising *hakīm*s in Oxford, but Pakistanis may travel to Birmingham or London to consult *hakīm*s there, including *hakīm*s from Pakistan visiting the U.K. who advertise their visits beforehand in the U.K. Urdu press. They may also consult *hakīm*s during return trips to Pakistan. That a *hakīm*'s qualifications are not recognized in Britain is not generally an issue; in rural Pakistan the local healer may or may not be a qualified *hakīm*. What usually matters more is that they know their clients, are accessible and, in comparison with a GP, give lengthy consultations. Treatments from a visiting *hakīm* may continue to be prescribed or purchased by post or through periodic return trips to Pakistan.

Folk Remedies

The principles of balancing *garmī* and *thand*, also operate in *desī* ('home' or 'folk') *ylāj* (remedies) for common ailments. Foods and remedies are classified as *garm* (hot) or *thand* (cold), a reflection of humoral qualities, not temperature (see Table 7.2). Meals are often prepared with the idea of balancing hot and cold properties in mind — a salad of yogurt and cucumber is often served with meat or pulses for its cooling effect[10]. Too much of a particular food, causing either excessive *garmī or* excessive *thand*, can cause illness. Toothache, upset stomachs and skin rashes are signs of excess *garmī* and increasing the proportion of cold foods in the diet or reducing the consumption of hot foods will redress the balance. Likewise, 'cooling' foods or Unani remedies may be taken alongside western medicines to counter the heating effects of the latter[11]. Menstrual symptoms such as sweating, stomach cramps, headaches and feelings of heaviness can be alleviated by taking a *desī* remedy (one involves drinking an egg stirred into hot milk) which 'gives heat' and stimulates menstruation which is a 'hot' condition. After giving birth, a woman is 'cold' and is given 'hot' foods (including a specially prepared sweet mixture of honey, flour, sugar, and pistachio nuts) to restore her humoral balance.

It is worth mentioning, too, the devices or marks that might occasionally be used to prevent illness or misfortune befalling someone or something that happens to be the object of *nazar* — of another person's envious gaze. The object of *nazar* might be a young bride, or a beautiful child, or someone about to take an exam, or a new building. A parent or other relative may procure a *tā'wīz* (amulet) for a child to wear around the neck or they may perform religious rituals on someone else's behalf as a protection against *nazar*. Occasionally *nazar* is invoked (usually by the older generation, such as a visiting grandmother) as a possible cause of a child's illness or other misfortune. *Nazar*, which literally means 'sight' or gaze' has in similar contexts been translated as 'the evil eye' and given a sociological explanation: Pocock argues that objects of *nazar* (or *najar*) in rural Gujarat in India exhibit 'desirable characteristics' in situations of scarcity; Srinivas considers that *nazar* practices in rural India reflect social distinctions[12]. Oxford Pakistanis may also make reference to *nazar* very lightheartedly, as a way of explaining bad luck — such as when losing at a game of cards.

The Use of 'traditional' Remedies in Britain

Some 'western' clinicians in Britain have expressed their concerns about the possible health implications for British Pakistanis of consulting *hakīm*s (and for British Hindus and Sikhs about consulting *vaid*s, the practitioners of Ayurvedic medicine). One

THE 'HOT' AND 'COLD' PROPERTIES OF SOME EVERYDAY FOODS (Note: there is variation in how some items are classified.)	
'HOT'	'COLD'
Meat and fish.	Spinach, potatoes, cucumber, cabbage.
Garlic, onions, aubergines, carrots, peas, cauliflower, okra.	
Coconut, figs, mangoes, melons grapes, lychees.	Citrus fruits, plums, watermelon, pineapple.
Dried fruits especially dates, figs and raisins.	
Most nuts.	
Most pulses.	
Butter, oil, eggs.	Cheese, yogurt.
Most spices.	Coriander.
Sugar, honey.	
Tea, coffee.	
	Table 7.2

issue is the possible health consequences of 'non-compliance' with western medicine, for a *hakīm* might advise a patient to stop taking drugs prescribed by their GP because of their 'heating' effects and the patient may choose to follow the *hakīm*'s advice. Another is the nutritional implications of the 'hot' and 'cold' food classification; for instance the avoidance of 'hot' foods during pregnancy may result in a protein deficient diet which might be linked to the generally lower birth weights of South Asian babies compared to their non-South Asian counterparts[13]. There has also been concern about the possible toxic effects of metals such as lead, mercury, silver, gold, arsenic and zinc in the tonics called *kushte*s which are used in Unani medicine, particularly if the tonics are taken in large amounts without the advice of a qualified *hakīm*[14]. Finally, there is the question of potentially harmful interactions between drugs prescribed by GPs and by *hakīm*s or *vaid*s[15].

Whether these are serious concerns depends on how and to what extent traditional systems are used; it is clearly important to distinguish theoretical knowledge of a particular system and actual use of it. One survey of 250 British South Asians found that 232 had consulted *hakīm*s in the past, in India or in Pakistan, and 202 still consulted *hakīm*s in Britain[16]. A DHS report suggests that there are traditional practitioners in all of Britain's main South Asian settlements, and patients often consult both a traditional practitioner and a GP[17]. On the other hand, the majority of south Asian respondents in a more recent survey did not consider 'traditional' remedies better than 'western' medicine for many conditions, and only 2% of them had consulted a *hakīm* or *vaid* in the year previously[18]. Similarly, a Glasgow study questions the proposition that use of traditional medicines presents significant health risks, because widespread theoretical knowledge of traditional systems co-exists with a fair amount of skepticism about their efficacy and an awareness of the potential dangers of metal-based remedies[19].

Survey data may of course reveal what people think the researcher wants to hear, rather than what actually happens. British South Asians may fell embarrassed to tell 'educated' researchers that they use traditional medicine, rather as some westerners may be ashamed to tell their GPs about visits to acupuncturists, aromatherapists, reflexologists, homeopaths or other 'alternative' practitioners. Alternative therapies are now increasingly recognized as 'complementary' in Britain, but 'complementary' does not automatically include traditional South Asian therapies.

I do not have quantitative data with which to discuss the extent to which Oxford Pakistanis use traditional remedies, but offer some comments on their significance. As in the Glasgow survey, many Oxford Pakistanis regard herbal remedies with some skepticism, and are aware of the dangers of some of them. A few have been vehemently critical, claiming English medicine is far superior. Yet even those who reject herbal remedies may know quite a lot about them and occasionally use them themselves, particularly for minor ailments. Homemade or South-Asian shop-bought herbal or mineral remedies (*desi ylāj*), such as *gulkānd* (made from rose petals), for example, may be taken for an upset stomach. An understanding of humoral principles may influence how information given by a GP is understood and may compete with it. The process of consulting a *hakīm* can also be important as a palliative, in enabling someone with a troubling condition to 'do' something for it, particularly if a GP's comment that 'it is nothing to worry about' has not been sufficient to dispel the concern.

Oxford Pakistanis may also favour and use homeopathic remedies for everyday ailments. They consider that western medicine is *garm* and can therefore have harmful side effects; homeopathic remedies, by contrast, have no such side effects. Homeopathic medicine was introduced to the Indian subcontinent in the 19th century and today has both trained and untrained practitioners in Pakistan. I met one schoolteacher who had retired to his natal village in Jhelum district bringing two suitcases of homeopathic remedies with which he treated villagers. In Oxford, I know of no practicing South Asian homeopaths but Pakistanis do consult English homeopaths, sometimes via the Asian Cultural Centre, though consider the consultation to be expensive. One woman suspected that the English homeopath's remedy was identical to, though more expensive than, the one she had obtained from her GP for the same condition. A few people also use the 'drop in' homeopathic clinic in east Oxford, where a consultation costs £5 rather than £25.

Prayer, Faith and Religious Ritual

Whereas the ideas and practice of Unani (and Ayurvedic) medicine, homeopathy and *desi ylāj* emphasize the correct balance of physical elements in the body and in the diet, religious beliefs and ritual practices emphasize the role of prayer, faith and religious ritual in the treatment and management of illness. Religious beliefs and practices associated with health and illness draw upon quite different theories of illness causality, but they are not viewed as incompatible with systems which emphasize a balance of physical elements in the body, including western medicine. For many Pakistanis, religious beliefs provide the ultimate or 'final-cause' explanation of illness. In rural Pakistan, the ritual practices associated with religious explanations of illness, particularly the ritual techniques used by *pīrs* (saints), provide the most accessible and widespread system for managing a wide range of illnesses and more generally for dealing with misfortune.

Ultimately, health, illness or misfortune is God-given, the consequence of God's will, and as such is to be endured. In cases of terminal or incurable illness this fatalism is itself a source of comfort. This does not mean that Pakistanis feel powerless when faced with illness, because they also believe in the efficacy of prayer and faith in response to illness and misfortune. Illness is perceived as a test of faith or as a sign of a deficiency in religious merit (*bartāb*) which ritual action can redress.

Most Pakistani Muslims believe that on The Day of Judgement souls will be reunited with their bodies and go for eternity to either paradise or hell, which, as one woman put it, is 'seventy times hotter than a gas fire turned up to maximum'. The judgement is based on the balance for each individual of good deeds, or *sawāb* (religious merit), against the bad. Prayer and performing one's duties as a Muslim build up the account of *sawāb*. The pilgrimage to Mecca (*hajj*) is believed to cleanse you of all your sins and make you 'as pure as a newborn baby'. Likewise, suffering during an illness may contribute towards perfecting the soul. Any cure is granted by the will of Allah, but piety, prayer and faith will be rewarded by forgiveness (*taubā*) if not as relief from suffering in this life, then in the next. Piety and prayers are also efficacious not only for one's own protection or alleviation from affliction but can be dedicated to another living person or else to someone whose soul is in the 'waiting room' prior to the day of judgement, in order to 'build up their *sawāb* account'. Prayers on someone else's behalf, on a Thursday or Friday, during the first 40 days and on the hundredth day after their death and annually thereafter will bring them *taubā*.

I should emphasize at this point that it is impossible to describe a unified 'traditional' South Asian or Pakistani Islam, for no such thing exists. South Asian Muslims share a belief in the five pillars of Islam and the Day of Judgement, and in the importance of prayer, fasting, pilgrimage to Mecca, and in not consuming alcohol or pork. Beyond these commonalities, however, South Asian Islam, like Islam elsewhere, is characterized by a diversity of traditions, which is in large measure a response to the impact of the colonial encounter and global processes[20].

It is in the context of beliefs about health and illness that competing versions of Islam find their most clear expression; one of the key issues is the role of religious ritual in healing. The beliefs of many, if not the majority, of Oxford Pakistanis can be located within the tradition of Sufism or Islamic mysticism, which continues to be influential across the Muslim world[21]. This tradition is also contested, locally and elsewhere (as I discuss in Chapter 9), particularly by those within the reformist traditions which reject aspects of Sufi Islam.

Central to the tradition of Islamic Sufism is a belief in the powers of *pīr*s or saints as spiritual intermediaries between ordinary people and Allah. Challenging this tradition, some Pakistani Muslims question the spiritual power of *pīr*s, regard their practices as 'backward' or not genuinely Islamic, and maintain that some *pīr*s are corrupt and exploitative. In Oxford, these ideological divisions encompass a range of different positions rather than a single ideological divide. Yet they are most often characterized as an opposition between 'Barelwi' beliefs in the power of *pīr*s on the one hand and 'Wahhabi' or 'Deobandi' beliefs which challenge the power of *pīr*s on the other. Among Oxford Pakistanis, of whom the majority is from rural Panjab where the *pīr* tradition is vibrant and thriving, an emphasis on the spiritual qualities of the prophet predominates in religious practice.

A *pīr*'s spiritual power (*baraka*) is linked to his being both a spiritual and a genealogical descendant of the Prophet or the Prophet's tribe. Thus, 'true' *pīr*s are Sayyed or Sheikh, though a close follower can himself become a *pīr*, without having a 'sacred' genealogy, and becoming a *pīr* may effect a claim to *ashraf* status. There is thus a hierarchy of 'greater' and 'lesser' *pīr*s, and within this varying claims to *ashraf* status are made[22]. The *pīr*s I met were all men and the shrines I have visited, heard or read about are all those of male saints, though I have twice been told about living women *pīr*s, in both Pakistan and Britain.

Through contact with a *pīr*, living or dead, ordinary people can have direct access to God's power. For access to this spiritual power, it may be enough to be in the *pīr*'s presence or in the same building, or to touch or lift a stone or take some soil from the shrine of a *pīr* who has died. (The stone or soil may then be tied in a cloth and worn around the neck like a charm). The *pīr*'s spiritual power enables healing and gives protection from affliction. It is sought for conditions which range from an out-break of pimples, the loss of a wristwatch and fear of failing examinations to eye troubles, back pain, infertility, the lack of a son, tuberculosis, high blood pressure and terminal or incurable illness.

Tombs of *pīr*s who have died are popular places of pilgrimage. One of the best known of these shrines in Pakistan is that of the eleventh-century Sufi, al-Hujwiri, popularly known as Data Ganj Baksh, in Lahore[23]. Another famous shrine is that of the thirteenth century Sufi Hazrat Farid al-Din, popularly known as Baba Farid, or Baba Farid Shakkar Ganj, near Pakpattan in the Panjab. At Baba Farid's death anniversary (*urs*) pilgrims queue to enter the southern door of his tomb, called the Gate of Heaven, which is only opened at this time[24]. Other shrines that Oxford Pakistanis visit include those of Baba Karam Shah and Pir Suleman Paras in Jhelum and Shah Dola, also known as Shah Dole Shah, in Gujrat. During a return trip to Pakistan in which they visited as many famous shrines as possible, one family also visited the shrine of Hazrat Mu'in al-din Chishti at Ajmer in Rajastan, India[25]. A *pīr*'s powers are explicitly supernatural and miraculous. Many popular stories reveal a *pīr*'s ability to transform nature; for example, not only may a *pīr* enable a woman to have a child, he may also have the power to transform the sex of a child, as the story Zahida told me shows:

> A woman who had no sons went to a *pīr*. Nine months later, a son was born. The woman decided to show the baby boy to the *pīr*, to thank him. On the way, she met another *pīr*, who asked her, 'What are you carrying? She replied, 'My baby'. He then asked, 'Is it a son or a daughter?' 'A son', she replied. 'Let me look, he said, and she showed him the baby. 'No', he said,' you've not got a son, you've got a daughter!' She looked, and he was right, she had a girl! She rushed on to her own *pīr* and told him she had given birth to a son, but had met a second *pīr* on the way who had said she'd got a daughter, and the baby had become a girl. Her *pīr* said. 'Let me look'. She showed him. 'No', he said, 'you've not got a daughter, you've got a son!' She looked and he was right, the child was a boy! She thanked him and set off home. On the way she saw the second *pīr* again. The same thing happened. So she went back to her own *pīr*. Returning home again, the same thing happened a third time. When she went back to her own *pīr* this time he said, 'Take a different route home!'

Contact with a living *pīr* is brief and highly ritualized. A *pīr*'s spiritual powers enable him to make a diagnosis on the basis of a generalized or brief statement of the problem; a *pīr* may in fact know what is troubling you even before you have said anything. Katherine Ewing argues that it is the ritualized nature of the encounter, and specifically the ritual activities performed by the *pīr*, rather than any personal relationship between the 'curer' and 'client' which is efficacious in this curing process; the *pīr* is an agent, facilitating supernatural transformations[26].

Writing an amulet (*tā'wīz*) is the standard technique of the curing process. A *pīr* is able to dispense *tā'wīz* because he knows which particular verse of the *Qur'ān* is appropriate for which complaint. The *Qur'ān* contains words suitable for every conceivable affliction, but their location is known only to Allah or to Allah's spiritual intermediaries (though I did, in Pakistan, buy a 'guide to writing *tā'wīz*'). A *pīr* writes on paper the words of the relevant Quranic verse. The paper is folded, enclosed in a metal or leather case and worn around the neck. Sometimes a *pīr* writes two copies of the relevant passage from the *Qur'ān*, one to be worn, the other to be dissolved in water and swallowed. The *pīr* may also offer some brief advice, perhaps that the *tā'wīz* should not be removed, or that it must be worn at night (in the case, for instance, of a *tā'wīz* to protect a child or a woman from night-fears). Sometimes he also recommends reciting a particular verse of the *Qur'ān*, or offers dietary advice or a herbal remedy, for some *pīrs* also practice as *hakīms*. A *pīr* consulted about missing objects or persons employs a method called *hasab* to ascertain whether they will return. I was told of one female *pīr* who used *hasab* to reassure a woman I knew that her lost kitten would return, which it did, a fortnight later. A *pīr* may also write a *tā'wīz* to ensure that a person who has run away after a quarrel returns safely.

A *pīr*'s methods may be various and idiosyncratic. Ewing notes from her observations of a *pīr* in Lahore that rather than writing a *tā'wīz*, a *pīr* may recite a verse of the *Qur'ān* and then blow on the patient in the general direction of their physical complaint. Or else he may recite a verse of the *Qur'ān* and blow on some water which is then given to the sick person. One *pīr* would blow on the patient, lick a piece of salt he had chipped from a large chunk, wrap it in paper and give it to the patient[27]. I heard of similar methods employed by a *fakīr*, who is a sort of wandering holy man who performs magical acts to benefit health. I witnessed one *fakīr* in Pakistan place some sugar on a piece of newspaper, blow on it, and advise the man who had consulted him to eat a little every day for a week in order to restore his health. But whereas a *pīr* is considered to be a living descendant of the Prophet Muhammad and is usually associated with the shrine of an ancestral *pīr*, a *fakīr* lacks these credentials and his spiritual powers are often regarded as suspect. (I was often told that the *fakīrs* who travel around villages giving magical remedies and claiming that the payment they receive will feed the poor at the shrines they come from are in fact fakes, merely lining their pockets).

Devotees of *pīrs* do consider that some so-called *pīrs* may be frauds, and say that a genuine *pīr* does not take money for his work, although in practice offerings of money or gifts are almost always made to the *pīr* or to the shrine with which he is associated. Alternatively, the supplicant may make a vow (*mannat*) that once their affliction has been cured or their wish granted they would make a particular gift to the shrine. Rashida presented a tongue made of silver at the shrine of Shah Dola, for instance, in fulfillment of *mannat*, when her child who had been diagnosed with 'learning difficulties' eventually began to talk.

Tā'wīz to influence other people may be used in the context of domestic power struggles — to harm an enemy or rival, such as a senior sister-in-law, to make someone agree with you, to make someone fall in love with you, to hide a love affair from parents, to control errant teenagers, to make a son accept a marriage he does not want, or to draw a husband's attentions, affections and duties towards yourself and your parents and away from your in-laws. These *tā'wīz* may be obtained in powder form to be put into food or drink, or may be left in a secret place, buried in the ground or put into a crack in a wall. However, they are regarded as *jādū* (magic) or 'bad magic' and potentially dangerous, even fatal: the recipient can become ill, go crazy, 'go like a cabbage', or become so weak that they die — like the twenty-five year old bride whose parents-in-law had procured a *tā'wīz* to make her more dutiful. Pakistanis acknowledge that *pīrs* can sometimes be bad and can give bad *tā'wīz* without you knowing. If you suspect bad magic you must see a good *pīr* and obtain a *tā'wīz* for protection.

Local debate about what constitutes 'genuine' or correct Islamic practice, particularly in the context of healing, is most often characterized as an opposition between 'Barelvi' beliefs, which are centered around devotion to the Prophet Muhammad and to *pīrs*, and the reformist 'Wahhabi' or 'Deobandi' traditions. In fact, the debate thrives within the Sufi tradition as well, for the devotees of particular *pīrs* may level criticism at the ritual and healing practices of other *pīrs*, particularly where money is involved, or where the custodians of a shrine in Pakistan or India benefit from the gifts of the pilgrims. This criticism also extends to another role of the *pīr*, as not just a healer but as also, occasionally, an exorcist.

Pīrs may be called upon to exorcise *jinn*, sometimes also called 'ghosts' or 'giants'. According to Panjabi Muslim cosmology, Allah created men, angels and *jinn*. *Jinn* are spirits made of fire (referred to in the last verses of the *Qur'ān*), which are invisible to humans and have great power, such as the ability to build mosques and heave stones, according to the story of their origin. Pakistanis say that the *jinn* were originally controlled by the Prophet Suleman (Solomon) by Arabic words written and recorded in his ring and that only the people closest to Solomon knew these words, passing them on, unwritten, over the generations. Today, only people who know these secret words have the power to control *jinn* and such people are called *āmil*s. A *pīr*, because of his spiritual power and closeness to God, may also have an *āmil*'s power, but an *āmil* is not necessarily a *pīr*; he is more like a magician and may order *jinn* to perform capricious acts like uprooting bushes.

*Jinn*s live in lonely, out of the way places, certain points in the road, or behind bushes. Usually they cause no harm, because they inhabit their own spirit world, which is separate from the human world. If they are disturbed, however, they can cross into the human world and cause accidents or possess people. In Pakistan, a farmer taking his bullock cart to town stopped to urinate, but unknowingly did so on a *jinn*'s house; as a result, he was afflicted with paralysis for two months. Another farmer's ploughshare dropped off the back of his tractor when he passed exactly the same point in the road where a year before a tractor had turned over and crushed its driver to death: 'A *jinn* must live at this point in the road', the farmer's neighbour said. Pakistani women in Oxford told me that a car accident between Chorley and Preston in which five Pakistani Muslims were killed but the English Muslim traveler survived was caused by a *jinn* who must have been in some way offended by the Pakistani travelers. Pakistani Muslim travelers now apparently avoid that route, or else do not stop or get out of their cars when passing that spot.

Jinn not only cause potentially fatal accidents, they can possess people and 'make them go crazy' (*pāgal*). Anyone may become possessed but the 'weak', that is, women, children and the elderly, are more likely to be afflicted. For example, Qudsia, a bride recently arrived from Pakistan, was possessed by a *jinn*. 'At night when she goes to the bathroom to urinate, a *jinn* takes her over; her hands are thrown up and down, then her body', Qudsia's mother-in-law said. Farid, a nine-year-old boy began to be troubled by *jinn* shortly after his arrival in Britain.

His parents think that just before coming to Britain he must have crossed some ground beside the pond outside their village where *jinn* children were playing and unknowingly broken their toys. As punishment, a *jinn* possesses him from time to time. 'The *jinn* usually comes at night when my son is sleeping', Farid's mother said, 'The *jinn* tells him beforehand by making a sound like knocking. Then the *jinn* enters and Farid struggles with it, his arms and legs thrash about and he shouts and cries in pain.'

Exorcising a *jinn* requires the *āmil* or *pīr* to say special Arabic words to communicate with the *jinn*. The *jinn* eventually agrees to leave the patient's body, shaking the *pīr*'s hand three times, a gesture which some say means the *jinn* will not return, but others are less sure. According to Ewing, a *pīr*'s control of *jinn* and hence of illness is symbolically effected primarily through the ritual power inherent in the Arabic words — the verses of the *Qur'ān* and the Attributes of God — uttered by the *pīr*. 'In the case of Muslim exorcism, the control of "God's words" by the exorcist gives him such a power over the demons'[28]. The *pīr*'s actions then symbolically 'trap' the *jinn*, bringing it under the *pīr*'s control, and bringing the exorcism to a successful conclusion.

In Pakistan, I was also told of other aspects of 'possession' in which the possessed person may speak in strange voices, the voices of 'ghosts', before the *jinn* finally departs and sometimes this possessed person subsequently has powers over *jinn*. The man paralyzed after urinating on a *jinn*'s house tried so many ways of asking the *jinn*'s forgiveness that eventually he could communicate with the *jinn* and control it. Able to cross the boundary into the world of the *jinn*, he is now an *āmil* whose services are sometimes required abroad. A woman who had previously herself been possessed would be called upon to act as a 'medium' in other cases of female possession and, during 'exorcisms' would also answer questions put to her by neighbours about the supernatural causes of other accidents or illnesses.

In Oxford, however, it is *pīr*s, rather than ordinary people who have themselves been possessed or other 'mediums', who are considered the most effective controllers of the *jinn*, because of their specific knowledge of verses of the *Qur'ān* effective in

Muslim exorcism. A Catholic priest was once called upon to exorcise a *jinn* that had possessed a schoolboy, but this exorcism was not considered successful. There is, as I have said, a hierarchy of *pīr*s, and thus of their efficacy in controlling *jinn*. Locally, several men are considered to have power over *jinn* but usually families seek exorcisms from the most renowned *pīr*s in Pakistan or from *pīr*s in London. Qudsia, the bride from Pakistan possessed by a *jinn*, was eventually cured by a *tā'wīz* obtained in Pakistan by her mother. Farid was taken to a famous *pīr* from Pakistan who was visiting London for the exorcism that finally cured him.

Purdah, *izzat* and the Reproduction of the *birādarī*

I now turn to consider the interplay of some of these ideas in the context of biological reproduction, a process critical to the social and cultural reproduction of the Pakistani *birādarī*. In Britain, GPs and the maternity services play a major part in this process, but Oxford Pakistanis also bring to it a background of cultural ideas about sexuality, purity and pollution, some of which draw upon aspects of the background medical systems in Pakistan. Women's experiences are particularly important here: not only do they have the babies, but, less prosaically, appropriate control of a woman's sexuality and childbearing is central to the *birādarī*'s honour (*izzat*).

Men, not women, are seen as perpetrators of *birādarī* 'blood' (despite the fact that husband and wife are often closely related). Female sexuality, if uncontrolled, can threaten the integrity of the *birādarī*; early close-kin marriage is one means of minimizing this risk. Marriage to a non-relative may be acceptable if the man and his family are regarded 'as if' they were *birādarī*, either through common 'caste' status or as a strategy for social mobility. However, if a woman has a sexual relationship with or marries someone outside the *birādarī*, especially if he is of another 'race', she threatens *birādarī* integrity to such an extent that in extreme cases she may be cut off altogether. The children of a woman who marries outside of the caste are regarded as having their father's caste (or 'racial') identity, not their mother's, whereas the children of a Pakistani father and an English or other non-Pakistani mother are regarded as belonging to their father's *birādarī*. The English mother may be incorporated into the *birādarī* or else may be asked to give her child or children over to the care of the father's parents or, if he is already married, to his Pakistani wife. Male sexuality may thus, in effect, extend the *birādarī*.

Cultural mechanisms which support these gender differences are established through socialization and upbringing; norms of 'appropriate' behaviour are instilled in girls from an early age and particularly as they approach puberty. Broadly, these norms are related to the ideals of *purdah*, which reflect its literal meaning as 'curtain' as well as its function as a system of social differentiation by gender and as a social and moral code[29]. Part of this moral code is to do with the control of female sexuality; women are seen as both in need of protection and a danger to men[30]. When a daughter reaches puberty, her potentially disruptive sexuality must be controlled to avoid disgrace to her natal family. She must dress and behave modestly, avoid meeting unrelated men and, ideally, marry early while still a virgin. After marriage, respectable behaviour and avoiding shame continues to be particularly important for women. Ideally, a new bride first lives with her husband in his parents' house. She must behave modestly, covering her body and the hair of her head and concealing the shameful fact of her sexual experience, while her husband will avoid relaxed or intimate contact with her while in the presence of his parents.

The control of female and to a lesser extent male sexual behaviour is also effected through purity and pollution beliefs associated with the loss of bodily fluids and substances. As has been noted in other Muslim societies, the loss of urine, faeces, semen and blood, as 'matter out of place', requires ritual control[31]. Ablutions before prayer remove the pollutions of urination and defaecation. Likewise, sexual intercourse is polluting for men and women and requires ritual ablution. Although sexual intercourse is expected between husband and wife, and children are desired, the sexual act is alluded to rarely and euphemistically, as a husband and wife 'doing work' or 'being together'. The verbs 'to beat inside' or 'to strike' (*mārnā*) or 'to connect' (*lagnā*) are used to refer to copulation in jocular usage, and the sexual organs are usually only mentioned as terms of abuse. After sexual intercourse, the husband and wife must take a ritual bath in which they should wash 'every hair of the head', and they can neither prepare nor consume food or drink until they have done so. One mosque-goer commented regretfully, 'where I work, it is easy for English men to have sex, during the lunch break, or in the back of a car. But for us it takes longer, because you have to bath afterwards. You have to make a proper programme'. Women complained in particular of the inconvenience in Britain's cold climate of having to wash their hair afterwards, for traditionally a woman's head hair is long and never cut. A daughter-in-law who washes her hair early in the morning in effect signals to the rest of the household, particularly to her mother-in-law who may take notice of such things, that sexual intercourse has taken place.

Hair is polluting in this and in other contexts, as Hershman has noted for Panjabi Sikhs[32]. Both sexes, I was told, should use depilatory substances (but not razors) to remove their pubic hair, for it is *nāpāk* (impure). A baby's head hair must be shaved soon after birth, because the first hair is *nāpāk* (impure), 'because it has been in the mother's stomach and in contact with blood, and other children will be frightened of it', as one mother explained. Women sometimes asked whether my children's first head hair had been shaved and advised that it should be, so that the second growth would be thick and strong. A woman's head hair should be carefully tended, sometimes oiled, always tied back and covered in the presence of unrelated men. That a woman's hair is also, ideally, never cut is a symbol, Hershman suggests, of the fact that a woman can never leave her state of impurity in relation to men; only widows, or female saints, may have shaven heads[33]. Among Oxford Pakistanis, hair cut short or uncovered and untied is associated with 'western' or 'uncontrolled' sexuality: a girl with a modern hair cut may be referred to insultingly as a *desī gorī* (home-made English girl). Chronically or terminally sick women, or women suffering from psychiatric illness or deafness, may have loose or cropped hair, partly for easy management, but also in denial of 'normal' female sexuality, for such women will not be married.

Processes which involve the loss of blood also require ritual control, or else are associated with specific dangers. Menstruation is simultaneously polluting and therefore dangerous and a necessary release of excessive *garmī* (heat); blood is hot and, as I was told, 'too much *garmī* may accumulate in the head and make a woman go mad'. A woman indicates her uncleanness at the onset of menstruation to the other members of her household by saying that her 'clothes are dirty' (*kapre plīt* or *kapre hogaie*) or that she has to 'wash her head' (*sir nahānā*) or 'wash her hair' (*bāl nahānā*). More direct references to menstruation are avoided, even in the presence of other women: I found that even the formal Urdu word, *mahvārī* (literally 'monthly') caused embarrassment, especially when senior women were present. One woman told me that during her most recent visit to her village, she noticed her sister and niece used an English word, 'menses', which she had never heard before, in preference to the Urdu one. A man avoids sexual relations with his wife during menstruation, 'because a woman's blood is dangerous and can make a man sick.' Menstruating women cannot pray, nor touch the *Qur'ān*, nor go to a mosque until they have had the ritual bath that marks the end of menstruation.

Pollution beliefs associated with loss of bodily fluids and substances also extend to childbirth. In rural Pakistan, a woman may return to her natal home for childbirth and be attended only by her closest female relatives and the village *dāī* (midwife). The *dāī* is traditionally of low caste status, as is appropriate for the defiling tasks of cutting the baby's umbilical cord at delivery and cleaning up the blood. In Britain, the polluting aspects of childbirth are contained through the fact that women prefer to give birth in hospital. After childbirth, a woman is considered polluted (*plīt*) for sixty days of the postpartum period, during which the couple should abstain from intercourse.

The birth of a child is the result of processes that involve much more than ideas about the polluting qualities of bodily substances, however. In considering some of these ideas, I hope to demonstrate the interplay of elements of the different 'systems' involved: the balance of hot and cold elements in the body, pollution beliefs, and the role of *hakīm*s, *tā'wīz*, and *pīr*s as well as the British N.H.S.

Fertility and Infertility

'Sadness after having a baby' is how the title of a leaflet produced in Urdu translates back into English. The leaflet is distributed by health visitors to newly-delivered Pakistani mothers because of concerns that the now clinically-recognized condition of post-natal depression, which apparently affects one in ten mothers, may be under-diagnosed among Pakistanis. My impression is that mostly the leaflet has been met with incomprehension, for it is almost inconceivable that for a young married woman, producing a baby could bring 'sadness'. The birth of a child is a cause for happiness (*khushī*) and great celebration, especially if the child is a boy. Usually, a new bride eagerly anticipates a first baby. Initially, a new daughter-in-law's housework and even her relationship with her husband may be scrutinized by her mother-in-law, and she must defer to her husband, his parents and any older brothers and their wives; only with a husband's younger brother and unmarried sisters can she be more relaxed. As she produces children, however, especially sons, a daughter-in-law gains status, respect and a degree of autonomy within her husband's parents' home, and eventually she and her husband may move with their children to a separate house.

If a bride does not show signs of pregnancy soon after marriage (the impurity of menstruation being difficult to conceal from a mother-in-law) questions may be raised about the adequacy of the sexual relationship or about the bride's health. Young brides from Pakistan living with their husband's parents may have little control over their fertility, and indeed not expect to control it, at least until after they have had their first child.

Failure to conceive or to produce live children can, in principle, result in divorce or in the husband taking a second wife, though in practice many other factors come into play. In Pakistan, Nusrat's first pregnancy miscarried at seven months. Her father-in-law consulted a *hakīm* on her behalf, and she was advised to avoid hot foods during the next pregnancy, for these can induce miscarriage, or 'cause a baby to fall'. Her second child died a few months after its birth. Eventually Nusrat was returned to her natal home. The failed marriage was attributed to Nusrat's childlessness, and as a result Nusrat's mother would spend long periods of time crying and would scarcely eat. Another childless marriage in the same village, however, did not break down. Khurshida had repeated miscarriages and stillbirths, but she and her husband took all the advice they could, visited the shrines of renowned *pīrs* and for years followed a chilli-free meat-free diet recommended by a *hakīm*. Men sometimes mocked Khurshida's husband's virility; 'He should have taken a second wife, but he is too weak', his cousin said, but women remarked that Khurshida's husband treated her with respect. Sixteen years later, I am told that this still childless couple are much respected members of the village who have helped Khurshida's widowed sister raise her children.

Given the attitudes to sexual intercourse outlined above, childless couples may be unwilling to go to GPs to discuss infertility problems. Women may prefer to consult a *pīr* or *hakīm* because no internal examination is involved, while dietary changes, other Unani remedies, or *tā'wīz* provide something 'to do' for the condition. However, producing children is such a crucial issue that a variety of avenues may be followed with equal intensity, particularly if the couple has been childless for some time, and the topic is generally approached in a pragmatic rather than a prurient spirit. Shamim, for instance, undertook extensive hospital investigations for infertility. She came to Britain in 1968 for marriage and a year later had one stillbirth, but failed to conceive again. Three years later, their GP referred the couple for infertility tests, all of which proved inconclusive. Shamim became very unhappy, suffering from a series of non-specific symptoms of ill health, which necessitated frequent visits to the GP. She is now resigned to childlessness, and although at times is very sad, she takes solace in prayer and in teaching the *Qur'ān* to her sisters' children and to other children in the neighbourhood. Her husband has not divorced her, nor taken another wife. At one point, a GP suggested adoption, but for Shamim this was out of the question, 'because the child would not be of the same blood'.

The avenues pursued vary to some extent with generation. A young couple brought up in England and aware of the treatments offered by the health service might more readily explain their problem to a GP than to a *hakīm*, though this does not necessarily follow. Bashir and Mina, first cousins married for ten years, were both raised in Britain, but have not had intensive N.H.S investigations for infertility. Two years after the marriage, Mina showed no signs of pregnancy, so during a return visit to Pakistan her in-laws took her to a *hakīm*, who asked for details of her irregular menstruation. Concluding from her appearance that Mina was weak and naturally rather phlegmatic, the *hakīm* advised that she increase her intake of warm foods, which would make her more receptive during sexual intercourse and would also regulate her menstruation. Later, she was taken to a *pīr*, who turned over her hands, examined her wrists, and wrote two *tā'wīz* for her: one to be dissolved in water and then drunk, the other to be worn constantly. However, these methods have not proved successful. They have now discussed with their GP the possibilities of fertility treatment, but Mina's mother-in-law considers such intervention would be wrong. Mina is currently bringing up her sister-in-law's daughter as her own.

Childlessness particularly affects the status of women, but the pressure to produce a child, or more than one or two children, or sons can also be considerably stressful for men. A woman in Pakistan once asked me, 'In England, can a wife whose husband is too weak to give her children divorce him?' This would be impossible, she said, in Pakistan. It is not fear of divorce that men may worry about, however, but their strength and potency.

These concerns are linked with ideas about maintaining the correct bodily balance of heat and coldness in relation to semen loss. Semen, which a boy's body begins to produce at puberty, is considered to be very concentrated blood. Since blood is *garm* (hot), accumulating semen could result in excessive *garmī* and possibly madness. Therefore, as for a woman, sexual intercourse protects a man from the effects of excessive *garmī*. However, excessive sexual intercourse or loss of semen by, for instance, masturbation weakens a man. 'Men lose more blood through intercourse than women lose monthly', I was told, 'because every drop of semen is made from 100 drops of blood. Just think what a lot of blood that is. That's why men get weak from sexual intercourse'. Unmarried men may worry about the weakening effects of masturbation, considered *thand* (cold) whereas intercourse is *garm*, despite the reassurances given by GPs or English friends. The sex of a child is also thought to result from the quality of a man's semen: thin or weak semen produces a girl, thick semen produces a boy. Semen becomes thin from excessive intercourse; once every two or three weeks, I was told, is ideal; newly married or particularly *garm* men may want it more frequently, but, as one mosque-goer said, 'they have to remember the inconvenience of the ablutions required afterwards'.

Some men consult both *hakīm*s and their GP during the same 'illness episode', about psychosexual problems: the effects of masturbation, impotence, premature ejaculation, 'sperm coming out when you are peeing' and infertility. 'If a *hakīm* came to Oxford' joked Saeed, 'men would queue up to see him'. I was told that the *hakīm* listens carefully to the man's account of his problem, prescribes a remedy, and offers advice. He has a list of prescriptions (*nuskhe*) for the various problems men have with a price for each remedy (*ilāj*). Remedies can also be obtained by sending payment for the prescription required. Some remedies have expensive ingredients such as gold, rare herbs and 'something from the navel of the black deer, which has a very strong smell'. The *hakīm*'s dietary advice usually involves the avoidance of hot foods, such as coffee, strong tea, meat and western medications, to allow strength and potency to be restored. He also counsels against masturbation while taking a remedy and at any other time because of its cooling and weakening effect.

Mazhar, married with two children, was very anxious that four years had elapsed since his wife had last conceived. He feared he was becoming weak through losing semen before intercourse took place. Accompanied by two Pakistani workmates, he consulted a renowned *hakīm* who was visiting Birmingham. The *hakīm* prescribed an expensive remedy and advised against hot foods. Still worried, however, Mazhar went a week later to his GP, an English woman to whom Mahzar bravely explained his problem 'with the help of gestures'. She reassured him that nothing was wrong, that losing semen would in any case not make him weak, and prescribed a relaxant. Mazhar now has seven children, and does not know which of the strategies he pursued made the most difference: 'My children are given by God', he says.

Producing a male child is often also a concern. Each child is considered a gift from God, but the birth of a son is generally more celebrated than that of a daughter. Pakistanis explain this by saying that a daughter brings worry and expense: she will eventually go to live in another household, she must be provided with a dowry or with evidence of a house and income if she is to bring a groom from Pakistan. Women who have had only daughters may desperately want a son. They may pray at the shrine of *pīr*s renowned for their powers to help women conceive male children, or they may obtain a *tā'wīz* 'for a male child' by visiting or writing to a *pīr*. They may seek advice about whom to consult from friends or from Urdu newspapers, which occasionally publish details of visiting *hakīm*s or *fakīr*s with remedies for the failure to produce sons.

Birth Control: Thwarting Allah's Will

Families in Britain have much easier access to information and resources for family planning than is generally the case in Pakistan. Health visitors or a woman's GP usually advise women who have recently had babies about the local family planning services. Sometimes this is how women who have come from Pakistan for, or following, marriage first hear about the local contraceptive services, but birth control is also much discussed among friends and relatives, both in Pakistan and in Britain.

In rural Pakistan, infant mortality is high and having more than two or three children is an insurance against the fact that some children will not survive to adulthood, so parents may be unwilling to limit the number of children they have. Parents often want male children because they regard boys as insurance for the future, as potential wage earners, whereas girls have to be given dowries at marriage. I have no information on the extent to which contraception is used in rural Pakistan. I was aware of government-promoted 'family education' and of the government-subsidized sale of condoms in some villages (small boys would buy them and blow them up as balloons). Several women, in Pakistan and in Britain, said that condoms have a drying effect on the vagina and uterus. My impression was that among women in Pakistan who already had a number of children and who also used birth control, the most popular methods were female sterilization (*nasbandī*) or the intrauterine device (IUD) or 'loop' (*chala*) for which women had to travel to the nearest town with a hospital.

Whether they used modern birth control methods or not, women in Pakistan would quite often discuss with me the 'ideal' family size and contraceptive techniques. They were also curious to discover whether their relatives in England had 'become English' by using contraception. In a village in Jhelum district, Zeban who has five children and her sister Zakia who has seven, both thought that two or three children would be ideal, 'otherwise you get ill and have headaches'. Zakia had used an IUD for five years after her sixth child but had very heavy periods. She stopped using it on her sister's advice, but became pregnant again. The midwife attending Zakia's seventh delivery asked me about special-care baby-units in Britain: 'in Pakistan, she said, 'babies are often weak because their mothers are weak from having too many babies, too many woman have babies every year'. It was therefore a good plan, she thought, to use birth control, but all the methods were unreliable or made women ill, 'except *nasbandī*, but *nasbandī* is sinful'.

Of the methods available, *nasbandī* (sterilization) was the least discussed but the subject of great curiosity. Kaniz's relatives in Pakistan asked me on several different occasions how many children Kaniz had, even though they knew the answer already. They also once asked whether she had had an 'operation' and 'become like the English'; only then did I realize that they wanted to know whether she had been sterilized. This scenario was repeated in a different village with Shahnaz's sisters. They knew Shahnaz had four children but asked me endlessly, 'has Shahnaz had any more children?' Once day, they pointed to a baby's bottle on the mantelpiece in a recent photograph from England, joking, 'look, she has had another baby'. I said that the baby's bottle in the photograph belonged to a visiting neighbour, but they persisted with their claim. Eventually, I told them that Shahnaz, who already had four children when she came to Britain in 1978, had been sterilized soon after. There was a long embarrassed silence: I had told them what they had wanted to know but did not want to hear.

It is perhaps the finality of sterilization that marks it out from other methods, though the critics of birth control consider all methods are in effect the murder of unborn children. In Oxford, the wife of an *imām* of the 'Barelwi' mosque commented on the Urdu phrase which means 'to make' a baby. 'It is wrong' she said, 'to think of children as being "made" by

their parents, for they come not as a result of their parents
actions or desires but of God's' will'. This is one of her many
cautionary tales, related as a true event:

> A woman in Preston had *nasbandī* after her third child.
> Three men, dressed in white, came to her house and asked
> her to go with them. 'I don't go anywhere without my
> husband's permission', she replied. They sought her
> husband's permission and the next day took her to a
> secluded place outside Preston, in the hills, and got out of
> the car and went over to a boulder. 'Turn over this
> boulder', the men ordered her. 'But I can't. Why should
> I?' she retorted. 'Because your children are under it.' 'No,
> 'she said, 'my three children are at home'. 'Turn it over
> and you will see,' they persuaded her. Eventually, she
> turned it over, and of course there was nothing there.
> 'Those are your children, the ones you have murdered',
> said the men.

While often wanting to space the births of their children,
women fear the loss of their fertility, which can become a powerful resource, with using modern birth control methods.
Abeda's husband wanted her to take oral contraceptives, but
Abeda, a young woman raised in Britain, explained her fears
about using contraceptive pills by telling me another cautionary
tale, again about sterilization:

> Three years ago, a Pakistani woman in Slough had her
> fourth baby, a boy. She was delighted to have four
> children, two boys and two girls, the perfect family. They
> distributed large amounts of *laddū*s after the birth. The
> mother then decided that now her family was perfect she
> would be sterilized. The day she returned from hospital,
> she received a phone-call saying that her elder boy had
> strangled to death while playing with swings, rope and
> tyres in a playground. She has been crying everyday since,
> saying, 'I am a young woman. If I had not been sterilized,
> I could have had another child. God can snatch our
> children away too. It is up to him'.

Women may also, sometimes, fear the disapproval or wrath of
a mother-in-law if they express a wish to space the births of
their children. Zahida would check her daughter-in-law's room

for contraceptive pills; her daughter-in-law eventually had an IUD fitted after her second child was born, but did not inform her mother-in-law. Women who have had two or three children may be more likely or willing to use contraception than newly married women. They may also not need to seek the permission of a mother-in-law or be chaperoned when they go out and may, therefore, have easier access to a GP or a clinic. Even so, they often remain considerably ambivalent about the various methods of birth control. Many women complain of the side effects and unreliability of the contraceptive pill. Some women consider that the reduced menstrual flow often associated with the use of contraceptive pills has a harmful effect, because it impedes the removal of excessive *garmī* from the body. The relatives in Pakistan of a woman who had died of cancer believed her illness had been caused by the 'drying' effect of contraceptive pills which, they said, her husband had made her take. The irregular bleeding and 'spotting' linked with use of the contraceptive pill also presents problems for ritual purity. Women may also consider the contraceptive pill to be unreliable. Amina reluctantly started taking oral contraceptives after her fourth child was born, because, contrary to her husband's wishes, she did not want to be sterilized, but she became pregnant again. 'Babies come when Allah wants', she said, 'You can get another baby even when you are taking pills; Allah decides.'

Some couples have never used modern birth control methods and have as many as eight or nine children, their births spaced as a result of the wife returning to Pakistan, alone or with children, for several months or a year or more at a time. Many Oxford Pakistanis say that the use of modern methods of contraception is 'against Allah's will', for Allah decides when to give or take a life, and that a person who attempts to thwart Allah's will by intervening in this process will be punished in the next life. Yet many women have, at some time, tried using one or another of the various available methods. They do so with considerable ambivalence, because of fears about the risks to their fertility and fears about wrongdoing. I know little of men's views on birth control. Several women who use the pill and the IUD said they would not want their husbands to have vasectomies; perhaps this indicates a desire to retain the ability to have another baby. Occasionally, women have tried to conceal the fact that they are using birth control from husbands who are opposed to it; in other cases, husbands have wanted unwilling wives to use oral contraceptives or be sterilized.

It is tempting to suggest that the most conservative views are mainly associated with those from rural backgrounds whose religious beliefs fall within the tradition of Islamic mysticism in the Indian subcontinent. In contrast, it may be those who favour a reformist or modernist Islam who are most likely to consider birth control to be compatible with Islamic belief. There is some evidence for this suggestion, at the level of public, stated views about birth control. In contrast to the conservative views of the wife of the *imām* at the 'Barelvi' mosque quoted earlier, whose husband supports the *pīr* tradition, the wife of another *imām* expressed a more liberal view on the use of birth control. This woman, a Gujarati-speaking Muslim from Karachi, whose husband was labelled a 'Wahhabi' by his critics (although he has a *pīr* in Karachi to whom he turns for spiritual guidance), considered that 'God gives you children in order that you should look after them properly, and having fewer children enables you to do this better'. It is therefore possible to distinguish different ideological positions, but this provides us with few necessary clues to contraceptive behaviour. In practice, many women, including those who say they are opposed to birth control or express ambivalence about it, have had some experience of using it. A mother who vehemently opposes contraception on religious grounds may nevertheless take her pregnant teenage daughter to a GP to arrange for an abortion, concealing her action from her relatives and friends. It is generally easier for a mother, or a daughter, to do this in Britain than in Pakistan, although there too women may use *desī* remedies and other techniques to induce abortion, or find some strategy for concealing an unmarried daughter's pregnancy from her prospective in-laws. Public statements advocating, or condemning, the use of modern birth control methods may therefore contradict private practice, in which people pursue strategies that are in keeping with *birādarī* interests.

NOTES

1. Lyon, 1991:145.
2. See also Minocha, 1980 (cited in Lyon, 1991:45).
3. See also Ewing, 1985.
4. Lyon, 1991.

5. Such presentation has been described as 'somatization' within transcultural psychiatry in an attempt to explain how, in the absence of specific words for 'depression' or 'anxiety', distress may be expressed in physical terms. For a discussion of the utility of the concept, see Mumford, 1993; Krause, 1989; Rack, 1982 and Kleinman, 1977 and, more recently, Kleinman, 1995.

6. See Basham, 1976.

7. Lewis and Young, 1992.

8. Qureshi, 1990:105.

9. Krause, 1989.

10. See Krause, 1989.

11. See also Nichter, 1996.

12. Pocock, 1973; Srinivas 1976.

13. Aslam, cited in Rack, 1982: 184.

14. Aslam, cited in Rack, 1982: 195-7.

15. Mays, 1981, and Aslam cited in Rack, 1982: 197.

16. Aslam, cited in Rack, 1982: 191-2.

17. Cited in Mays, 1981.

18. Johnson, 1986.

19. Bhopal, 1986.

20. Lewis, 1994 (b):36-47.

21. Schimmel, 1975.

22. Sherani, 1991.

23. See Lewis 1994(b):27-30.

24. Lewis, 1994 (b):32; Eaton, 1984.

25. See also Currie, 1978.

26. Ewing, 1985.

27. Ewing, 1985:110.

28. Ewing, 1985:111.

29. Papanek, 1973; Jeffery, 1979.

30. See Mernissi, 1975, for an exposition of the view that heterosexual love threatens Allah's order; purdah is a strategy for containing this threat.

31. Douglas, 1966; Boddy, 1989 and Gardner, 1995:248.

32. Hershman, 1974.

33. Hershman, 1974.

8 TAKING AND GIVING: DOMESTIC RITUALS AND FEMALE NETWORKS

If you are born into an east Oxford Pakistani family, then it is very likely that the person you will marry and the people with whom you will have life-long kinship obligations will be relatives from the extended family, *birādarī* or caste. Within this framework, however, there is a degree of flexibility, because while marriages take place preferentially with kin, socio-economic considerations are paramount in shaping particular marriage choices. In such circumstances, the concept of *birādarī*, which often invokes the notion of shared 'blood', may be loosely invoked to justify marriage between people even where there is no known genealogical relationship. In these situations, the participants themselves consider the nature of the relationship between household to be more important than any precise genealogical kinship. In effect, they are stressing the principle of 'fraternal solidarity'[1] rather than that of genealogical descent in their justification of such marriage.

The notion of reciprocity is central to understanding this sentiment of fraternal solidarity. Reciprocity is expressed in a number of ways. It underlies the giving and receiving of mutual aid between households. It is explicitly and ritually expressed in a system of gift exchange called *lenā-denā* (literally 'taking-giving'). It is also, in a rather different way, central to the performance of a religious ritual called the *khatmī-Qur'ān* (the 'completion' or the 'sealing' of the *Qur'ān)*. These expressions of reciprocity involve *birādarī* members, friends and neighbours; they reflect both kinship relationships and 'fraternal solidarity' between kin and non-kin. And it is through their competitive participation in these rituals that families continually assess their relationships with one another and may, potentially at least, effect changes in *birādarī* structure.

As in rural Pakistan, it is women rather than men who play the major role in sustaining these relationships of informal reciprocity and in managing more formal relationships of gift exchange between households. In this way, women's roles have important implications for the standing of a household, both locally, in relation to other Pakistani families in Oxford and Britain and in relation to kin in Pakistan.

Gift exchange between friends, neighbours and kin

Gift giving 'when something happens' (at what anthropologists call a 'life-cycle' event) in a household is a striking feature of relationships between Pakistani women in east Oxford. Women give each other gifts such as notes of money to the value of between £5 and £30, *jorā*s (women's 'suits' — a *jorā* is the *shalwār-qamīs* and *dupattā*), handbags, and men's shirts and socks. Women guests give gifts to the women of a household celebrating a birth, a boy's circumcision, a child's birthday, a child's first completed reading of the *Qur'ān* or a marriage. Hosts give gifts to guests when they invite to dinner relatives or friends in whose household someone has just been married or someone has recently arrived from or is about to depart for abroad.

This practice of gift-exchange is not unique to east Oxford Pakistanis, but has been noted in rural Pakistan, where it is usually called *vartan bhanji* and is a feature of women's participation in domestic life-cycle rituals[2]. In many other societies too — perhaps in all societies — gifts supposedly 'freely' given, such as wedding or birthday presents or dinner invitations are in fact given with some expectation of return, for the very fact of 'giving' creates an obligation to 'receive' and to 'return'[3]. In *lenā-denā*, the expectation of return is explicit; the term itself implies obligation. The recipient of a gift feels obliged to return a similar gift on the next appropriate occasion, and gifts are viewed in terms of goods or sums of money that are 'owing'. Women make a mental note of the value and amount of gifts given or write down these details in a notebook or ledger, so that they can return a similar gift or gifts on the next appropriate occasion.

The process of returning *lenā-denā* gifts illustrates this inherent obligation, for a return gift should be similar in kind and value to the gift received, but worth slightly more, so that while the original debt is 'cancelled' another is created. The difference between the gifts given and received, perhaps £5, £10 or £15 or one suit, plus a small increment, then determines the value of the next gift and enables *lenā-denā* to continue.

In east Oxford, *lenā-denā* relationships often seem to be just as intense between friends and neighbours as they are between kin. In fact, for some families whose closest kin live elsewhere in Britain or are in Pakistan, *lenā-denā* exchanges between close friends seem more intense that between kin. As Zekiye Eglar notes for a village in Gujrat district in Pakistan, *lenā-denā* seems to be a way of maintaining good relationships with kin and non-kin alike[4]. In east Oxford, as in rural Gujrat, participation in *lenā-denā* includes kin and non-kin, irrespective of caste boundaries. At a child's first *Qur'ān* reading, a wedding and at a *khatmī-Qur'ān*, for example (Tables 8.1, 8.2 and 8.3), the guests were not only *birādarī* but also people from different castes, even across the *zamīndār/kammī* divide. Pakistanis are sometimes explicit that reciprocities can cross this divide. Manzoor, a Jhelumi and a Jat, spoke in this way about his relationship with a fellow Jhelumi who is a Mochi:

> Whenever any of his family goes to or comes from Pakistan, we invite them to dinner and they invite us to dinner. I call him *chachā* (father's brother), because he is the same age as my father, and his children call me *bhaī* (brother). We don't care that he is a Mochi. It's the same with another friend who calls himself Khan and I call him Khan. In fact, we address each other as *bhaī*. But he is not a Pathan. In fact, he is a Tarkan, but don't tell him that I know.

Sohrab, a Gujar, described a similar relationship with the household of a fellow villager who is a Kumhar (potter):

> You know Abdul who was at the wedding. Actually he is low caste. Please don't ask him or say that I told you because he would feel embarrassed and ashamed, because of his background. He is a Kumhar, but they tend to call themselves Malik now. (Malik is a title of respect, meaning 'owner'.) But we don't treat him and his family as inferiors, while we are living here. We are all the same here. He has been to my house three or four times. We invited him to dinner after our daughter's wedding. He invited us to dinner when his niece returned from Pakistan, and after his son's wedding.

Relationship to host	Caste	Current Residence	Origin in Pakistan	Gifts given by women
1 Elder brother And wife	Jat	Glasgow	Village in Sahiwal	Unknown
2 Younger brother, Arif And wife	Jat	E. Oxford	Village in Sahiwal	£20
3 Friend (Iqbal's younger brother's wife's brother; formerly Iqbal and Arif's neighbour; his sister married to Arif) And wife	Rajput	Gloucester	Village in Sahiwal	£20
4 Manzoor. Iqbal and Arif's friend since early days in Oxford And wife	Arain	E. Oxford	Village in Sahiwal	Suit for Iqbal's wife; 3 sweaters for their sons
5 Matloob. Cousin of Manzoor And wife	Arain	E. Oxford	Village in Sahiwal	Suit for Iqbal's wife; 3 sweaters for their sons
6 Friend (a widow, Iqbal's neighbour)	Dogor	E. Oxford	Village in Faisalabad	Suit for Iqbal's wife.
7 Friend And wife	Kashmiri	E. Oxford	Village in Jhelum	Suit for Iqbal's wife; shirts for sons
8 Friend (widow, lodged with Iqbal and his wife when first moved to Oxford) and daughter	Chaudhuri	Headington, Oxford	Rawalpindi (and East Africa)	Suit and shawl for Iqbal's wife

Relationship to host	Caste	Current Residence	Origin in Pakistan	Gifts given by women
9 Friend and wife (a close friend of Arif's wife) Jehangir, friend of Iqbal, Arif,	Jat	E. Oxford	Village in Jhelum	Suit for Iqbal's wife
10 Manzoor and Matloob from early years in Oxford Jehangir, friend of Iqbal, Arif, Manzoor and Matloob from early years in Oxford Jehangir's daughter In addition, nine women	Tarkan	Surrey	Same village as 4 and 5	£20
neighbours of the host				

Table 8.1

Relationship to host	Caste	Current Residence	Origin in Pakistan
1 Bilqis	Qureshi	Oxford	Village, Gujrat.
2 Bilqis's mother-in-law. Lives with son and daughter-in-law.	Qureshi	Sandford, near Oxford	Village, Gujrat, near that of 1.
3 Bilqis's husband's brother's daughter.	Qureshi	Oxford, adjacent street to 1.	Village, Gujrat, near that of 1.
4 Bilqis's next door neighbour. Works with father of 3. at Sandford.	Jat	Oxford, same street as 1.	Village, Faisalabad.
5 Next door neighbour, (other side to 4.)	Arain	Oxford, Same street as 1.	Same village as 4.
6 Friend. Husband works with Bilqis' husband at British Leyland.	Arain	Oxford, parallel street to 1.	Same village as 4.
7 Daughter of 6.	Arain	Oxford, parallel street to 1.	Born here.
8 Friend. Same *biradari* as 5 and 6. Husband at B.L.	Arain	Oxford, street near 1.	Village, Sahiwal.
9 Sister-in-law to 6.	Arain	Oxford, parallel street to 1.	Same village as 4.
10 Daughter of 6's husband's brother.	Arain	Oxford, adjacent street to 1.	Born here.
11 Friend. Husband at B. L.	Arain	Oxford, adjacent street to 1.	Village, Faisalabad.
12 Friend. Husband at B. L.	Nai	Oxford, same street as 11.	Village, Jhelum.

Relationship to host	Caste	Current Residence	Origin in Pakistan
13 Friend. Husband at B. L.	Rajput	Oxford same street as 6.	Village, Gujrat.
14 Friend. Used to live on same street as 11 and 12	Chaudhari	Headington	Ugandan Asian, born in Pakistan.
15 Friend. Husband at B. L.	Jat	Oxford, adjacent street to 1.	Village, Jhelum.
16 Sister of 15.	Jat	Oxford, lives near 1	Same village as 15.
17 Sister-in-law of 15	Pathan	Oxford, same street as 7.	Same village as 15.
18 Friend. Husband is a well-known shopkeeper.	Pathan	Oxford, Parallel street to 1.	Abbotabad city
19 Friend	Pathan	Oxford, parallel street to 7 and 17.	Village, Attock.
20 Sister-in-law of 19	Pathan	Oxford, same street as 19	Same village as 19.
21 Imam's wife	Patel	Oxford, same street as 18.	Karachi. Before 1947, village in Gujerat, India.
22 Friend. Husband at B. L.	Unknown	Visiting Oxford	Has returned to. live in Lahore.
23 Convener of 'first' khatami-Quran.	Pathan	Oxford, same street as 18.	Attock city.

Table 8.2 (Continued)

Relationship to groom	Caste	Origin in Pakistan	Gifts given
Female Guests			
1 Neighbour, and her 4 children.	Dogor	Village, Faisalabad	£5 *salami*.
2 Sister-in-law of 1.	Dogor	Village, Faisalabad	£10 *salami*, suit.
3 Friend.	Mochi	Village near	£20, suit.
4 Friend.	Gujar	Village near groom's family	groom's family £5, shirt, socks tie for groom suit for bride.
5 Friend.	Gujar	Same village as 3.	£15, 2 men's shirts, socks, 2 suits.
6 Daughter-in-law of 5.	Gujar	Same village as 3.	£10
7 Wife of man with whom groom's father lodged in 1960s.	Kashmiri	Kashmir	£10, suit.
8 Daughter-in-law of 7.	Kashmiri	Kashmir	£5 *salami*.
9 Wife of groom's father's workmate.	Unknown	Mirpur	Cardigan, 1 suit.
10 Neighbour.	Indian Panjabi Christian		2 suits.

Relationship to groom	Caste	Origin in Pakistan	Gifts given
11 Daughter-in-law of 10.	Indian Panjabi Christian		3 suits.
12 English neighbour.			
13 Daughter of 12.			
Male guests			
14–20 Husbands of 3 to 9 and 12 above. Apparently all men (except husband of 12) gave £5 *salami* after groom had signed the *nikah*.			
21 Bengali neighbour.			
22 Jhelumi workmate, here without his family.			

Table 8.3 (*Continued*)

Sometimes common caste membership appears to influence participation in domestic rituals; Arain women, at least, tend to invite other Oxford Arain whether or not they are related or from the same village in Pakistan. Generally, though, it seems that *lenā-denā* can be started with anyone (even an interested anthropologist). Nazira described how *lenā-denā* with someone new might start:

> First you might meet someone in your street. You find out she lives near. You discover she is also from your area in Pakistan. You like the way she talks. You invite her to your house for tea. You start visiting her. Then you invite her and her husband and children to your house for dinner and you give her £20 for *khushī* (happiness). That is how *lenā-denā* starts. Then she might give you a gift if something happens in your house.

The initiation of *lenā-denā* involves a small gift, but if the participants intend the relationship to continue, they will willingly increase the amount and value of goods exchanged. Zarina, for example, described how she and her husband began and continued *lenā-denā* with a new household, that of one of her husband's work-mates:

> When I first arrived in Oxford, one of my husband's friends from work invited us both to supper and gave me a handbag. That started *lenā-denā*. When my first baby was born, they gave £5. When our second child was born, they gave another £5. Then when their son was married, I gave £10 to the bride as *salāmī* and my husband gave £10 to the groom. Altogether we have given £10 more than what they have given us. You don't give back the same; you give more, to keep *lenā-denā* going. Tonight we are having dinner with them. They have called us because, as is our custom, after there has been a wedding in your house, you should call your friends to dinner. When we go, we will take this suit as a present for the new bride. Now the groom's sister is in hospital, because she has just had a baby and so we have given her £5. But our *lenā-denā* with her is separate.

Generally people avoid returning gifts of exactly the same amount, for it creates bad feeling: it indicates that the recipient of the initial gift does not want the relationship to continue and this is tantamount to refusing a gift in the first place. As Nazira said:

> You can stop *lenā-denā* if you want to by giving back exactly what you owe. If, for example, I give you £2 and next time you give £2, then it is finished. But usually we don't do this. We keep *lenā-denā* going for *khushī* (happiness). It means you have a good relationship.

Once a *lenā-denā* relationship is established, the intensity with which is it continues is a matter of negotiation. The extent of *lenā-denā* between two households reflects the nature of the relationship between them and provides a means for assessing this relationship. Pakistanis expect support in times of need from their close friends as well as from relatives; if this is not forthcoming, *lenā-denā* exchanges and participation in life-cycle rituals may decline or cease. Likewise, in the event of a dispute between families, those on both sides of it may stop attending each other's family rituals and discontinue gift exchange.

In theory, *lenā-denā* occurs between equals, but in practice it contains an element of competition. Since giving a gift creates a debt or obligation, giving in excess of what you expect can be returned is generally frowned upon. Even so, occasionally women may competitively give larger and more valuable gifts in order make others indebted to them and thus demonstrate their superior status. One 'community representative' attempted to cultivate 'friendships' with three households of people who were impressed by her ability to speak English, her knowledge of British society and by the fact that her children were attending private schools. Dressed finely, she visited these families at the celebrations of *īdu'l-fitr* and *īdu'l-zohā* (the two main Islamic festivals) bringing lavish presents of suits, cardigans and shirts. The recipients, already involved in *lenā-denā* with other close friends and relatives, felt obliged to reciprocate on the next appropriate occasion, but they could not afford to return the full value of these gifts. Two of these families accepted that the resulting imbalance put them under this woman's patronage. The third family concluded that this woman was exploiting their sense of obligation for her own political purposes. They discontinued the relationship after returning the first gift, by refusing to accept a further one.

The type and value of gifts given

The gifts given in *lenā-denā* are goods, mainly sweets, money and clothes and, more generally, hospitality, the type of gift depending to some extent on the occasion for *lenā-denā*. Particular kinds of gifts are associated with certain occasions. Sweets are associated with birth, for instance, though friends also give gifts of money and other goods; gifts of money called *salāmī* are given at particular stages of the marriage ceremony, and small gifts of money called *īdī* are given to children at *īdu'l-fitr* and *īdu'l-zohā*.

When a child is born, the parents' friends and relatives give gifts, 'for *mubārak* (congratulations)', such as £5, £10 or £20, which the mother, for 'good luck', first places among the blankets wrapping the baby. They may also give baby clothes, cot blankets, nappies and talcum powder. The child's parents may also mark the birth by distributing boxes of sweets — traditionally *laddū*s (round and yellow), or else a mixture of different types — to everyone with whom they have (as well as, sometimes, to initiate) *lenā-denā*. Sweets are almost invariably distributed if a son is born, but only sometimes if a daughter is born, because the birth of a son is a greater cause for celebration. As Zarina said:

> When our son was born, my husband ordered £125 worth of sweets in boxes from the Ambala sweet centre in Drummond Street, in London. And he brought me home from the hospital in a hired Rolls Royce. We distributed all the sweets locally, except for several boxes that we kept for our relatives in Birmingham. We give sweets for *khushī*. Later, when our daughter was born, we were happy, but not as happy as we would have been with another boy, and we didn't order any sweets.

Gifts of money called *salāmī* are associated with specific stages of the marriage celebrations. The marriage rituals usually take place over several days and involve a number of distinct ritual events that ensure the safe transition of the bride from the status of 'daughter' to that of 'wife'[5]. These ritual stages

include: the 'preparation' of the bride with oil and henna
(*tel menhdī*); the arrival of the groom's party (the *bārāt*) on the
day of the *nikāh* (the signing of the marriage contract); the
giving by the bride's family of a reception dinner for the *bārāt*
and the *rukhsatī* (departure of the bride). The bride's arrival at
the groom's parents' house involves another reception dinner,
this time provided by the groom's family.

On the day of the *nikāh* (signing of the marriage contract), the
bārāt (groom's party) arrives while the dowry is on display and
is usually taken to a separate room in the bride's parents'
home. Here, before the *imām* arrives for the *nikāh*, the groom
is decorated with a garland of tinsel and money (now usually
made of £5 notes with a centrepiece of £10 or £20) and his
friends and relatives (the members of the *bārāt*) give *salāmī*.
Salāmī gifts are now usually of £10, £15, or £20 notes, in
keeping with inflation[6]. The groom then signs the marriage contract in the presence of the *imām* or other religious expert, and
three male witnesses. He is asked to repeat the principles of
Islam and some prayers and is asked three times whether he
agrees to the marriage. The *imām* and three witnesses (who
generally include a close male relative from the bride's side and
one from the groom's) then take the contract to the bride, who
is waiting in a separate room. The men kneel in front of the
bride while she states her agreement to the marriage and signs
the contract. The contract is returned to the groom, the *imām*
leads a short prayer, and then the groom is congratulated and
again given *salāmī*.

After the *nikāh*, sweets including *laddū*s and pastries are
distributed first to the men present and later to the women
guests (in a separate room) and the groom again receives gifts
of money, £5 or £10, as *salāmī*. This time the bride's relatives
and friends give *salāmī*, which may total between £40 and
£100, and sometimes also gifts such as rings or wristwatches.
The bride's family then provides an elaborate reception dinner,
often in a hired hall, for the *bārāt* and all other guests who may
number up to several hundred people. After the reception, there
is the *rukhsatī* (the bride's 'send-off') at which the bride's
relatives and friends give *salāmī*, while her mother notes the
amounts given and by whom (so that appropriate returns can
be made in the future). The groom's party then takes the bride
and her dowry to the groom's house. On her arrival, the

bride is usually first taken into a room where the dowry is arranged and displayed. Her mother-in-law gives her sweets to eat and milk to drink and her husband's relatives and friends give *salāmī* (while the groom's mother takes note). The groom's family then provides a second reception dinner for all the people who arrived with the bride's party.

Smaller sums of money, called *īdī*, not *salāmī*, are given by parents and parents' friends to children at *īdu'l-fitr* and *īdu'l-zohā*, as 'pocket money'. At *īdu'l-fitr*, families may also send Id cards, parents may give children new clothes, and friends and relatives visit one another, serve bowls of at least one of the various sweet dishes of *halwā*, *seviān* and sweet rice.

Particular kinds of gifts may in this way be associated with certain occasions, but the occasion itself does not always determine the type of gift given; different kinds of gifts may be given on the same occasion. Probably the most commonly given gifts are £5, £10, or £20 banknotes and women's 'suits' (*jorā*s). For instance, to celebrate a child's first completed reading of the *Qur'ān*, the child's parents invite relatives and friends to a dinner, and on this occasion too the guests give gifts of 'suits' or cash to their host or hostess (see Table 8.1). After the dinner, the child whose first completed *Qur'ān* reading is being celebrated usually recites a page or two of the *Qur'ān* to the assembled guests, and then the *imām* presents the child with an Arabic *Qur'ān*.

The gifts given at any particular occasion also reflect what is currently 'owing'. Nazira received in total eighteen 'suits' when she left for Pakistan, including one from Bilqis. After her return, she gave gifts to Bilqis when Bilqis' son was born and later when he was circumcised, in response to the obligation created by Bilqis' earlier gifts:

> When I was leaving for Pakistan, all my close friends invited us both to dinner and gave me a suit, and some friends gave other things too. Eight relatives gave me one suit, and my sister gave two. Bilqis and my sister's next-door neighbour also gave suits; altogether I received eighteen suits. Then when I returned from Pakistan three months later, these same people invited us to dinner and again gave presents. Now I have to give gifts to the people

who have given them to me. When Bilqis' son was born, just five and a half weeks ago, I gave her a suit, a shirt and socks for her husband and three new outfits, some baby talcum powder and some feeding bottles for the baby. Then at the circumcision I gave another suit for the baby and I gave £5 to Bilqis' elder son. The next occasion for gift giving is the fortieth day after a birth. So now Bilqis will have to give suits to all the people who have given her one.

Some socio-economic implications of *lenā-denā*

Women say that *lenā-denā* brings direct practical advantages, in the form of extra cash or goods at times of need, when a child is born, for instance, or when a family are about to travel abroad. You give at these events because you know that you will receive at the next similar occasion in your own household. Giving in *lenā-denā* can therefore be viewed as a form of rotating credit, though with a less predictably timed outcome. From this perspective, the ritual occasions at which *lenā-denā* occurs are but vehicles which enable *lenā-denā* to continue.

Some life-cycle rituals have changed in form in east Oxford, while others have been added to the repertoire, extending the occasions for *lenā-denā*. For example, although a Nai (barber) sometimes performs a boy's circumcision in the 'traditional' way at home, usually six or seven days after the birth at the same time as the shaving of the first head-hair, circumcision is now more frequently performed in hospital. Irrespective of this, however, friends of the boy's parents give gifts in *lenā-denā* for the boy, his siblings and his mother. On the other hand, a child's birthday (*sāl girāh*) is not traditionally celebrated in rural Panjab, but has become increasingly popular in east Oxford. Parents may hold a small party for the child, sometimes with a birthday cake, and give small presents and cards. Unlike most 'English' children's birthday parties, however, the focus of celebration is at least as much upon the adults as upon the child. The guests are usually women with whom the child's mother has *lenā-denā* and who give her gifts of banknotes and clothes. Usually, the guests must not leave without being given a full two or three course meal like the meal given at dinner invitations, at the celebration of a child's first reading of the *Qur'ān* and at a *khatmī-Qur'ān*.

The money women invest in *lenā-denā* has a variety of sources. Mostly *lenā-denā* is financed by men's earnings and requires the co-operation of husbands, though women also use money from their own part-time earnings, from 'piecework' done at home for local factories, and from saving in *kametī*s (rotating credit associations). Twenty women may each pay £20 a week to a *kametī* organizer who gives the full amount collected weekly to one of the donors, so that each woman, when it is her turn, receives £400. Women who put money into *kametī*s consider this form of credit useful in the events of a marriage or travel abroad. In fact, in anticipation of a particular life-cycle event, donors may specifically request that their turn to receive the full amount falls on a particular week.

Husbands even with low-incomes generally regard their wives' *lenā-denā* with other households to be necessary for good neighbourly relations and to maintain the honour of the household. Furthermore, families generally recoup much of this investment when their turn comes to be the recipients of *lenā-denā* gifts at life-cycle events in their own household. This is shown most dramatically at marriage.

Lenā-denā and marriage expenses

The reciprocity that underlies much of the social and religious activity of east Oxford women is especially important at marriage. Zekiye Eglar, discussing the ritual stages of the wedding ceremony in rural Gujrat, Pakistan, sees in marriage ceremonies the climax of gift exchange[7]. In Oxford too, the gifts given at marriage more than at any other life-cycle ritual represent the culmination of *lenā-denā* obligations between friends and relatives. Weddings are the most elaborate of all the life-cycle rituals, and (with, sometimes, the possible exception of funerals) draw the largest number of guests. Whereas a fraction of all potential guests attend other occasions for *lenā-denā*, at a wedding virtually all of a family's friends and relatives are invited, including, sometimes, English friends and neighbours. Guests may come not only from Oxford but also from other parts of Britain and from Pakistan, and Oxford Pakistanis may travel to Pakistan specially in order to be present at the marriage of a close relative or friend. The presence of a large number of friends and relatives is important as a public display of the extent of the goodwill and status with which a family is regarded. Since friends and relatives are also those with whom a family is involved in *lenā-denā*, the goods and money given at each stage of the ritual may make an important contribution to the overall cost of a wedding, especially for the bride's family.

Formally, the gifts given at the various stages of a marriage fall are either 'contractual' gifts or *lenā-denā* gifts. The context and value of 'contractual' gifts, which are exchanged between the two parties to a marriage, are usually specified in advance. These include *mangnī* (engagement) presents, the *mahr* payment and the bride's dowry (*jahez*). *Mangnī* presents, usually suits and sometimes also jewellery, are given by the groom's family to the bride and her mother. The *mahr* is a sum of money specified in advance of the marriage and written into the marriage contract; Islamic law requires the groom to pay *mahr* to the bride or to promise to pay in the event of a divorce. Traditionally, *mahr* is a small symbolic sum, and older married women say that as a symbol of trust and faith in one's husband and his family, particularly if they are close kin, a 'good' wife will excuse her husband of the duty to pay *mahr*. However some younger brides in Britain, and in Pakistan, are demanding quite large amounts of *mahr* to be paid into a bank account when the marriage takes place, particularly if the marriage is between non-relatives. If a large sum is demanded, the groom's family expects to be compensated with a large dowry. The bride's dowry typically includes household goods, clothes, jewellery and a financial payment.

The friends and relatives of the respective parties to a marriage give *lenā-denā* gifts such as *salāmī* at the particular stages of the marriage ritual. While, however, it is possible to distinguish these two categories of marriage gifts, they are not in practice entirely separate, because generally much of the dowry consists of gifts given in *lenā-denā* by the relatives and friends of the bride and her parents. The bride's family expects to receive these gifts in return for gifts they themselves will have given on earlier occasions (and they will be expected to return similar gifts to their friends and relatives on future occasions). The bride's family displays all these gifts when they show the dowry to the wedding guests, before it is taken with the bride to the groom's home. In this public display, one of the bride's relatives announces the type, amount and value of gifts given towards the dowry by each guest, and enters the details into a notebook or the traditional ledger used for this purpose. This display represents the culmination of obligations between people in *lenā-denā* and as such indicates a family's standing among its relatives and friends. It is shameful to have received only a few gifts from others. If a bride's family does not receive the gifts expected and owing in *lenā-denā*, they may feel dissatisfied and shamed in much the same way that groom's family feels dissatisfied if they do not receive the dowry they expect.

Lenā-denā gifts and *salāmī* given by relatives and friends to the bride's family can thus make a substantial practical contribution towards the bride's family's marriage expenses, which can be considerable. When Iffat, a Gujar girl from Slough, married her cousin — her father's brother's son — from east Oxford, Iffat's parents estimated that their total expenditure exceeded £8,000, but they recouped over £1,000 of this in *lenā-denā* gifts and *salāmī* payments from relatives and friends (Figure 8.1). Sometimes, in Oxford, not all of the customary elements of the marriage rites are performed in full or 'correctly'. At one wedding, the bride's family asked me to take part in the bride's *tel-menhdī* (the smearing of oil on the bride's hair and the decoration of her hands and feet with henna). They expected that, having recently returned from Pakistan, I would have a better memory than they had of what exactly should be done. There was no such amnesia when it came to announcing and recording the gifts of suits, goods and *salāmī* given at the various stages of the marriage.

Gifts in *lenā-denā* from friends can also compensate for the lack of relatives in Oxford. At one wedding in which the bride's parents and siblings were in Pakistan and the bride (the groom's father's brother's daughter) had come to Britain as a fiancée, the only kin present were the groom's parents and siblings (Figure 8.2). His mother's married sister in Reading did not attend because of a long-standing and unresolved family dispute. In this case, in a departure from 'custom', the groom's family gave the dowry. The groom's father said this was because his brother in Pakistan was poorer than he was and

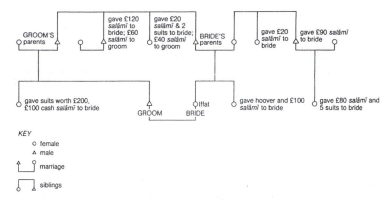

Figure 8.1   Iffat's marriage. The figure shows gifts given by relatives other than the bride's parents and the groom's parents. Gifts from the groom's parents included the bridal outfit and jewellery worth £500. They also provided the house. Dowry gifts from the bride's parents included a television, tape recorder, furniture, crockery, £3,000 in cash (amount specified in advance), £3,000 worth of jewellery and ten suits for the bride. They also gave suits for each female member of the groom's family. The bride's family estimated their total expenditure to be over £8,000, including £3,000 for the cost of reception. they recouped about £1,000 in *lenā-denā* gifts, which included thirty suits, a toaster, an electric iron and £4,000 in *salāmī*.

because 'the bride is my brother's daughter, so she is my daughter'. He gave the bride jewellery worth £4,000, which included a ring for which the gold cost £450, and he paid for the bride's fare to Britain. The bride's family sent a gold ring for the groom, a set of jewellery for the bride including earrings, necklace and rings, and the bridal outfit. (This is provided by the groom's family, but the bride's family had it made in Pakistan and the bride brought it with her when she came to Britain). The groom's family estimated their total expenditure to be £6,000. They also said that although no other relatives attended who would have given gifts, they had received from the wedding guests, who were all friends living locally (Table 8.3), at least £125 in cash, and twelve suits.

Cycles of Qur'ān readings

Recipients of *lenā-denā* gifts must wait until the next appropriate occasion in order to return a gift, with the result that gift-exchange tends to occur over a fairly long time-scale and

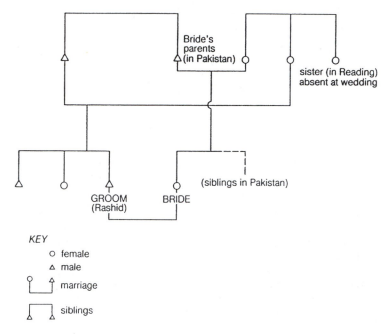

Figure 8.2   Rashid's marriage.

the gifts given on any one occasion are not discrete but part of continuing cycles of exchange. Similarly, women's performance of a religious ritual called the *khatmī-Qur'ān* tends to be cyclical and involve reciprocity. In east Oxford, women do not attend the mosque, nor, generally, do they observe strict purdah in the sense of veiling; their religious observance involves, primarily, prayer and the performance of the *khatmī-Qur'ān*.

In this ritual, the entire *Qur'ān* is read at one sitting; this is the 'completion' or 'sealing' of the *Qur'ān* (*khatm* means 'finish'). The task is a communal one: the woman convening the ritual asks her friends and neighbours to participate. She designates one room of her house, usually the front room or an upstairs bedroom, for the purpose. The women participants must remove their shoes before entering the room and must have performed their ritual ablutions. Each participant receives an allocated number of *sipārā*s, which are the thirty sections of roughly equal length into which the *Qur'ān* is divided — thirty participants will each read one *sipārā*; fewer participants will each read more. In this way, the entire *Qur'ān* can be read in a short space of time and women say that there is considerable religious merit in doing this. When the reading is complete, an *imām*'s wife may lead prayers for the convener and her family, and then all guests are given a meal before they depart.

Women usually perform the *khatmī-Qur'ān* on Thursday or Friday afternoons, while husbands are at work; Friday is the day of congregational prayer, Thursday the 'eve' of Friday. *Khatmī-Qur'ān*s are also sometimes held on Sundays, when husbands and sons may be invited not to read the *Qur'ān* but to partake of the food provided afterwards. In this case, men sit separately in a backroom, smoking, chatting and drinking tea while the *Qur'ān* reading is going on, and the convener's husband and sons, who may be helping in the kitchen, will bring them food when the *Qur'ān* recitation is complete. Afterwards, any remaining food is distributed by car to the homes of those of the women guests whose husbands and sons did not attend. Sometimes the ritual is not performed in the convener's home, but instead, all of the participants, dedicating their reading to the convener, recite a pre-arranged number of *sipārā*s in their own homes. In this case, the convener always prepares food for the participants and distributes it to their homes afterwards.

The food afterwards is an important element of the ritual, and just as giving presents in *lenā-denā* puts the recipient in debt to the donor, so too the host's hospitality at a *khatmī-Qur'ān* involves putting guests under obligation to the convener. A guest reciprocates if she can, by convening a *khatmī-Qur'ān* in her own house on the next appropriate occasion. Women who cannot afford to host a *khatmī-Qur'ān* and dinner remain indebted to the convener for her hospitality, for the meal provided is usually elaborate. It includes a number of large bowls of chicken or other kinds of meat curry, kebabs, huge dishes of savory rice and sometimes *paratha*s (*chapātī*s made with butter, sometimes containing minced meat), dishes of sliced cucumber, tomatoes and onions, bowls of chutney and yogurt, and dishes of sweet rice and *halwā* containing nuts and raisins. The food alone may cost between £40 and £60 and take several hours to prepare.

The obligation to attend and convene *khatmī-Qur'ān*s extends over time with the effect that, as with other forms of *lenā-denā*, *khatmī-Qur'ān*s tend to be performed in cycles. Some women convene *khatmī-Qur'ān*s with astonishing regularity and are invariably guests at other women's *Qur'ān* readings, while some guests never reciprocate by holding their own *khatmī-Qur'ān*. In one such cycle, the first *khatmī-Qur'ān* I attended was followed by three others in the space of four weeks and the convener of each was present as a guest at the other *khatmī-Qur'ān*s:

The first *khatmī-Qur'ān* in this cycle took place on a Friday afternoon in the home of a woman from Attock city, and was arranged because the convener's husband was about to sit an important examination. Six women were present: the convener, a friend of hers from Lahore (considered very respectable by the other women present), the *imām*'s wife and women from villages in Faisalabad, Gujrat, and Sahiwal districts, one with her thirteen year-old daughter. The second *khatmī-Qur'ān* took place a week later in a nearby street, arranged because the convener's son was in hospital. The convener, Bilqis, was one of the guests at the *khatmī-Qur'ān* held the previous week, a woman considered 'educated' because she had been to school in England and spoke English well. Over twenty women and numerous small children were present, including all those who had been at the *khatmī-Qur'ān* the week before (Table 8.2). The third *khatmī-Qur'ān* took place the following Sunday, convened by the woman from Lahore who had attended the previous two *khatmī-Qur'ān*s. This time, the *Qur'ān* reading was held to secure Allah's protection on moving to a new house on the Cowley Road. About twenty women were present, including the convener, most of the guests of the previous week's gathering, one of the convener's new neighbours, with her three well made-up and bejewelled daughters, and an English woman married to a Pakistani (who sat with her two daughters in the kitchen throughout the proceedings). The *imām*'s wife was absent so a woman guest who had attended the previous week's gathering led the prayers. A week later, the convener of the first *khatmī-Qur'ān* held another, for the same reason as before. Twenty-seven women were present including seven who had not been at the previous gatherings. The *imām*'s wife was again absent and so the woman who had led the prayers the week before did so again, aided by the convener herself, who, together with her daughter, had written prayers especially to ask for Allah's blessing for her family.

Qurān readings for 'blessing' or 'to show off'?

Women say they hold the ritual when they need Allah's intervention or protection, when someone in their family is ill, or in danger, or, in the case of funerary *khatmī-Qur'ān*s, in need of blessing to secure a place in heaven. The parents of a girl with leukemia followed the advice of a *pīr* by holding a *khatmī-Qur'ān* for her before her father took her on pilgrimage to Mecca. Bilqis held a *khatmī-Qur'ān* before her son's hip operation and again during his convalescence. Another woman held a *khatmī-Qur'ān* in fulfillment of a vow (*mannat*) made to Allah that she would do so if her child recovered from illness.

The religious benefit or blessing (*sawāb*) of holding a *khatmī-Qur'ān* on these occasions arises from the recitation of the Arabic in which the *Qur'ān* in written; 'the *Qur'ān*' means 'The recital'[8]. The emphasis is on the correct recitation of the Arabic, not on understanding it. The *Qur'ān* is revered as the word of Allah revealed to the Prophet Muhammad by the Angel Gabriel and a person must be ritually pure before touching it. After reciting from the *Qur'ān*, a person must wrap the book carefully in a cloth cover and keep it in the highest place in the room. As Zarina explained:

> The Arabic in which the *Qur'ān* is written has a special power and reading it brings *sawāb* which is good for the soul, especially in the next life. For this reason, we must keep the *Qur'ān* in the highest part of the room and a person who has not washed before touching the *Qur'ān* will be harmed. A translation does not have this power, and reading it does not bring *sawāb*, so you don't have to wash first to touch a translation and you do not have to keep it in a high place.

The recitation of the entire *Qur'ān* is considered particularly efficacious in time of illness, risk or danger, times at which

Allah's blessing, intervention and protection is most required, because the *Qur'ān* is believed to contain an appropriate passage for every occasion. The recitation of Ya Sin (Sura 36), for instance, is considered beneficial for someone who has died. But, people say, a person cannot generally know which passages suit which occasions, for the location and meaning of passages efficacious in particular situations is known only to Allah, and, some believe, to *pīrs*. People recite the entire *Qur'ān* to be sure that they are reciting the correct passage. Sometimes, in a feat that is considered particularly meritorious, the *Qur'ān* is read not once but twice in one sitting.

Pakistani women say you must attend a neighbour's *khatmī-Qur'ān*, if invited, to show that you are a good neighbour. You must also attend because if you pray for Allah to bestow *sawāb* (religious merit) upon the convener and her family, then she will pray for Allah to give blessing to you and your family on the next appropriate occasion in your household. This is considered particularly important when someone dies. Offering condolences and reading the *Qur'ān* at a death is regarded as a moral and religious duty, even if you did not know the deceased or his or her family well. When someone dies, Oxford Pakistanis expect that all friends and even mere acquaintances to go the home of the bereaved family, even if this involves travelling to other parts of Britain or even to Pakistan, as soon as they hear of the death. On hearing of the death of a friend, for instance, several carloads of people set off to Oxford from Bradford. On arrival at the bereaved family's home, the women offering condolences (*afsos*) go either to the backroom or to an upstairs bedroom to sit with the women of the households, while men go to the front room, or if it is time for prayer, to the mosque. There is usually no cooking done in the house for ten days after a death; neighbours bring tea in thermos flasks and share the cooking for the bereaved family. During this time, those who have come to offer condolences will say prayers for the deceased person and recite the *Qur'ān,* dedicating their reading to the deceased. The religious importance of these mortuary rituals is that they are to ensure Allah's forgiveness for the dead person's sins and to accumulate *sawāb* for his or her soul so that it may go to heaven, not hell. Pakistanis believe that *sawāb* can be transferred by proxy to the 'account' of the deceased, for the balance of one's good deeds during one's lifetime is not final but subject to revision until the Last Judgement. Funerary *khatmī-Qur'ān*s are held on the third, tenth and fortieth day after the death, and relatives may also recite particular sections of the *Qur'ān* for the benefit of the deceased at any time between these intervals and annually thereafter.

Likewise, at a *khatmī-Qur'ān* the religious benefit which the *Qur'an* recitation generates accrues to the convener and her family, to whom the prayers are dedicated; friends, neighbours and relatives thus have a certain shared responsibility in accumulated *sawāb* for one another. There is some ambiguity, however, in the hospitality, in the form of the meal that is provided after the *Qur'ān* reading is complete. While the women readers are still assembled in the front room or an upstairs bedroom, the *imām*'s wife or another woman leading the prayers may pray over a portion of the food, dedicating her prayers to the convener and her household. Some women say that part of this food should be given to the poor, 'but there are no poor people in Oxford'[9]. The same is sometimes said of the sacrificial meat in two other religious rituals observed by Oxford Pakistanis, *qurbānī* and, occasionally, *'aqīqa*.

Several aspects of Islamic religious ritual involve giving to the poor. One pillar of Islam is *zakāt* or almsgiving — the giving of a proportion of one's income to the poor as a 'sacrifice' to please God. Another central sacrifice is *qurbānī*, the sacrifice of an animal at *īdu'l-zohā* to commemorate Ibrahim's (Abraham's) sacrifice of his son Ishmael (Isaac). In Pakistan, at *īdu'l-zohā*, families usually sacrifice a goat (*bakrā*) or a sheep. The *qurbānī* (sacrificial) meat is then divided equally into three parts, one part consumed by the sacrificer's family, another given to friends and neighbours and the third part given to the poor. In Britain, *qurbānī* sacrifice is generally of a sheep, arranged through the local *halāl* butcher. The sacrificer himself should go with the butcher to the abattoir, in order to select a sheep and touch it before it is slaughtered. I was told that this is to ensure that the sheep is healthy, because God will not accept the sacrifice of a defective, injured or very old animal. Likewise, the sacrificer should not argue over the price of the sacrificial beast, for then it will not be a sacrifice. Some families simply order their *qurbānī* meat from the butcher, rather than going themselves to inspect the beast; they say they hope Allah will forgive them for this, for what matters, they say, is their intention (*niyat*). There is a further ambiguity over the validity of the *qurbānī* sacrifice in Britain because British Pakistanis cannot easily identify a group of poor people to whom to give a portion of the meat. In their villages of origin, most Oxford Pakistanis know exactly who constitutes 'the poor', for these are usually low status *kammī* families or refugees; in contrast, they say, 'there are no poor people in Britain, everyone is rich'. Thus, the portion of the meat that should go to the poor is divided among family, friends and neighbours, that is, among other Pakistani Muslims who are considered equally 'rich'.

The same ambiguity over the validity of the ritual surrounds another sacrifice called *'aqīqa*, which, in Pakistan, parents sometimes perform after a child is born. In *'aqīqa*, usually two goats or sheep are slaughtered for a boy, one for a girl, and a third of the sacrificial meat is distributed among family and friends, while the remaining two-thirds should be given to the poor as a form of almsgiving. Manchester Pakistanis perform *'aqīqa*[10], but Oxford Pakistanis rarely do so; the only performance of *'aqīqa* that I know any details of was done by a woman whose friends debated whether or not she had performed the ritual properly. Some said that the blood and bones of the sacrificed animal should have been put, or washed, into a hole in the earth — 'but what would the neighbours say if they saw you burying bones in the garden — they would think you had murdered someone!' Most discussion was about the fate of the meat; in this case, all of the meat was distributed among friends and neighbours. Critics observed that some if not all of it should have been consumed within the home of the sacrificer, to ensure that the meat was eaten and not thrown away by people who did not need it.

In Pakistan, there is a third type of animal sacrifice called *sādqā* in which all of the meat of the sacrificed animal must be given to the poor and none of it consumed by the sacrificer's family; the term *sādqā* also means 'charity or almsgiving'. *Sādqā* is performed at times of extreme or incurable illness, or exceptional danger. Zafar's wife told me she held *sādqā* sacrifices for her husband every week during a war with India. She has also performed *sādqā* for her mentally ill daughter on several return trips to Pakistan. She says she cannot perform *sādqā* in Oxford, however, because all of

the meat must be given to the poor. I have not heard of *sādqā*
ever having been performed in Britain.

Some Pakistanis consider that the performance of *qurbānī* or
'aqīqa in Britain might not properly constitute a sacrifice,
because 'there are no poor people' and so the ritual may not
bring religious merit (*sawāb*). To avoid this ambiguity, they
may only perform these sacrifices in Pakistan. Oxford
Pakistanis quite often send money to have the *qurbānī* sacrifice
performed in Pakistan by proxy. Parents may sometimes send
money for *'aqīqa* to be done by proxy, but they usually wait
until returning to Pakistan themselves because *'aqīqa*, unlike
qurbānī, can be performed at any time.

Despite these ambiguities, *qurbānī* sacrifices are quite regularly
performed at *īdu'l-zohā*. Critics say that the distribution of the
meat among friends and kin is simply a means of displaying
wealth; it is indeed an indication of status in that not all families
can afford to slaughter a sheep at *īdu'l-zohā*. In much the same
way, the *khatmī-Qur'ān* is considered by some to be a means of
'showing off'. Afraz, a Mirpuri woman whose husband has been
unemployed since the closure of the Osney bakery, commented
critically that *khatmī-Qur'ān*s were held 'to show off'. My
enquiry about whether she had attended a *khatmī-Qur'ān* held
on a Sunday in a shop that a couple expanding their cloth business had just bought prompted this remark:

> First I have a *khatmī-Qur'ān*, then you have one, and you
> invite more people than I did, and you cook more food
> than I did, and then people talk, and it goes on like this,
> the showing off.

'But', I countered, 'there are religious reasons for holding a
khatmī-Qur'ān. People say you need Allah's protection on
moving to a new house or on starting a new business'. To this,
Afraz retorted:

> Yes, but in Pakistan who can afford a new house or a
> new business? Who can afford to feed her neighbours
> every time she applies new mud to her roof? They (the
> rituals) have been started here by people who want to
> show that they are rich people or are about to become
> professionals. You have to cook more food than your

household would eat in a week and it costs you at least
£40. Then you and all your guests must wear your best
suits. Women make new suits specially. These suits that I
am sewing are for Imrana, who needs them by Sunday,
when Sakina is holding a *khatmī-Qur'ān*. That suit and
those two girls' dresses are for Khalda who is going to
Imrana's sister's wedding next week. The men complain
that all their money goes on new suits and that women
waste so much time in the cloth shops choosing new
designs. Each suit costs at least £15 for the cloth, and
sometimes £20 or more, and then there's £3 or £4 for
the sewing, and some women, like Mahmuda, charge £5.
I take £4 per suit.

While there always is a religious justification for *khatmī-
Qur'āns*, the ritual does indeed sometimes seem to be an excuse
for 'showing off', as the critics say. The woman who had convened the first and the fourth *khatmī-Qur'āns* in the cycle
described above, did so on both occasions to ensure Allah's
protection for her husband who was, apparently, about to sit
an examination to become a pilot with Pakistan International
Airlines. She said the second *khatmī-Qur'ān* was necessary
because after the first *khatmī-Qur'ān* her husband was too
unwell to take his examination the following day,

> because too many people were looking at him. The
> women I invited to read the *Qur'ān* must have gone home
> and gossiped about us, saying 'look at them, how clever
> they are becoming, taking exams for entry into a profes-
> sion. They think they are becoming superior to the rest of
> us'. It is from people's gaze (*nazar*, i.e. the evil eye) that
> he got sick.

So a second *Qur'ān* reading was necessary just before he finally
took his examination in order to protect this man from the
danger of *nazar*, of 'being in people's gaze' as a result of the
first *Qur'ān* reading. Several women agreed with Afraz by commenting critically that this convener too was performing the
ritual not 'for Allah' but 'to show off'.

Khatmī-Qur'āns do seem to be performed in Oxford with far
more frequency than in rural Pakistan. In the Pakistani villages
I visited, women, individually or gathered in someone's house,

would sometimes read the *Qur'ān* when someone had died, and this was always done by men as part of the funerary rites, while women prepared food to be served afterwards. While I was there, no woman convened a *khatmī-Qur'ān* for any other reason. East Oxford women also say that in Pakistan women's *khatmī-Qur'āns* are rarely convened other than at deaths. Moreover, I could find no mention of women's *khatmī-Qur'āns* in the literature on rural Pakistan; it is possibly more specifically associated with wealthier city women. Several of the conveners of the most intense cycles of *khatmī-Qur'āns* in Oxford are from the cities in Pakistan, and consider themselves superior to the 'villagers', although most of the participants are of rural origin. The ritual seems only relatively recently to have become an important aspect of women's social life in east Oxford, and elsewhere in Britain. Given the ambiguity over its 'sacrificial' aspects, the ritual's function as a mechanism for competitively assessing and displaying status is particularly apparent, in both the cyclical nature of the ritual itself and in the hospitality provided afterwards.

Conclusion

In her study of a village in Gujrat, Pakistan, Zekiye Eglar writes that gift exchange is a means of maintaining goodwill with kin and non-kin alike, irrespective of caste boundaries[11]. By contrast, Hamza Alavi, in his analysis of Rajput *birādarī* structure in Sahiwal district, considers it important to distinguish *pakki* (firm) from *katchi* (sic) (temporary) gift exchange. 'Firm' gift exchange defines one's 'immediate' *birādarī* where social interaction is most intense, whereas 'temporary' gift exchange indicates a courtesy relationship between friends and neighbours but involves not permanent obligation[12]. In this view, to consider gift exchange as a means of maintaining goodwill with kin and non-kin alike is to miss its structural significance in demarcating *birādarī* structure, for it is within the *birādarī* that gift-exchange relationships are most enduring.

In principle, however, *lenā-denā* provides a mechanism for forming new relationships of an enduring nature with non-kin, through the networks of continuing obligations that it creates. In the context of labour migration, the most intense gift-exchange may take place among non-kin, who become, in effect, a 'temporary' *birādarī*. It is also logically possible that such relationships may develop to the extent that, within the constraints of 'caste' (Chapter 4), they lead to an arranged marriage. In at least one case, close ties of reciprocity between household of non-kin have eventually led to a link of marriage between them (Chapter 5).

In the case of marriages arranged between non-relatives, *lenā-denā* is nearly always established subsequently. Pakistani women have sometimes attempted to initiate *lenā-denā* with the English or European wives of Pakistani men. One Italian wife told me that several women from her husband's village brought her gifts when her first child was born. She was, however, so offended when one of the women visitors then said that the baby looked Chinese, not Pakistani, that she returned the presents a few days later and had no further contact with those 'rude gossiping peasant women'. There are, on the other hand, a few English wives are now thoroughly involved in *lenā-denā*. They have 'become' Pakistani, in their dress, their demeanour, by becoming Muslim and through their active participation in domestic rituals and *lenā-denā*; all of this effectively validates their incorporation into husbands' *birādarī*s.

Lenā-denā, the cyclical exchange of gifts managed by women on ceremonial occasions, explicitly expresses the reciprocity that underlies formal and informal social activity in east Oxford. Women's exchanges of goods and services in effect binds the participants and their households into complex social and moral networks. In this respect, they are like the '*total* social phenomena' described by Marcel Mauss in his book 'The Gift', for within them 'all kinds of institutions find simultaneous expression: religious, legal, moral, and economic'[13]. These reciprocities in effect exert a form of social and moral control, for the exchanges provide a mechanism for assessing the status of individuals and households, and the occasions provide opportunities for the exchange of news and gossip, about marriage prospects, or the 'scandal' of someone's daughter's behaviour, or an issue of dispute at one of the mosques.

At the same time, *lenā-denā* as an expression of the reciprocity that underlies social life does not merely reproduce in Oxford a Panjabi tradition, because new occasions for it have been incorporated into the ritual repertoire. The celebration of children's birthdays, for instance, may indicate 'aspirations towards cultural change and even assimilation', as Gerd Baumann has noted among families of South Asian (and predominantly Sikh) backgrounds in Southall[14]. Oxford Pakistanis have incorporated the celebration of a child's birthday as a new element within a distinctly 'traditional' Pakistani system of inter-household exchange. Another novel feature of this competitive reciprocity between east Oxford households is the intensity with which women perform the *khatmī-Qur'ān*, a relatively simple Islamic ritual which, in comparison with rural Panjab, has clearly gained in significance locally as a vehicle of status competition. Nor does the process merely affirm *birādarī* boundaries because, as I have shown, it enables Pakistanis to create new relationships and to engineer and consolidate changes in *birādarī* structure that may have long-term implications.

The centrality of women's roles in this process also raises issues relevant to discussions of the status of Pakistani women and of women generally[15]. How well a woman conducts domestic rituals has implications for the standing of her husband and her household in relation to neighbours and relatives. In western societies, a woman's status is most often assessed in relation to whether she has paid work outside the home, that is, in a large measure, to her socio-economic autonomy. Many Pakistani women do not participate directly in the wage economy; they create and maintain status in relation to other Pakistani women primarily though their networks of reciprocity. Yet in exchanging goods and services, in building up networks of obligation, they create 'value'[16] which is only partly of a financial nature, but which certainly has socio-economic implications. The gradual increase in intensity of social exchange managed by women since their arrival in Britain is testament of the strength and vitality of some of the structural and cultural processes that maintain 'ethnic distinctiveness'. Moreover, these networks are not confined to women of the pioneer generation, and must not been seen as simply a function of the fact that it is still the case that most first-generation women do not have paid work outside the home. Participants in *lenā-denā* today include younger women raised in Britain and women who earn full or part-time wages. These younger women may use part of their wages towards their participation in 'traditional' ritual activities; the process has parallels with that described for east African origin Sikh women who convert wages into dowry[17]. For such women, maintenance of distinctive forms of social exchange is indeed compatible with participation in the wage economy.

NOTES

1. Alavi, 1972.
2. Eglar, 1960; Alavi, 1972; Naveed-I-Rahat, 1981, and Donnan, 1988.
3. Mauss, 1954.
4. Eglar, 1960:176.
5. See Werbner, 1990:259–296, for an analysis of the symbolism behind the sequence of the wedding rituals.
6. In 1982, *salāmī* gifts were generally of £1 and £5 notes. Werbner suggests that the increase in *salāmī* gifts in Manchester over the years reflects not only inflation but migrants' raised expectations as they have become wealthier (1990:243).
7. Eglar, 1060:143–172.
8. Dawood, 1974:9.
9. See also the discussion in Werbner, 1990:156–165.
10. Werbner, 1990:161 and 163.
11. Eglar, 1960:176.
12. Alavi, 1972:8–9; 13–14 and 16.
13. Mauss, 1954:1.
14. Baumann, 1992:109.
15. On the status of South Asian women, see for example: Bhachu, 1988; Shaw, 1997 and Werbner,1988.
16. Weiner, 1976.
17. Bhachu, 1985.

9 PUBLIC FACES: LEADERSHIP, RELIGIOUS ISSUES AND POLITICAL MOBILIZATION

I once had to interpret in court for Muhammad Anees who had been charged with shoplifting. He had been in England for over fifteen years but his knowledge of English was poor. Under cross-examination he had to answer one main question. Was there some sort of commotion going on in the street outside the shop, and if so what? Anees replied that he thought something might have been happening but he could not remember what. At this point the court adjourned, and Anees, his solicitor and I withdrew to a private room. The solicitor then explained, with unmasked irritation, that Anees had just contradicted his written statement given to the court the day before. This statement said that some youths fighting in the street outside the shop had distracted Anees' attention just as he was going to pay for his goods. The solicitor then asked Anees why he had just contradicted in court the previous day's statement. It emerged that Anees had relied upon a Pakistani community representative from a local welfare association to give the original statement, the details of which Anees did not know. In view of Anees' contradictory evidence, the solicitor now advised Anees to change his plea to guilty. Anees accepted this. The court reconvened and Anees was fined.

Afterwards, I felt that I had somehow let Anees down, that had I known more about the case beforehand I might have helped him steer his way through the proceedings. However, Anees said, in a somewhat condescending tone, that I was worrying unnecessarily because things did not happen that way. He had already done all that he could by approaching a community representative who was a 'big man' (barā ādmī), capable of getting him let off. He seemed to have assumed that this patron would ensure charges were dropped by providing a story, of which the details did not really matter, and, more importantly, by negotiating with the solicitor and other members of the court. This had obviously not happened. Even though Anees had been let down by his patron, who, by not furnishing Anees with the details of the story, had allowed him to contradict himself and thus worsen his case, Anees bore his patron no grudge. Anees felt that he had been unlucky this time, but this did not cause him to question the procedure he had followed. For him, the case had already been decided by the ability of his patron to negotiate with the solicitor. He felt that this had been unsuccessful because of his choice of a patron, not because of the procedure he had adopted. If his patron had had sufficient influence and if the court had liked him, he would have been let off anyway and it would not have mattered that he had contra-dicted himself. He protested his innocence in the eyes of God and seemed quite unconcerned about how the English court viewed him, as if he did not believe in justice on earth. This incident, contradictory and confusing to the lawyer and the court, only makes sense in the light of experiences of law and justice in Pakistan.

Patronage in Pakistan

To understand Anees' case, and many like it, we need to con-sider the significance of authority and leadership in Pakistan; the following picture is drawn from incidents and conversations with villagers there. Villagers frequently spoke of police corrup-tion. In particular, they described how the rich bribe the police when someone has to be charged for a crime, and induce them or compel them to charge an innocent party who cannot afford to bribe. One bank-clerk reported that police had arrested a colleague of his while he was travelling on a train and had imprisoned him for a crime someone else had committed. For such people, survival lies in strengthening their *birādarī*s. This means extending the network of people bound to each other by mutual obligations and doing favours for people with authority to ensure the return of a favour when necessary; the *birādarī* network is trusted rather than the system of police or the law. An individual will not go to court until he has found someone, such as a barrister, ideally from within his own *birādarī*, who has some obligation to him and would be sure to win the case or get it withdrawn.

One man had been involved in a quarrel at work that had developed into a fight with knives. It ended with him killing one of his opponents. He was lying low in a photostudio until his friends had secured contacts who would ensure his defence in court. Having such contacts can mean that sentences are reduced or withdrawn. Another man, the murderer of the husband of a woman with whom he had planned to elope, had his sentence reduced as the result of having influential and wealthy relatives. In another case, a young man had been in jail four times for assault, including two assaults on policemen, in incidents in which he saw himself as seeking revenge for injustices. On each occasion he had been released because he had an influential uncle in the army. Indeed, knowing that his uncle had influence seemed to explain this young man's readiness to become involved in such incidents. Influential *birādarī* contacts may also mean that people can escape punishment for a crime that *birādarī* members may themselves have set up.

Many villagers regard the wealthy owners of land, villages, or factories, government officials or army officers as being in a position to dispense patronage; as a result they are treated with deference and respect. One landlord, who had recently returned to Faisalabad district after spending twenty years in Glasgow where his sons still run businesses, had bought a large farm, with a large *pakkā* house (built of kiln-baked bricks and mortar), a tube-well and tractors with money earned in Britain. He had also purchased an ice factory in town and given his brother the task of running it. He now employs landless labourers from a nearby *kachchā* settlement (built of mud bricks) who treat him with respect and subservience; on one occasion an employee knelt at his feet to ask a favour. As the landlord himself proudly pointed out, they now also call him *chaudharī*, a title or respectable form of address, which literally means 'head man'.

There is a similar attitude to tax officials in the villages that they serve. A landlord may give the tax official free accommodation in the village and each year at *Id* villagers may give him sacks of corn, goats, buffaloes, money and dinner invitations; the villagers expect the official to do favours for them in return. Other 'big' officials are treated in the same way; for instance, a police commissioner may receive annual gifts of *ghī* (butter), buffaloes, goats, cash and grain at *Id* from villagers. This gift-giving creates obligations like those produced by *lenā-denā* within the *birādarī*, but which extend beyond it to landlords, police, and government officials. It may produce important results, not just for individuals but for an entire village. For instance, one village had electricity while surrounding villages did not because one of its *birādarī*s contained a brigadier in the army without whose patronage the village would be like the surrounding villages, still waiting for electricity. Influential individuals do not necessarily seek these roles; they may be compelled to act in this way by *birādarī* members and fellow villagers who need an influential person to act on their behalf because they cannot rely on the bureaucracy.

Nepotism and patronage thus have a far more explicit role in public life and in how institutions work than they have in Britain. In Pakistan, one cannot appeal to the justice of the system, to the rules and principles embedded in the bureau- cracy, to deal with a problem. It is important to have and to maintain personal contacts with people in positions of author- ity and influence. Each official is seen first as a member of someone's *birādarī* and only second as an official. Business will be attended to if an official is a *birādarī* member; if he is not, he may have to be bribed, or some other *birādarī* member may have to exert his influence.

Britain: local politics and patronage

In Pakistan, for those without influence or relatives in positions of authority, legal and government institutions are to be avoided. It is different for people with influential contacts. As one young man boasted to me, 'If a policeman tells me to come to prison but I refuse, what can he do? His superiors are my father's friends. He can do nothing'. It is therefore not surpris- ing that the pioneer generation migrants of rural backgrounds have often assumed that their first recourse, in dealing with British authorities, must be to enlist the aid of a patron. We might expect that such attitudes would, however, disappear after a few years of living in Britain, but on the contrary, such attitudes have in a large part persisted. Part of the explanation for this is to do with the fact that, for many men, in the early years of settlement a patron's aid was necessary to cope with life in England.

When Pakistani men first came to Britain, the majority of them had a very poor knowledge of English and had great difficulty in circumventing racial discrimination in finding accommoda- tion and employment, in handling the D.H.S.S. and so on. The

British economy needed labour in the late 1950s and early 1960s, but the government, while encouraging immigration, made no concessions to accommodating and meeting the needs of the immigrants once they were here. Migrants therefore turned to those of their *birādarī* members or fellow villagers of relatively well-educated backgrounds in Pakistan, who had reasonably good English and seemed able to communicate effectively with local British institutions, such as the departments of the local council, and with the Pakistan Embassy. In this way, 'ordinary' migrants would place in a position of influence and authority someone who appeared educated or at least able to offer them they help they needed. Individuals who attained this status would generally confine their welfare activities to members of their own *birādarī*s and through these patrons *birādarī*s would in effect compete with each other for resources.

The first Pakistan Welfare Association in Oxford, co-founded by two men, a Pakistani and a Bangladeshi, arose from this genuine need for welfare in the early 1960s. Since then several other Welfare Associations have arisen, but have often been fairly short-lived, with influence confined to a relatively small circle of friends, kin and fellow-villagers. These Associations are in theory open to all and sometimes the members elect their office holders, yet the key office holder seems usually to operate as a patron does in Pakistan.

The first Pakistan Welfare Association in Oxford, founded in 1961, provided a free and popular welfare service, which included negotiating with the Home Office and the Pakistan Embassy and filling in tax forms. Its founders also played a central role in the founding of the mosque in 1965 (see Chapter 2). By the mid-1980s, elections had been held twice for the post of president and secretary. On both occasions Khurshid was elected president, though there have been different secretaries. Khurshid is from a village in Jhelum district but is unusual is that he studied politics and local history in Pakistan and is respected among fellow Jhelumis for his knowledge of English and Urdu. Non-Jhelumis regard the Pakistan Welfare Association as a primarily Jhelumi organization, mainly because Jhelumis, they say, are the beneficiaries. Khurshid has also raised funds from friends and fellow-villagers in Britain for improvements to his village in

Pakistan. These improvements, which included a paved road, two schools, a community centre, a dispensary and a wall round the cemetery, would not have been made without Khurshid's effort and influence.

Shamim, a woman from Karachi, established another shorter-lived association of which she was president and which, she claimed, was a local branch of All Pakistan Women's Association. She provided free welfare services by interpreting for women in hospitals, taking up discrimination cases, contacting the housing department over housing problems and helping people complete forms. Her organization was nominally democratic, for Shamim chose the other office holders from among her close friends; its sphere of influence was limited to a small number of families from Jhelum and Faisalabad, obliged to Shamim by the debt incurred from accepting her services.

The threat to Islamic values

Today, the majority of families manage reasonably well in their dealings with British institutions, in some cases older parents relying upon the assistance of sons and daughters educated and raised in Britain. Given that this particular need for patrons such as Khurshid and Shamim has diminished, we might expect traditional attitudes to people in authority to have changed in consequence. In fact, however, many of the pioneer generation, at least, still hold attitudes that, I have suggested, are linked with the political background in Pakistan; such attitudes do not necessarily change overnight, or without good reason. Most migrants retain contacts within Pakistan and some hope to return one day, although they are aware that having become used to a less 'corrupt' bureaucracy, re-adapting to life in Pakistan may be difficult indeed. And individuals who have the status of 'community representatives' have appealed to a newly perceived 'community' need, articulated from time to time in relation to the younger generations growing up in Britain — the need for protection from the threat of western values. By appealing to fears about the erosion of Islamic culture in the west, certain individuals have come to acquire in the eyes of some Pakistanis a status akin to that of a patron in Pakistan.

Pakistanis hold ambivalent views about English society. I was aware, in Pakistan, that Britain is admired for its wealth, education and health services. Comparing Britain with Pakistan, people often commented on the apparent absence of nepotism and bribery in politics and administration, and praised the health and social services. 'England' one man said 'is the most civilized country in the world.' In Pakistan, people spoke with pride of the role of the British administration in organizing the building of the canals, irrigation and settlement of the canal colonies. A number of migrants have, since living in Britain, pioneered changes in the provision of services or facilities in their villages of origin. Khurshid, the president of the Pakistan Welfare Association, was so impressed by the fact that British cities have community centres and British cemeteries have walls around them that he arranged for these improvements to be made to his village in Pakistan. British goods are much sought after in Pakistan, and in general anything man-made or 'from abroad' (*valāyatī*) is more highly valued than local (*desī*) or 'home-made' goods. Silky man-made colourfast fabrics, for instance, are considered superior to locally produced cotton. English is compulsory in higher education in Pakistan and the high-status schools, modeled to some extent on British private schools, have English as the medium of instruction. British professional qualifications are highly regarded in Pakistan, and many of the pioneer generation of migrants want their sons and daughters to obtain professional qualifications in Britain for this reason.

The admiration of things 'English' or 'Western' also has racial connotations. In Pakistan, fairness of skin is coveted; it is desired in a bride and associated with high caste status and with those who can afford to keep women in purdah. Women's magazines show pink, round-faced babies in advertisements for dried milk and pale-faced women in advertisements for creams to lighten skin colour. Relatives of families in Oxford sometimes asked me about the skin colour of their relatives in England, for they expected it to lighten in Britain, and mine to darken in Pakistan. Pakistanis sometimes refer to themselves as *kale log* (black people), in contrast to the *gore log* (white people), whose skin colour confers a higher status. Within the *kale* category too, there are important gradations of colour: darker skins are associated with low caste status and 'inferior' racial origins. One man described people of *kammī* status as 'black' and of a different 'race', (using the English word). On the same grounds, east Oxford Pakistanis consider Bangladeshis inferior to them, while people of Afro-Caribbean origins rank lowest. The word *habshī*, usually translated as 'negro', is in east Oxford occasionally used as an insult to describe Afro-Caribbeans.

British Pakistanis, however, often regard English people ambivalently. They may admire many aspects of 'English' society and 'western civilization' but consider that the British administrative and political system is one that hunts down immigrants, has betrayed their rights as British subjects by successive changes in immigration and nationality laws and treats them as inferior. While only some of the first generation speak openly of racial discrimination, many of the second generation born in Britain speak bitterly of it. The term for 'white' when used to refer to people can be ambivalent and even insulting (*gorā*, of a man, *gori*, of a woman, *gore*, of people). For many Pakistanis, especially of the pioneer generation, this ambivalence is located in what Pakistanis perceive as a stark contrast between 'English' social and sexual mores on the one hand and 'Islamic' values of purdah and sexual segregation on the other.

Many Pakistanis hold a low opinion of western social and sexual morality and particularly of the position of women in western society. They consider that the western system permits free sexual relations and even encourages women to dress revealingly and to provoke men. They often cite Britain's high divorce rate and the increasing proportion of illegitimate births as evidence of the low moral standards of the west. Pakistanis women are often suspicious of English women, including, at times, myself; sometimes their husbands have or have had English girlfriends or wives. The women I know well have always been curious about my views on the position of women and on Islam, and remain concerned that I will 'burn in hell' for the sin of not believing in God and for other sins such as preventing pregnancy.

Initiatives to establish institutions to meet the 'needs' of the 'Muslim community' in Oxford usually appeal to these feelings about Western values, contrasting them with Islamic ones. In the 1970s, for instance, the Pakistan Welfare Association appealed to the heads of Muslim states for money to build an Islamic Cultural Centre in Oxford. This project was to include a mosque, a hostel, an auditorium, an Islamic library and a

Muslim Mission school. The appeal was made on the basis of the emotive issue of the perceived threat of western influences, as the following extract from this letter shows:

You are well aware that the Muslim minority in Britain is in the grip of a materialistic culture, cut adrift from its moral moorings. The entire media of instruction champions the cause of a bestially nude society which considers all ethnical *(sic)* values outdated. The academic policy of this country is not based on faith and it never aims at building and completing our character. The ideas of virtue and sin in this country have merged into one dark spot, too hazy to recognize. We consider it our duty to realize and express our fears that if the present Muslim generation remain blind to its duty and responsibility, and fail to keep abreast of the time, there won't be a single Muslim in Britain beyond the next two generations. A healthy continuation of the new generation, nursed and nurtured in the Islamic traditions, can only be ensured by establishing a Muslim mission school in a place like Oxford.

I have mentioned in my earlier letters that various other communities of the World, who are smaller in number and size than the Muslim community living here, sensing the wind of change towards religion in the West, are zealously establishing their religious and national centres in Oxford to propagate their creeds and secure a grip over the minds of the young generation here. Muslims have settled down in Britain in large numbers and have established as many as 350 Mosques in this country. But, due to the absence of any propagation of Islam and appropriate religious instructions if the future generations remain ignorant of Islam's glorious teachings and are, consequently, absorbed in the mighty currents of the western civilization, the entire present day generation would be held responsible by the future historian. To safeguard against these horrific possibilities the establishment of an Islamic Cultural Centre in Oxford is the need of the hour.

Muslim students from all over the World flock to the intellectual heaven of Oxford in search of knowledge since *(sic)* centuries. But, it has been observed that in most cases they return totally dyed in western hues. Has anyone ever pondered over the cause of this phenomenon? Since the advent of the science and technology and a trend towards learning English literature hordes of Muslim students are converging in Oxford. Due to the shortage of residential facilities they have to bank upon the accommodation provided by people of the other religions, very much like their predecessors. This constant practice has made them total slaves to the alien culture, beyond all rectifications. Like their precursors, they have been rendered worthless, incapable of doing any good to the Muslim community. The responsibility of stemming this evil tide rests entirely on your shoulders. If you choose to turn a deaf ear to this call of the hour and a blind eye to these stark realities every student that you send here for education may carry back with himself the seeds of destruction of the society and values that you cherish. These students may fall a prey to all sorts of conspiratorial activities which may endanger the whole fabric of your political and moral existence. It is, therefore, essential that all Muslim students studying in Oxford should assemble in a single centre to collectively devise ways and means for amelioration of their lot in the light of Islamic traditions.

Pakistan Welfare Association, Oxford, after prolonged study and consideration, has sought your assistance in the establishment of an Islamic Cultural Centre encompassing a Mosque, a hostel, an auditorium, Islamic Museum, Islamic Library and a Muslim mission school. The centre is expected to fire the imagination of the Muslims of this Country for all times to come. It will make Oxford a cradle of Islam. You are the guardian of the faith and Allah almighty has showered his blessings upon you in abundance. If you care to assist the Pakistan Welfare Association, Oxford, in the realization of this project it can materialize in a matter of hours. You are, therefore, requested to render all possible help in enabling us to keep the banner of Islam high and fluttering in this part of the World[1].

Over the years, the issue of protecting young Muslims from the pernicious influences of the west and of defending Islamic values has at times generated very strong feelings; locally, political support can be mobilized if the need for it is expressed within these terms. In the early 1980s, the local authority proposed that they close Milham Ford school, the only all-girls state secondary school in the city, which many, though not all, east Oxford Muslim girls attend. A Community Relations Council survey had shown that while most Pakistani Muslim parents sent their daughters to Milham Ford because it was single sex, there were also parents who sent their daughters to the local mixed secondary school because they thought the education there was better. For these parents, the religious question at that stage was not as important as the quality of the education that their daughters were receiving. When, however, the proposal was seen as a threat to Islamic values, many of the parents of girls attending the co-educational school sided with those campaigning to maintain the all-girls' school.

A 'community representative' with some influence among fellow migrants or wishing to acquire local support may take up issues like these. In the early 1980s, perhaps the single most emotive local 'community' issue was that of protecting young Muslim women from pernicious western values. This issue figured prominently in Shamim's community relations role, for instance. She once organized an *Id* celebration for women in a hired hall, at which she addressed all the women present about their duty to ensure that their daughters keep their hair tied up and covered with a scarf, wear the *shalwār* or at least trousers rather than skirts, and do not wear make-up. At another communal gathering, she referred insultingly to someone's daughter as a *desī gorī* (a 'home-made English girl'), and warned mothers to take care that their daughters do not become *desī gorīs* too. (The phrase is used as a term of abuse for a girl who wears jeans, make-up, cuts her hair short and may work or go to college). However, it was her objections to Urdu classes for Pakistani girls held at Milham Ford school that brought her most prominently into the 'public' eye. Through the local media, she maintained that the classes were 'brainwashing' the girls, 'trying to break our culture and religion and encouraging the children to be members of the permissive society'. The girls, reports claimed, were being shown 'sexy' Indian films that depict people who 'dance in very thin clothes and hold each other's hands' and 'show the girls how to meet men without their parents knowing.' Reports also claimed that during the Urdu classes, the teacher 'discussed subjects like arranged marriages with the girls, and by implication urged them to rebel against their parents'.

Community representatives as patrons

Taking a public stance as defender of the values of 'the community' or of Islam does not of itself make a person into a patron in the way that they might operate in Pakistan. How much power or authority do such individuals in fact have? 'Ordinary' Pakistani Muslims might view their community representatives as patrons, but it does not necessarily follow that these patrons are successful in securing resources from the Arab states, for instance, or from British local authorities or other funding agencies, for community projects. In Oxford, as in other British cities, the individuals who have become office holders of welfare associations or other voluntary organizations and who may, as a result, be seen by local statutory and voluntary agencies as community leaders or representatives, are not necessarily wholly typical of ordinary Pakistanis (that it, if it possible to define a typical 'ordinary' Pakistani). They are a heterogeneous category, from a variety of backgrounds and often in some respects peripheral to the communities they purport to represent[2]. Some have been described as 'integrationists' in that they are of urban origin, committed to western values and regarded with suspicion by the 'mass of rural uneducated Pakistanis', even though they may have official status in the eyes of the British authorities[3]. On the other hand, most might better be described 'accommodationists', drawn from the educated but poor middle classes who are 'culturally aligned with the uneducated peasantry'[4]. Of the 'Asian immigrant brokers' who organize the welfare societies in Manchester, 'the majority tended to be less religious and to have certain exceptional attributes (of regional or denominational affiliation) which set them apart from the Punjabi Sunni majority. In other respects, however, they were very much of the "centre"'[5]. In Oxford, most community leaders share broadly the same backgrounds as their fellow migrants, and may have relatives locally, but certain specific features of their individual circumstances and experiences have propelled them towards becoming community representatives[6]. Most 'ordinary' Pakistanis have not become members of the local Community Relations Council (CRC) (affiliated to the Commission for Racial Equality) and have neither the time nor the inclination to become involved.

Two features of the role of such leaders are striking. One is the frequency and intensity of competition between them for posi-

tions on welfare associations or as community representatives
on the executive committees of local CRCs, both in Oxford and
elsewhere. In Oxford, this has involved, for example, accusations and counter accusations of elections having been rigged.
The other is that once elected or co-opted, successful candidates
rarely attend meetings and do very little work for their council
(in the case of the CRCs, the day-to-day work is done by paid
officers); much of their role, as Werbner notes, is 'validatory
and symbolic'[7]. Why, then should such positions be so sought
after? A part of the answer, lies in the fact that very often both
'leaders' and 'ordinary' Pakistanis do indeed view these positions in much the same way that they would view them in
Pakistan, that is, in terms of the influence they may gain and
the patronage they may dispense. This is apparent in many
aspects of the behaviour of leaders in or aspiring towards
prominent positions, and in the attitudes of ordinary Pakistanis
towards such people.

For example, when Akram Ali stood for election at the CRC,
many other migrants commented that he was doing so to get
benefits for his family, in the form of paid work or other
favours, through his contacts with local councillors. Akram
Ali's competitors also said that he would be 'getting something
for nothing' if elected. A man called Arshad who had been
taken into police custody believed that he was released soon
after, with no charges made against him, only as a result of
Akram Ali's intervention. Akram Ali's involvement in this case
was unclear, but two days later he invited Arshad and his wife
to dinner at his house and impressed the couple with his deep
concern to help his 'community'. Arshad assumed that the
British system was like Pakistan and that to be released one
needed to have a patron and Akram Ali certainly seemed to be
behaving as if he has such powers.

In a similar, earlier incident, Shamim brought to the attention of
the local press the case of a Pakistani family living in a council
house with a badly leaking roof, promising the family that they
would be allocated a better house as a result of the publicity. The
grateful family gave her a dinner invitation and *Id* presents. As it
turned out, the family were re-housed eighteen months later as a
matter of course, but this did not alter their conviction that
without Shamim's intervention they would never have been
moved. Community representatives like these may be keen to

impress upon fellow migrants that they do indeed have influence. They might drop into conversation the names of Pakistan Embassy officials or local English councillors in order to impress fellow Pakistanis with their apparent power and influence. One such leader claimed to be from one of Pakistan's twelve largest business families, with influential contacts in Pakistan's government. In conversations with fellow Pakistanis from rural backgrounds, he would talk of recent visits to the Pakistan Embassy in London and of personal telephone calls from the Pakistan Ambassador and even from the President of Pakistan himself. This name dropping, and the ambition to hold office in the welfare associations, is, as one ordinary Pakistani put it 'for status, so that when he (a community representative) walks into a meeting, everyone will treat him with respect, even the elders who are his seniors'.

But how successful have these community representatives been? They may have achieved some status in the eyes of the fellow Pakistanis they have assisted, especially their kin, but do they wield any real power? Often, in fact, the competition between rival community representatives has effectively curtailed their projects. The appeal to Muslim states for funds to establish an Islamic cultural centre, for instance, generated so much rivalry between competing associations that the project was never realized. The Arab states apparently promised £50,000, subject to the guarantee of proper premises and assurance that the money be used for its intended purpose only. This promise prompted local competition for the control of funds, through the office of president of the Pakistan Welfare Association. A rival Pakistan Welfare Association was established as a breakaway group because, its members claimed, the election that had returned Khurshid as the original association's president was irregular. This new rival group claimed that they comprised the 'real' Pakistan Welfare Association primarily, it seems, because they wanted to receive and control the funds that had been promised to the PWA. The situation resulted in the promise of funding from the Arab states being withdrawn.

Ordinary Pakistanis themselves do not always offer uncritical support of their community representatives. Shamim's objections to the Urdu classes at Milham Ford School brought her into contact with the local authority and the media. Her objections caused deep concern to the teachers who had introduced the pilot mother-tongue teaching scheme intending to give a positive value to the home language and culture of Pakistani Muslim girls in school. For a while, the issue was emotive and contentious, and did pose a real threat to the classes. Previously, the parents had given written permission for their daughters to attend the classes and to watch one Indian film at the end of the summer term. At the time of the press reports, however, some girls were absent from the classes while their parents investigated the rumours circulating among their neighbours and friends. The Urdu teacher, herself a Pakistani Muslim, explained that in class the girls themselves had brought up the subjects of marriage and the role of women, and because these subjects were important to them she felt she had no right to stop them being discussed. In the end, however, none of the parents of the girls who attended the classes wanted them stopped and the classes have continued. Urdu is now a popular GCSE and A level choice for Pakistani pupils, and not only at Milham Ford School.

In this case, Shamim's intervention was not, in the end, particularly effective. She had previously attempted to forge links with local city councillors, the Lord Mayor, barristers and head teachers by sending them Christmas gifts such as china, cut glass and other goods, bought with money received from other Pakistanis in *lenā-denā* or saved in *kametī*s. However, her influence was mainly restricted to a network of friends and exerted through circles of *lenā-denā* and *Khatmī-Qur'ān*s.

Sometimes, however, attempts to forge links with local councillors do bear fruit. Since the late 1960s, some local authorities have been administering two schemes funded by the central government to 'meet the needs' of 'ethnic communities'. In Oxford, the county council has administered section 11 funding, mainly for English language and mother-tongue teaching, while the city council and the CRC have administered Urban Aid grants for particular ethnic minority projects under the urban renewal programme. City and county council staff or councillors may be aware of the inadequacies of existing provision state provision; for example, there may be no interpreters in the housing department. At the same time, they may have few contacts within the 'ethnic communities', and so be glad to draw in community representatives to work with them towards meeting these needs.

For the community representatives, ethnic minority representation on the executive committee of the local community relations has been the main route towards building up links with statutory agencies and local councillors. This route has provided access to committees of other bodies where ethnic minority representation is required, such as on the police liaison committee or on the City Council's housing committee. Once in position, individuals may use their positions to demonstrate to fellow migrants their apparent power and authority, making it appear that others, such as the paid staff of the CRC, are beholden to them for appointments. They may therefore gain status, in the short term at least, in the eyes of fellow migrants. Through their links with particular councillors, they may also promote themselves or their relatives as applicants for posts in community relations, sometimes securing paid posts in this way. However, their expectations of their position and their styles of management sometimes conflict with the expectations of staff and volunteers. Oxford is not unique for having had central government funding withdrawn as a consequence of grievances against a succession of Pakistani chairmen of the executive committee of the CRC. Elsewhere too, competition for community representation is a political struggle over the distribution of scarce resources[9].

Non-Asian journalists, bureaucrats and politicians, when confronted by Pakistani community representatives intent on presenting themselves as the spokespersons for their community's needs, do not of course have to establish whether they are 'truly' representative. The process does nevertheless reinforce the image which prevails in both local and national politics and media that 'ethnic minorities' are 'communities' defined by a set of cultural characteristics, from which particular social and cultural 'needs' arise. Yet the very concept of community representation is quite alien to many Pakistanis from rural Pakistan where the favours of powerful patrons or relatives in government positions are competed for in order to secure resources or justice.

Influence of the mosque

For the majority of Pakistanis in Oxford, the disputes involving community representatives are of passing interest only, unless they involve a close friend or *birādarī* member. Ahmed's response to my question about whether he would vote in an OCCR election is typical of many Pakistanis who are not members of the local CRC. 'If it was something that affected my family and children', Ahmed said, 'then I would go and vote; but these people are only in it for themselves, and one is as bad as the other.' The issues tackled by OCCR and voiced by community representatives (for instance housing shortages, school cutbacks and racism in its various forms) of course ones that might well affect Ahmed and his family. However, for Ahmed and many like him, combating racism is of less direct interest than the question of, for instance, which Islamic sect the local *imām* belongs to.

In Oxford in the early 1980s, an incident that generated very strong feelings among east Oxford Muslims and captured local media interest was a dispute within the first established mosque. This dispute was essentially a doctrinal one. Such disputes are not unique to Oxford but have occurred in other British cities where Pakistani Muslims have settled. The dispute in Oxford ran on for two years and was only to some extent resolved by 1984. The issues at stake and the emotions this dispute generated illustrate several processes in the establishment of the Muslim presence in Britain; essentially, it drew attention to the emotion generated by perceived attacks on Islam. A closer look at the main elements in this dispute sheds light on why, a few years later, Salman Rushdie's *The Satanic Verses* was to cause such deep offence to many ordinary Muslims, most of whom had not read the book.

There are at present four mosques in the city, all within east Oxford. The first mosque was opened in 1965 in a converted warehouse in Bath Street, St. Clements, and was recognized in 1971 as a Trust by the Charity Commission. It remained Oxford's only mosque until 1984. Previously called the Oxford Mosque and now called the Oxford Sunni Mosque, it still serves the largest proportion of the Pakistani Muslim population in Oxford. The second mosque, called the Muslim Welfare House/Mosque was founded in 1984 in a house in Stanley Road. Sunni Muslims, who make up the overwhelming majority of Oxford's Pakistani Muslims, may attend either of these mosques, but this second mosque was established as a consequence of sectarian and regional divisions which I discuss below.

There are also a few Shia Muslims in Oxford, who, although not formally excluded from the mosques, tend not to attend them. The third mosque, established in the mid-1980s, belongs to the Ahmadiyya community, which in Oxford numbers some twenty households[10]. The fourth and most recently founded mosque is the Bangladeshi mosque, established in a converted shop on the Cowley Road. East Oxford Muslims have also recently obtained planning permission from the local city council for a purpose-built mosque on a prestigious east Oxford site that they have purchased. They are currently raising money for the building to start. The gradual proliferation of mosques over the years follows on a smaller scale the process of fission and segmentation broadly along the lines of kinship, village of origin and sectarian differences that Philip Lewis describes for Bradford[11]. Quite independently of these developments, the Oxford University Islamic society is currently seeking planning permission for a purpose-built mosque in the city.

Most Pakistani Muslim men in Oxford attend a mosque at specific prayer times; the mosques produce monthly timetables of the daily prayers because these times change daily according to the position of the sun. Some men go to a mosque if not at all five prayers then at least for the evening prayer. More men attend once a week on Fridays for the *jum'ā* or main congregational prayer at noon; at each of the two main mosques between 50 and 100 men may be present for *jum'ā* prayers. Even more men attend the prayers at both *Id* celebrations, *īdu'l-zohā* and *īdu'l-fitr*. If an *Id* festival falls at a weekend when the majority of men are not at work, then in the early afternoon an observer might see distinctive groups of Muslim men wearing the traditional *shalwār-qamīs* returning from the midday prayers at the mosques. Regular mosque-going also provides a form of welfare, because fellow worshippers will notice if a regular worshipper is absent. The mosques also provide forums for raising matters of 'community' welfare, especially through the mosque committees. Women do not attend the east Oxford mosques; they express their faith through prayer at home and through convening *khatmi-Qur'an*s (see Chapter 8) — although the plans for the new purpose-built mosque include a women's gallery, with a separate entrance and separate washing facilities for ablutions. Women also supplement the teaching at the mosque school by supervising children reading the *Qur'ān* at home in the evenings and at weekends.

Over the years, east Oxford Muslims have become increasingly concerned to pass on their knowledge of Islam to their
children. In both of the main mosques, the mosque committee
employs an *imām* not only to lead prayers in the mosque but
also to hold *Qur'ān* classes there for children. In the late
1980s, during one week over 300 children would attend
Qur'ān classes at the Bath Street mosque and about 150 children would attend the Stanley Road mosque. These numbers
have increased over the past decade. The classes are open to
boys and to girls under about 12 years of age; older girls do
not go to the mosque but generally receive Islamic instruction
from adult women in their own or in a neighbour's home. At
the mosque classes, boys and girls are divided into separate
groups and taught by traditional methods and with strict discipline to recite the *Qur'ān* First, they learn to recite the
sounds of each letter of the Arabic script and then learn the
sounds of letters joined to each other. They then proceed to
learn to recite the Arabic of the *Qur'ān* itself, aiming to learn
it by heart. They are also taught the basic principles of Islam
and how to perform *namāz* (prayer).

The committee of each main mosque also employs a part-time
driver for their mosque van which, every evening, transports
children from their homes to the mosque and back. The
mosque committee also collects three-monthly subscriptions
from the members of each Mosque Society. These subscriptions pay the *imām*'s salary, the van driver and maintain the
mosque building and the van. At the Ahmadiyya mosque subscriptions are not a fixed amount but those who can afford it
give donations to the mosque committee to pay for the *imām*
and the upkeep of the mosque building.

Most Pakistani Muslims also subscribe to one of the Muslim
Funeral Committees. Two of these funeral committees are
organized through Oxford Sunni Mosque Society and the
Muslim Welfare House/Mosque. A third, smaller funeral committee, the Oxford Kashmiri Funeral Committee, is run by
people from Mirpur and adjoining parts of Azad (Free)
Kashmir who support the Kashmiri independence movement;
they regard themselves as Kashmiris rather than Pakistanis.
The Ahmadiyyas also have a funeral committee, organized
centrally from London. Members' subscriptions to a funeral
committee are paid after someone had died and cover the

costs of buying a coffin, washing a corpse, bringing it to be viewed by bereaved relatives and friends and taking it to Heathrow to be sent to relatives in Pakistan. These costs may amount to £5–6,000. Strictly speaking, this 'insurance' extends only to those who pay subscriptions, though sometimes when someone dies who was not a member and had few relatives locally, friends collect money to help the bereaved family return the body to Pakistan.

The mosques play an important role in the day-to-day lives of most families. Men attend prayers at the mosques on at least some occasions if not on a weekly or daily basis; children attend classes for instruction in Arabic and in reciting the *Qur'ān*, and the funeral committees provide insurance for sending corpses to Pakistan. These functions of the mosque have remained largely hidden from the non-Muslim public view. Although community representatives from time to time raise issues of concern to Muslim parents such as that of single-sex education or sex education in schools, on the whole questions of religious faith have been perceived by 'outsiders', such as local councillors, teachers, journalists and others, as internal matters for the 'Muslim community' to resolve by itself. This perception is linked, in part with another, that of the local Muslim community as a homogeneous and united entity. In Oxford, between 1982 and 1984 disputes took place in the largest mosque in Bath Street were to challenge these views.

Factional and ideological divisions

According to local press reports, a dispute in the Bath Street mosque had in 1982 'split the 1,000 strong practising Muslim community in the city' and a year later had 'torn the city's Moslem population in two'. The dispute involved a series of violent incidents and on several occasions the police were called to the mosque. One police officer later remarked that the police had been unable to understand what was happening. Disputes had occurred before, but this particular dispute was to have a particularly far-reaching effect, for it resulted in the founding of the second mosque in 1984. Similar disputes have occurred elsewhere in Britain where they have also involved sometimes violent confrontations.

The Bath Street mosque dispute focused on the services of the *imām* whom the mosque committee had employed on a permanent basis since early 1981. The mosque committee members had begun to feel that they were losing control of their *imām*'s activities. They considered that he had acted without their authority in buying a house with money donated to the Mosque Society for purchasing a property for the *imām*'s use. They said that he had imposed a new system of instruction for children without consulting them. They thought his preaching was divisive: he was too outspoken about his own religious convictions, which represented the beliefs of the Barelwi sect, and he had not taken care to adopt a 'middle road approach' that would be acceptable to all Muslims. In fact, they considered that once his status in Britain had been secured, by his having permanent employment and suitable accommodation, the *imām* had used his position to create ideological divisions within the Muslim community by preaching against other sects.

The committee had apparently given the *imām* several warnings that if he did not stop his divisive preaching, he would be sacked and as a consequence deported, because his remaining in Britain depended on his continuing employment as the *imām*. When the *imām* failed to alter his behaviour, the mosque committee wrote to the Home Office. On the first day of the Muslim month of Ramadan, the mosque committee president announced in the mosque that the *imām* had been sacked and that the Home Office had issued a deportation order on the grounds that the *imām* was longer qualified to remain in Britain.

Dismissal of an *imām* is, of itself, not necessarily sufficient to precipitate a fight; the mosque committee had sacked the previous *imām* for returning late from his annual leave and there had been no public outcry. However, in this case, there was an immediate, emotional and violent response within the mosque itself at evening prayers and a fight broke out which resulted in the police being summoned.

Emotions running high, the *imām*'s supporters called on the Community Relations Officer at the local CRC for help. They sacked the mosque committee and elected a new one at a meeting held in the local CRC offices with the support of the community relations officer. The new mosque committee then took control of the existing mosque and re-instated the *imām*. The *imām*'s supporters circulated a petition for signatures and sent it to the Home Office, and *imām*'s position in Britain was eventually confirmed.

Why did the *imām*'s dismissal lead to such a fierce dispute? The dispute touched upon sectarian and political differences within Sunni Islam in South Asia. Contemporary South Asian Islam has a number of distinctive expressions, the main strands of which are alive in Britain today — as Philip Lewis' excellent overview of the dynamics of the Muslim presence shows. Disputes in the first main Oxford mosque have focussed mainly upon the opposition between the 'reformist' Deobandis the 'conservative and populist' Barelwis[12]. In the 1982 dispute, the *imām*'s supporters claimed that 'Wahhabis' or 'Deobandis' were trying to seize control of the mosque. They viewed the mosque committee that had attempted to sack the *imām* as comprising men of the 'Deobandi' or 'Wahhabi' reformist tradition, whereas the *imām*'s religious beliefs, in contrast, are those of the Barelwi tradition. The ideological differences between these traditions focus in particular on beliefs in the power of *pīr*s.

Beliefs in the power of *pīr*s (saints) as spiritual intermediaries between man and God are central to the tradition of Islamic Sufism. A *pīr*'s followers (*murīd*) generally ascribe supernatural powers both to the Prophet Muhammad and to *pīr*s. Ordinary people have access to this spiritual power through contact with living *pīr*s or through worship at the tombs of deceased *pīr*s. As one young member of the *imām*'s following explained:

> Barelwi is the right way. We believe in God and that we can reach God by knowing his Prophet. We believe that *pīr*s can help you to learn to know the Prophet, because you can reach God's power through a *pīr*. A great *pīr* can help you more than a lesser *pīr*, because great *pīr*s give power to lesser *pīr*s. There is a hierarchy of *pīr*s. It is like having a Prime Minister whose power is dispersed through government officials down to the local level so that eventually the power reaches ordinary people. That is how we reach God's power and how God's power reaches

us: through the *pīrs*.

And as older woman from Attock district explained:

> *Pīrs* are there to help us because man is so weak that he
> cannot reach God without guidance. People need *pīrs* to
> guide them on the right path, just as you took names and
> addresses when you went to Pakistan.

A *pīr*'s spiritual power enables him to provide treatment for
and protection from numerous minor and serious ailments and
afflictions, usually by preparing *tā'wīz* (see Chapter 7). It is not
only living *pīrs* who have power over the natural world, for
deceased *pīrs* may continue to exert their supernatural capabili-
ties from their tombs, which are often places of pilgrimage.
Saleem explained this by describing an incident he had
experienced:

> In 1963 I was travelling to Pakistan by road with a Shia
> cousin who lives in London. We spent three weeks in Iran
> and my cousin especially wanted to visit the tomb of Ali
> Reza, a Sufi saint, buried in the old capital of Iran. I had
> terrible teeth trouble at that time; my gums were bleeding.
> At the shrine I was told to buy some sugar which would
> cure my trouble. I wasn't convinced, but eventually
> bought some, and my teeth and gums recovered. It may
> have been due to a change in water or diet, but I believe it
> was because of the *pīr*.

These beliefs in the power of *pīrs* and in the spiritual qualities of
the Prophet Muhammad are associated with the Barelwi Islamic
tradition, which takes its name from the religious school
(*madrāsa*) founded by Ahmad Raza Khan in the late nineteenth
century at Bareilly, Uttar Pradesh (in northern India). While many
east Oxford Pakistanis, including the *imām* and his supporters, do
describe themselves as Barelwis, not everyone who holds beliefs of
this sort is necessarily familiar with the term 'Barelwi' and may
simply describe themselves as 'Sunni' Muslims. Nevertheless, such
beliefs are characteristically held by a majority of east Oxford
Pakistanis.

Those who challenge the beliefs of this tradition are referred to
as 'Deobandis' or, in more derogatory local usage, as

'Wahhabis', though they may not themselves use these labels, but simply describe themselves as Sunni Muslims. The term 'Deobandi' is taken from the name of a reformist seminary, founded by the Muslim scholars Muhammad Qasim Nanautawi and Rashid Ahmad Gangohi, in 1867 at Deoband, also in Uttar Pradesh. These founders were concerned to purify Islam of practices which they regarded as unIslamic, particularly the beliefs in the efficacy of *pīrs*, worship at tombs and the ascription of special qualities to the Prophet. The work of the Deobandi school was later complemented by that of the Tablighi Jama'at, a twentieth-century proselytizing movement which in Britain has close links with the Deobandi mosques. Not all of those with Deobandi-type beliefs among east Oxford Pakistanis would necessarily label themselves as Deobandis but would describe themselves simply as Sunni Muslims. In dubbing them 'Wahhabis', their opponents are making reference to the Wahhabi movement, which, although of the same general character as the Deobandi movement, originated in Arabia in the eighteenth century. Many Deobandis strongly resent being called Wahhabis.

> Earlier this century, differences between the Barelwis and Deobandis resulted in 'a *fatwa* war' in which Barelwis and Deobandis: declared each other non-Muslim, *kāfir*, and sought endorsement of their respective anathemas from religious scholars in the Hijaz, the heartlands of Islam in western Arabia. It is hardly surprising that Tablighi Jama'at activities are banned in Barelwi mosques. Mutual antipathy between Deobandi and Barelwi can still flare up into open conflict today'[13].

Locally, people whose beliefs reflect the Barelwi tradition perceive Deobandi or 'Wahhabi' criticism as an attack on Islam itself, for the criticism attacks the central belief of devotional South Asian Islam that God's power can reach ordinary people via devotion to the Prophet. The *imām* whom the mosque committee had tried unsuccessfully to dismiss in 1982 was himself a charismatic Barelwi leader, with connections with other *pīrs* and Barelwi dignitaries in Pakistan and Britain. He had spoken against the Deobandis and the Tablighi Jama'at, for instance, and the issue of whether touring Tablighi Jama'at preachers should be allowed to stay in the mosque was a matter of continuous dispute. By accusing the committee that had sought to remove the *imām* of 'Wahhabism' the *imām* supporters were guaranteed a large following.

At the time of the mosque dispute, many east Oxford Pakistanis spoke in vivid terms of the evils of Wahhabism. Here is one account from a woman whose husband and sons were staunch supporters of the *imām*:

> The Wahhabis are a minority and too puritanical. They believe that Mohammed was just a man like the rest, who lived and died, even though he was the last prophet. They believe that there is no benefit in praying to him and that you must pray direct to God. That's not what we believe. We believe Muhammad is not dead but lives with Allah and we can reach Allah by praying to Mohammed and to the *pīr*s who are Muhammad's descendants. But Wahhabis say *pīr*s have no special powers. It is like the difference between Protestants and Catholics.

She went on to explain why this difference was more than a question of belief:

> There was a man from Walsall who became a Wahhabi. One year he returned to his village in Azad Kashmir. There was the tomb of a *pīr* in the courtyard of his house. Maintaining that a Muslim should not follow *pīr*s, he insisted that the grave be removed. Although his relatives tried to stop him, one evening he started to shovel the earth away. But as soon as his spade hit the earth, he saw the courtyard suddenly fill with thousands of snakes. Screaming and terrified, he ran indoors, warning his family that snakes were filling the courtyard. He couldn't escape the snakes, which were also in the rooms and climbing up onto the beds, jumping from one to another. His relatives gradually persuaded him that there were no snakes in the room, but, terrified, he vowed never to touch the tomb again and to this day he has never gone back to Wahhabism.

During our conversation, a visiting neighbour added:

> The previous *imām* was a Wahhabi and most of our people don't like Wahhabi views, but he didn't preach

and for eight years people thought he was all right. But when the new *imām* came, they realized they could have a proper religious education, for adults and children, and so we decided to employ him permanently. The old *imām* lost his job, not only because he was late returning from Pakistan, but also because the majority decided they didn't like his beliefs and wanted the new *imām*. And that's how the trouble started. The Wahhabis who supported the previous *imām* then tried to throw out the new *imām*.

The previous *imām* — the one ousted for overstaying his leave — was indeed not 'typical' of most east Oxford Pakistanis; he was a Gujarati Muslim from Karachi, with relatives in Dewsbury where, since 1982, there has been a Deobandi seminary[14]. He was a mild-mannered man who held moderate views, and, although the supporters of the new *imām* considered him a 'Wahhabi', he told me he did himself visit a *pīr* in Karachi, for spiritual guidance. He did not preach, but was simply a *hāfiz*, who is someone who has memorized the entire *Qur'ān*. The new Barelwi *imām*, a charismatic and outspoken personality, was, like most east Oxford Pakistanis, from the Panjab province of Pakistan, and was in this respect generally considered 'one of our people'. For most Oxford Pakistanis, the *pīr* tradition is still vital, pervading more than just the spiritual life of east Oxford Pakistanis, and the new *imām*'s teaching touched these feelings directly. The committee which had sacked the previous 'Deobandi' *imām*, and then later attempted to sack the Barelwi *imām*, in fact comprised individuals who were not all strictly speaking Deobandis, yet it had been quite easy for the new *imām*'s supporters to make the accusation of Wahhabism stick.

The opposition of Deobandi and Barelwi beliefs was the central idiom through which the dispute in 1982 was expressed, and it resulted in 1984 in a second mosque being established, the Muslim Welfare House/Mosque. Today, although this mosque is associated with the Deobandi tradition, many of those who attend on a day-to-day basis do hold beliefs in the power of *pīr*s; it is only in disputes that these oppositions come to the fore. It is through this combination of fission and expansion that the Muslim presence in east Oxford has developed.

The perceived attack upon Islam, in this case in the form of 'Wahhabi' activity, generated a strength of feeling that was to be given fuller expression, at a national level, with another perceived assault on Islam in the subsequent 'Rushdie Affair'. While the protest against the publication of Salman Rushdie's *The Satanic Verses* was a 'genuinely populist response which caught up almost everyone in the Muslim community', Oxford Pakistanis did not take to the streets in public protest; this was the prerogative of larger, more self-confident settlements[15]. Yet most 'ordinary' Pakistani Muslims were indeed deeply hurt by what they understood as Rushdie's insulting portrayal of the character of the Prophet Muhammad, and, by implication, their tradition of devotion to the Prophet and to *pīr*s. The reaction of most British Muslims to the *Satanic Verses* was not about 'Islamic fundamentalism', as alleged in the media, so much as an expression of the love of the Prophet characteristic of, but not exclusive to, the Barelwi devotional tradition. 'All the religious zealots had to do was simply quote from the SV (sic) for anger, shame and hurt to be felt'[16]. At the same time, the protest demonstrated the political power of a perceived threat to Islam among ordinary Muslims. In this way, it has fuelled the process through which Islam has become increasingly important in the identities of British Pakistanis[17].

NOTES

1. Reproduced with permission from the President of the Pakistan Welfare Association, Oxford.
2. Scott, 1972–3, Saifullah-Khan, 1976. See also Aurora, 1967 and R. Ballard and C. Ballard, 1977.
3. Saifullah-Khan, 1976.
4. Aurora, 1967.
5. Werbner, 1991
6. Shaw, 1991.
7. See, for instance, Shaw, 1991 and Werbner, 1991.
8. Werbner, 1991:20.
9. Eade, 1989; Kalka, 1991 (a); P. Werbner, 1991 and Baumann, 1996.
10. The Ahmadiyyas believe that the founder of their movement, Mirza Ghulam Ahmad, who was born in 1835 in Qadian in India, was the promised messiah and final leader of the Muslims. The centre of the Ahmadiyya community and mission was at Qadian, India, until Partition in 1947, but moved to Rabwah, in Pakistan. Muslim critics consider the belief in Mirza Ghulam Ahmad as a final prophet to be a heresy, one for which Ahmadiyyas have been heavily persecuted. In 1984, the present leader of the Ahmadiyya community fled to south London, where the

community has a well-organized centre. In Oxford, many Pakistani Muslims are strongly opposed to the Ahmadiyyas, regarding them as non-Muslims.

11. In Bradford, there were 30 mosques by 1989, but then Bradford's Muslim population was at least 10 times bigger. See Lewis, 1994:56–62.
12. Philip Lewis, 1994:36.
13. Lewis, 1994:40.
14. Lewis, 1994:90–2.
15. Werbner, 1991(b).
16. Tariq Modood, 1990.
17. See also Shaw, 1994.

10 CONCLUSIONS

In January 1989, several hundred Bradford Muslims gathered as copies of Salman Rushdie's *The Satanic Verses*, published in September 1988, were set alight in front of the town hall. Not long after, British Muslims demonstrated at Hyde Park in central London, petitioned Penguin books to withdraw Rushdie's book and called upon the British government to extend the scope of the blasphemy laws. The protesters felt their demands were justified because of the deep offence that Rushdie's insulting portrayal of the Prophet Muhammad had caused them; their motive was devotion to the Prophet and to Islam. They were not calling for Rushdie's death, and shortly after the Ayatollah Khomeni pronounced a *fatwa* on Salman Rushdie on 14th February 1989, a number of British Muslim leaders, claiming to represent 90% of the mosques and the majority of Britain's 1.5 million Muslims, publicly dissociated themselves from it[1]. By the autumn of that year, however, the anti-Rushdie campaign had gained considerable momentum; Khomeni's *fatwa*, best understood in relation to Iranian politics and the politics of the Muslim world, had become a central issue in inter-Muslim rivalry[2]. There is no doubt that these events generated a sense of political crisis in Britain, and a shadow fell upon liberal circles in which multiculturalism was celebrated. This was why some pronounced the Rushdie affair to have been 'the death of multiculturalism'....

Of course Britain is and has long been a multi-cultural society. The British are among the most diverse of the Europeans, comprising groups of various origins and heritages, different kinds of families, marriage practices, health beliefs, ways of socializing, religious beliefs, and so on. The list of immigrants to the British isles includes, in the first ten centuries, Celts Romans, Anglo-Saxons, Vikings and Normans; in the nineteenth century Irish, Jews, Germans, Poles and Italians, and even before the first World War, Afro-Caribbeans and Chinese. And there is no doubt that contemporary multiculturalism in the form of the liberal educational theory of the 1970s and 1980s, which celebrates cultural diversity and proclaims that the values of 'minority cultures' should be respected, is still alive and well, with reference to at least some characteristics of ethnic minorities. But it is also true that the furore over *The Satanic Verses* highlighted the limits of extreme multiculturalism in the modern British context. It raised difficult questions about how, and under what constraints, people of different cultural backgrounds can co-exist within a single nation-state.

These were certainly not new considerations, for in Britain the presence of immigrants has raised concerns about national identity and stability for at least as long as the idea of a nation has existed. The Irish, for example, despite belonging to Britain under the 1801 Act of Union, were recorded as the largest 'immigrant' population in the 1871 Census and were in the course of the previous century often perceived as trouble-makers and religious fanatics[3]. The very idea of a nation is, in most modern or nineteenth century formulations, based upon the idea of citizens having a particular pattern of social organization in common, sharing moral or religious principles and the sense of a common heritage. This concept of a nation precludes cultural or ethnic diversity; such diversity is seen as inimical to national stability. Yet it is equally a feature of the modern post-colonial world that ethnic and cultural diversity has increased dramatically through internal and international migration, as a consequence of the very same processes of industrial and technological change that generated nineteenth century nation-building[4]. In Britain, the implications of this diversity for notions such as citizenship and for public policy have for some time been and still are matters for negotiation.

The arrival of immigrants from the Indian subcontinent and the Caribbean after the second world war prompted a series of British 'race relations' studies, in the 1950s and 1960s, that were on the whole concerned with documenting 'assimilation', in a reflection of the prevailing laissez-faire style assimilation policy adopted by the state at that time[5]. Assimilation — the process whereby immigrants adopt the language, social structures and values of the majority population — could be more or less measured, it was assumed, along a scale of structural and cultural variables. Before long, however, it was apparent that such confident assumptions about the inevitability of assimilation were unjustified; forces towards assimilation were indeed at work, but certain groups were tenaciously retaining old ways, and there was no apparent unity in these processes. Since the 1970s, sociologists and anthropologists have offered explanations for these varying trajectories, with different degrees of success. Sociological analyses, which emphasize racism or class, usefully highlight the roles of socio-economic disadvantage and racial exclusion, but tend to ignore the dynamics of migrants' socio-economic networks — which may even divert to the sending countries resources that might otherwise fuel social advancement in British terms — and may overlook the power of religious beliefs to influence and justify action[6]. Ethnographic or cultural accounts, on the other hand, which emphasize the internal dynamics of migrant communities, give a central place to the meanings migrants themselves attribute to these processes but can be accused of underplaying the wider socio-economic and political constraints on people's lives and thus of blaming non-assimilation upon 'culture'[7].

Many of these accounts also employ the concept of ethnicity, a term which, in most of its anthropological incarnations, refers to a common social structure, shared moral or religious principles and a sense of shared ancestry, usually in relation to a particular place and sometimes with reference to particular biological characteristics[8]. In most formulations, these characteristics of ethnicity are, following Frederik Barth's model, articulated in relation to others — that is, in the construction of 'ethnic boundaries'[9]. The concern is with identifying exactly what makes one group different from another — is it who they socialize with, or what they see as their long-term life plans, or is it their religious beliefs, or some combination of factors such as these?

The concept of ethnicity, however, is not confined to academic circles; in Britain it is invoked in many non-academic contexts too. Ethnic allegiances are often treated by the media as natural qualities of human groups, that may, as in nationalist ideologies, justify separatist movements. Ethnicity is frequently, too, a euphemism for race: in the 1991 Census, 'ethnic group' refers to colour categories of 'black' and 'Asian' and 'white' with relatively little attention given to differences within the first two of these categories and none given to the undifferentiated 'white'. (The justification for the Census classification is that despite its shortcomings, it provides a means of monitoring racism[10]). In my view, these diverse uses of ethnicity undermine the analytical value of the term, but perhaps the larger problem with subsuming particular constellations of 'cultural' characteristics — social structures, economic activities, religious beliefs, health beliefs, and so on — under the label 'ethnicity' or in some overall explanation of 'difference' or of 'boundary maintenance' is that it may be difficult to disentangle which particular characteristics are salient, at any given point in time, and which ones change. Some recent accounts, including mine, have avoided the term, and instead attempt to show that what characterizes a particular group of people and indeed what defines them as a group may alter over time as circumstances change.

Pakistani settlement in Oxford — and elsewhere in Britain — can be described in terms of several distinct phases. The migration itself was generally regarded as a means of improving the status of a circle of close kin 'at home' rather than as a route to individual social advancement. Men in unskilled or semi-skilled work remitted money home for this purpose and valued frugality and saving. They also played down status distinctions derived from the background in Pakistan. With time, however, locally derived socio-economic differences emerged as particular men became landlords or moved into shopkeeping or other business enterprises, these distinctions sometimes over-riding, or competing with, differences such as caste status derived from Pakistan. The arrival of women and children in the late 1960s and early 1970s intensified status competition and accelerated the re-creation of patterns of social behaviour derived from Pakistan. Women's networks of exchange, including gift exchange on ceremonial occasions and the convening of *khatmi Qur'āns*, were well established by the time of my first fieldwork in the early 1980s. It was clear that for most Pakistanis the prospect of a permanent return to Pakistan was becoming increasingly unrealistic, even while some migrants at least continued to dream of returning home and making good there.

Over the past fifteen years, there have been several significant local socio-economic changes: factory jobs have been lost, men of the pioneer generation have retired, become unemployed or moved into self-employment and the proportion of women in paid work and of young adults, especially women, in further or higher education has increased. Yet there has been no very marked change across the generations in the type of work taken up by young men and even those who have obtained professional qualifications often favour self employment. Women continue to organize and participate in *Qur'ān* readings and other distinctive domestic and religious rituals, and arranged marriage remains both expected and common, though it has its critics. Ideas about health and illness continue to be drawn from the background of diverse medical systems in Pakistan and sometimes influence health-seeking behaviour, despite widespread use of GPs and the National Health Service. Many British Pakistanis continue to revere *pīr*s, within a contested Islamic tradition that is best understood in relation to the heterogeneity of Islam in the Indian subcontinent. Disputes that occur from time to time in the mosques very often reflect these ideological divisions; in Oxford in the 1980s one such dispute resulted in a new mosque being established. In recent years, concerns over maintaining an Islamic identity in the context of a secular state have gained importance. These are now perhaps the most pressing contemporary issues for British Pakistanis especially of the younger generation. Indeed, concerns with aspects of their Muslim identity have displaced the 'myth of return' as a defining characteristic of Pakistani settlement in Britain[11].

British Pakistanis are a heterogeneous category, and regional, religious, class and caste differences derived from Pakistan affect the forms of their adaptation to British society and their assimilation of western norms and values. But whatever their other differences, the majority of Pakistanis are of small-scale, middle or low ranking landowning backgrounds. They are all of course city dwellers now, by virtue of their migration to Britain and because they may also have moved to cities in Pakistan, but for the majority these are only recent developments. As Tariq Modood writes in the context of understanding the British Muslim response to *The Satanic Verses*, it is important 'to recognise that we are talking about a semi-industrialised, newly urbanised working class community that is only one generation away from rural peasantry'[12]. And these links to the peasant world are still significant. Many Oxford Pakistanis have close relatives in Pakistan who are small-scale farmers, producing, with varying degrees of success and mainly for home-consumption, crops such as wheat or (in the canal colonies) sugar cane, or livestock such as buffaloes and chickens. Relatives in Britain have often financed extensions to these enterprises and maintain some form of commitment towards them, despite the immigration controls and despite the fact that families with children, grandchildren, properties and businesses in Britain have proportionally less money to remit to Pakistan. Travel and communication between Pakistan and Britain is on-going, and maintained in particular through the immigration of men and women as spouses of young British-born Pakistanis.

In short, most migrants retain, to varying extents, social ties with relatives in Pakistan that are often bound up with their interests in land and property there, despite the fact that they now also have socio-economic commitments in Britain. Migrants are, as Pnina Werbner puts it, 'double-rooted'. And this dual allegiance would not have been possible to anything like the same extent without the particular form of Pakistani social organization known as the *birādarī*, which means, literally, 'kinsmen', 'brotherhood' or 'relatives'. *Birādarī* membership brings with it distinctive patterns of authority and particular ways of thinking about relationships with kin; and it invokes concepts such as honour *(izzat)* and shame, especially as they affect gender roles and sexuality.

Many aspects of the lives of east Oxford Pakistanis are best understood in terms of these *birādarī* interests. Oxford *birādarī*s are first and foremost outposts of *birādarī*s in Pakistan that exist in competitive relationships with one another and are competitively driven from within; this explains the rifts and realignments in *birādarī* membership over time. Migrants have accommodated very many material changes in living standard arising from their migration to Britain, but many of their ways of thinking reveal the persistence of attitudes rooted in *birādarī* membership. Indeed, material progress is rooted in *birādarī* values. Most of the more recent adaptations of the past fifteen years, in household organization, family structure and employment patterns, such as the increase in the proportion of 'nuclear' households, the move to the suburbs and the increasing number of women in paid work, can still be interpreted in terms of the desire to acquire property and status in traditional terms, even when they might appear to indicate the contrary.

Arranged marriage continues to maintain and draw upon *birādarī* allegiances. Most marriages take place within the *birādarī*, and there is some evidence that over the past fifteen years the rate of consanguineous marriage has in fact increased. Marriages are typically with cousins and often entail the migration from Pakistan of sons or daughters of siblings of pioneer migrants. But migrants do not simply follow a 'rule' of preferential first-cousin marriage. They weigh up their interests in a way that permits changes within *birādarī* structures, and the flexibility of this process reveals how migrants have adapted to their new circumstance without necessarily assimilating individualistic values. Through this process, some elements of dissent and dissatisfaction are contained; there are marriages of Pakistani men to English women, and arranged 'love marriages' between young adults who meet at college and then inform their parents.

My account therefore emphasizes the adaptive role of the *birādarī* in the processes of establishing the Pakistani presence in Britain. But I do not want to imply that Pakistani kinship is the sole cause of Pakistani non-assimilation. It is crucial to consider other factors in understanding the continuing significance of Pakistani kinship in Britain. British Pakistanis started out on the lowest rung of the ladder of structural assimilation, because of their relatively limited competence in English and their lack of professional qualifications. They lacked financial resources to fall back upon (in contrast with the east African Asians, for instance, who arrived in Britain in the 1970s). They also faced racial hostility and discrimination from the natives, a fact that was acknowledged as an impediment to assimilation when the British government, from 1965, passed a series of Acts to outlaw racial discrimination in public places, housing and employment. In view of these major structural constraints, kinship has been, and continues to be, British Pakistanis' most powerful resource.

Men who move into taxi-driving, shopkeeping or other small businesses are taking advantage of a niche that is open when others are closed, often drawing upon the support of kin or friends in the process. They see such moves as in keeping with *birādarī* interests and easily adapted to family needs. But viewed from outside, their socio-economic position in Britain is heavily dependent upon kinship networks and the social activities and obligations which sustain them. Migrants themselves sometimes acknowledge this vulnerability: when,

Oxford families have experienced racist attacks or business failures, their relatives in Pakistan have sometimes tried to persuade them to return. Recent fears of increasing hostility towards British Muslims have exacerbated these insecurities. As one man said, 'We keep links with Pakistan, because you never know, what happened to the Ugandan Asians might happen to us.' It is, then, a combination of factors, of migrants' continuing socio-economic links in Pakistan and their limited socio-economic resources — their relative socio-economic insecurity, their low starting point on the ladder of assimilation in Britain, their vulnerability to racial discrimination — that accounts for the findings of surveys intended to monitor the progress of Britain's ethnic minorities. The most recent of these shows that Pakistani (and Bangladeshi) Muslims have fared the least well of all ethnic groups in Britain, in terms of income, employment and housing[13].

Set against these structural constraints, the Pakistani *birādarī* has without doubt played a positive role in facilitating Pakistani migration and settlement in Britain. And viewing the process of settlement and adaptation from the perspective of the Pakistani *birādarī* suggests that the 'problem' of non-assimilation tells us more about the assumptions of the 'host' society than about the concerns of Pakistanis themselves. However, while the Pakistani *birādarī*, with its roots in Pakistan, has eased adaptation to life in Britain, I do not wish to paint too rosy a picture of it. While there are very many admirable aspects of Pakistani social life, especially the hospitality and generosity that people show towards both kin and non-kin, in certain contexts and in some families, the competitive aspects of the concerns for property and status and property, and migrants' readiness to take revenge for honour slighted, have sometimes worked against their interests in Britain.

The pioneer generation was clearly motivated by a desire to improve its lot in Pakistan, and although many of the younger generation raised here share this drive for property and status, it is not sustained by the same sense of purpose. 'They think they are kings', said one father, commenting of the 'easy' life of his unemployed sons, one of whom is serving a prison sentence on drugs charges. Fathers might 'blame' someone else's son for leading their sons astray, but some of the parents of the young men who have recently become involved in semi-legal or illegal activities including drug-dealing have accepted the extra income, or its benefits and 'turned a blind eye', only to find that their sons, later, are serving prison sentences.

In extreme circumstances, men and sometimes women have 'taken the law into their own hands' in their attempts to salvage honour or damaged reputation, following perceived insults to a wife or daughter, in the event of daughter or sister's elopement, if a marriage has failed, if money has not been returned or paid, or if someone's son has been charged with some offence or imprisoned, and so on. These attempts to salvage honour have included physical or mental abuse, physical assault, and even murder. I have heard, for example, of women putting ground glass into *samosā*s to be eaten the next day, of brothers using hockey sticks to beat up a lodger not paying rent, and of an enraged husband attacking an adulterous wife with an axe. An arson attack upon a family in which two children burned to death was motivated not by 'race' but by 'inter-ethnic revenge' in connection with drugs charges. The revenge-seekers may then themselves be arrested, detained by the police or face prison sentences as a result. Of course, incidents like these are not typical — they take place when individuals or households are under extreme pressures. And they are not confined to Pakistanis; the values or sentiments that motivate them by no means unique to Pakistanis. But, as the nationally publicized case of a mother and son jailed for life for murdering a daughter who 'dis-honoured' her family shows, the doctrine of multiculturalism in modern Britain has its limits. Protection of, and respect for, minority values and customs does not extend to ideas and practices that contradict civil rights[14].

Incidents such as elopements, brothers pursuing an errant sister, 'bounty hunters' and even honour killings can be under-stood, I have shown, within the 'traditional' framework of the structure and values of *birādarī*s in Pakistan, and it is import-ant to realize that such conflicts occur there as well as in Britain. They are therefore not simply a symptom of western versus South Asian 'culture clash'. There is, however, an important difference between Pakistan and Britain in the ways in which, in most cases, these conflicts are expressed and resolved. In Pakistan, domestic violence, particularly against

women, is, for the most part, socially sanctioned, backed up by
the ideas and values that shape relationships between men and
women. 'Honour' killings rarely reach the courts, and there is
little trust in the criminal justice system[15]. In Britain, by contrast, civil rights, (some of which are very recent or are under
negotiation) particularly in relation to domestic violence are
now protected in law. Although much domestic violence,
emotional blackmail or sexual abuse remains unreported in all
sections of British society (and the implementation of the law is
itself affected by deeply entrenched values and ideas concerning
gender) the state now recognizes a responsibility to protect all
of its citizens. A couple 'on the run' can reasonably expect
some police protection; a woman seeking to escape a violent
husband or in-laws may be re-housed outside the area by her
local council; a divorced woman has, in principle, economic
autonomy and the freedom to re-marry.

One of the problems with the media portrayal of 'culture clash'
is that it suggests that minority cultures are uniform and
unchanging, that one case is typical of all. While the most dramatic of these cases — the ones which make local or national
newspaper headlines — do indeed highlight some fundamental
differences in values, many of the kinds of conflict I have
described are resolved eventually with some form of reconcilia-
tion or adaptation to a new situation[16]. Such adaptation and
accommodation, in what is perhaps a typically British com-
promise from both sides of the culture divide, has been taking
place ever since the beginnings of Pakistani settlement in
Britain.

From the 1960s, to counter fears about the political consequences of racial tension and non-assimilation, anti-racist
legislation has addressed discrimination in public places, employment and housing. But cultural matters such as religious belief
also have public consequences, in the workplace, for instance,
and in the schools — where various surveys have shown 'ethnic
minority' pupils to be particularly disadvantaged. In the 1970s,
multicultural educational policies were introduced in areas of
substantial 'ethnicity' in order to address the disadvantage faced
by pupils of different linguistic and cultural backgrounds — in
direct contrast to the earlier *laissez-faire* approach to assimilation. In addition, local authority and central government funds
were administered through community relations councils (local

branches of the Commission for Racial Equality) for 'ethnic' youth and community projects to promote good 'community relations'. (I was myself employed at the Oxfordshire Council for Community Relations in the mid 1980s to run one such project, teaching Urdu to mainly English adults and training native-speakers as teachers of Urdu in adult education). A number of changes in statutory and educational provision have been negotiated, for example in exempting Muslim pupils from aspect of physical, religious and sex education and in permitting Muslim dress in school. In Bradford, in the mid-1980s, the Council for Mosques lobbied the education authority to retain two single-sex upper schools and to provide *halāl* meat in school dinners for Muslim pupils; these provisions have continued despite racist backlash and protests from animal rights activists[17]. In Oxford, the threat of the closure of the only all-girls state secondary school was capable of mobilizing a response from an apparently united Muslim community well before the furore over *The Satanic Verses*.

Most east Oxford Pakistanis of the first generation have not become involved in these public issues, the men concentrating instead on working long and anti-social hours in order to make gradual improvements to the standard of living of their families. Yet 'community' issues, mainly to do with Muslim identity, have gradually been pressed forward, in the early years by individuals acting as 'cultural brokers' and later, in the 1970s and 80s, through statutory processes of ethnic minority consultation. Locally, these processes have both raised the profile of 'ethnic minorities' and served to increase inter- and intra-ethnic competition for access to funds[18]. Occasionally, too, issues of mosque politics and of doctrinal difference surfaced in these arenas. In Oxford, in the early 1980s, following the outcry at the prospect of the charismatic Barelwi *imām* being sacked and consequently deported, both young and older men among the *imām*'s supporters called upon the community relations officer (CRO), a lawyer of Pakistani origin, to help them negotiate a 'democratic' solution. The CRO became actively involved in this process, reconvening a committee that reinstated the *imām*, organizing a petition and writing to the Home Office. There were those who, at the time, considered that the CRO's duties should not extend to resolving mosque disputes, but there is little doubt that experiences such as this have served to increase confidence in pressing local interests through the democratic processes of British civil society.

Viewed from the perspective of this gradual accommodation within British political and civic structures, the protest about *The Satanic Verses* and the demand to extend the blasphemy laws to protect minority religious interests is less startling. In Oxford, perceived attacks upon Islam had already proved effective in mustering popular support. The intensity of the emotions generated can also be understood to some extent in terms of the particular and contested 'Barelwi' tradition of Sufi Islam that is popular among a majority of British Pakistani Muslims. For those who revere the Prophet as a man of superhuman qualities, Rushdie's portrayal of the Prophet as not only an ordinary mortal but also as corrupt and licentious was deeply offensive. The prophet's life, is, for many Muslims, exemplary. Thus, as Tariq Modood writes, 'the truth is that all the religious zealots had to do was simply quote from SV (*The Satanic Verses*) for anger, shame and hurt to be felt[19].

But why, then, did the Muslim response take on the proportions of a major national crisis? The prospect of Muslims taking to the streets in violent protest awakened earlier fears about political stability. The 1962 Commonwealth Immigrants Act, which ended primary immigration from the Indian subcontinent and the Caribbean, was primarily a response to the first major post-war outbreaks of racial tension — in the 1958 riots in Nottingham and Notting Hill Gate. Yet it failed to dispel the belief of Enoch Powell, among others, that the presence of culturally and religiously distinct settlements of immigrants and their descendants, occupying 'whole areas, towns and parts of England' would be inimical to national political unity[20]. The Rushdie affair touched upon these insecurities. Ten days after the Ayatollah's *fatwa* on 14th February the Home Secretary Douglas Hurd spoke at a gathering of British Muslims and underlined the importance of integration while retaining religious traditions and refraining from violence; then in July 1989 the Under Secretary John Patten addressed British Muslims on what 'being British' entails. Their statements gave multiculturalism and tolerance of cultural and religious difference a central place, but added that such tolerance must be accompanied by an understanding of democratic processes[21].

The fear that Muslims would take to the streets in frenzied protest should also be understood in relation to current national political concerns. 'National' unity was already in question, with civil war in Northern Ireland, Scottish and Welsh nationalisms, and the prospect of European union. In this contest, the vision of a separatist 'Islamic' movement, perhaps with connections across the Muslim world, was threatening indeed.

On the other hand, left-wing and liberal circles in Britain were disturbed because the Muslim protest over *The Satanic Verses* used the 'liberal language of equal rights in rational argument against the secular British elite' to demand the extension of the blasphemy laws to protect Islamic sensibilities and thus to institute 'their own strongly held religious traditions'[22]. Among non-Muslims, this demand conjured up images of British Muslims as uniformly 'fundamentalist', and as fanatics of rigid and unchanging beliefs — an image that has a long history in the Islam of the European imagination[23].

The Muslim demand to extend the blasphemy laws was not met, and one effect of the campaign has been to increase pressure to abolish these archaic laws (which in any case fail to protect non-Christians and atheists)[24]. Other effects of the Rushdie affair have stretched further and have on the whole worked against Muslim interests in Britain. As Malise Ruthven writes, 'there can be no doubt that the publication of the book, followed by the Ayatollah's *fatwa* against its author combined to produce a major setback to community relations in Britain'[25]. The events have, in some quarters, reinforced racist sentiment and fuelled fears about Muslims as fanatics wishing to wage holy war (*jihad*) and to impose Islamic law within a secular state. 'Islamophobia' is apparently on the increase, and a recent report calls for legislation to protect people from discrimination on the grounds of religion[26]. A further effect has been the defensive response of a small and disillusioned 'fundamentalist' or 'separatist' minority of young British Muslims[27]....

Multiculturalism teaches us to value and respect cultural difference. This doctrine generally depends upon particular ideas of what constitutes cultural difference. With respect to British Pakistanis, this, at first, seems obvious: there are distinctive kinship structures, particular ways of socializing, certain ideas about health, honour, gender, authority and power and so on, which are broadly derived from the background in Pakistan; such characteristics might also be described as ethnic differences. Yet a closer look reveals considerable heterogeneity in these characteristics, cross-cutting allegiances, disputed identities and contested traditions; the problem then is one of understanding what matters in which context.

As the Rushdie affair has shown, it is in the particular context of British civil rights (which have themselves been, and are being, negotiated in relation to current social and political concerns and earlier social and political changes, especially of the past century) that some of the limitations of the doctrine of extreme multiculturalism become obvious. A particular cultural notion such as honour might explain why murder is socially approved in some sections of Pakistani society, but in the context of British civil rights, murder is condemned and the murderer punished. Indeed, issues of human rights that might govern though civic law the ways in which we live together are more and more matters of political debate across the world.

In the public debates about cultural difference that concern British Pakistanis, what has most consistently been at issue — apart from the current debate over 'arranged' or 'forced' marriage, and the civil rights issues this raises — is their religious identity. And increasingly, young British Pakistanis are turning to Islam as a more significant source of identity than ethnicity, especially because of its universal appeal, and because it does indeed appear to offer absolutes[28]. In doing so, however, they are questioning some of the 'Islamic' practices of their parents, distinguishing religious practice from tradition or custom, and using modern styles of argument in referring to and or re-interpreting 'Islamic' sources to justify their positions. Many young Muslims are uneasy, too, about the popular image of Muslims as intolerant and fanatical. They may point to the humanist elements within Islamic traditions, for example to the sentiment that completing the 'rituals' of Islam is meaningless unless it is accompanied by actions which do not harm other people. It is likely that debates of this sort will be on the agenda for the future.

NOTES

1. The Guardian, Tuesday February 21st, 1989.
2. See, for instance, the discussion in Ruthven, 1990.
3. Holmes, 1991:16–17.
4. McNeill, 1985; on the origins of nationalism, see Gellner, 1983 and Anderson, 1983.
5. Castles, 1995.
6. See, for example, Castles and Kosack, 1973 and the critique in Watson, 1977.
7. For instance, Jeffery,   1976; Tambs-Lyche, 1980; Shaw, 1988 and Werbner, 1990.
8. See, eg. Banks, 1996.
9. Barth, 1969. And see Jeffery 1976 and Tambs-Lyche 1980 for two applications of Barth's model.
10. For a detailed discussion of the Census classifications, see Ballard 1996 (a) and 1997.
11. See Shaw, 1994.
12. Modood, 1990:145.
13. Modood et al., 1997. Earlier surveys have been published as Daniel, 1968; Smith, 1976 and Brown, 1884.
14. The Independent, 26th May 1999.
15. See, for instance, 'A question of honour', The Guardian, 27th May, 1999.
16. 'Anguish, 'rape' and family break before divorce, The Guardian, 27th May 1999.
17. Lewis, 1994:149.
18. See Kalka, 1991 (b) and Shaw, 1991.
19. Modood, 1990:154.
20. Smithies and Fiddick (eds.) 1969.
21. For a detailed discussion of Patten's texts and an analysis of the British government's response to the Rushdie Affair, see Asad, 1993.
22. Asad, 1993:267.
23. As an example of the secular liberal attack on Islam, see Weldon 1989. For an historical analysis of Islam in the European imagination, see Ballard 1996 (b).
24. See Russell, 1999 and Lee, 1990.
25. Ruthven, 1990:157.
26. Islamophobia: a challenge for us all, London: Runnymede Trust, 1999.
27. A militant youth group (Hizbut-Tahrir) is active in some British universities, the Pakistani students I know have been frightened by its anti-western, anti-semitic and anti-homosexual propaganda.
28. Jacobson, 1998.

BIBLIOGRAPHY

Ahmad, I. (1966), 'The Ashraf-Ajlaf distinction in Muslim social structure in India', *Indian Economic and Social History Review*, 3:268–278.

Ahmad, I. (ed.) (1976), *Family, kinship and marriage among Muslims in India*, Delhi: Manohar Book Service.

Ahmad, I. (ed.) (1978), (1973), *Caste and social stratification among the Muslims*, Delhi: Manohar Book Service.

Ahmad, I. (1978), (1973), 'Endogamy and status mobility among the Siddique Sheiks of Allahabad, Uttar Pradesh', in *Caste and social stratification among the Muslims*, I. Ahmad, (ed.), Delhi: Manohar Book Service: 157–194.

Ahmad, S. (1971), 'Social Stratification in a Panjabi Village', *Contributions to Indian Sociology*, New Series, 4:105–125.

Ahmad, S. (1977), *Class and Power in a Punjab Village*, Monthly Review Press.

Ahmad, Z. (1962), 'Muslim caste in Uttar Pradesh', *The Economic Weekly*, 14:325–366.

Aggarwal, P.C. (1971), *Caste religion and power: an Indian case study*, New Delhi: Shri Rana Centre for Industrial Relations.

Aggarwal, P.C. (1976), 'Kinship and marriage among the Meos of Rajasthan', in Ahmed, I. (ed.), *Family, kinship and marriage among Muslims in India*.

Alavi, H. (1972), 'Kinship in West Punjabi villages', *Contributions to Indian Sociology*, New Series, Vol. 14, No. 6: pp. 1–27.

Anderson, B. (1973), *Imagined communities: reflections on the origins and spread of nationalism*, London: Verso.

Anwar, M. (1979), *The myth of the return: Pakistanis in Britain*, London: Heinemann Educational.

Ansari, G. (1960), 'Muslim caste in Uttar Pradesh: a study of cultural contact', *Eastern Anthropologist*, 13, (Dec. 1959 — Jan. 1960) pp. 1–83.

Ardener, S. (1984), 'The comparative study of rotating credit associations', *Journal of the Royal Anthropological Institute*, 94:201–29.

Asad, T. (1993), *Genealogies of Religion: Discipline and reasons of power in Christianity and Islam*, Baltimore: The Johns Hopkins University Press.

Aurora, G.S. (1967), *The New Frontiersmen*, Bombay: Popular Prakashan.

Ballard, R. and Ballard, C. (1977), 'The Sikhs', in J.L. Watson (ed.), *Between Two Cultures*, Oxford: Basil Blackwell: 21–56.

Ballard, R. (1983), 'The context and consequences of migration: Jullundur and Mirpur Compared', *New Community*, Vol. X1, Nos. 1–2, pp. 117–136.

Ballard, R. (1990), 'Migration and Kinship: the differential effect of marriage rules on the processes of Punjabi migration to Britain', in Clarke, C., Peach, C. and Vertovec, S. (eds.), *South Asians Overseas: migration and ethnicity*, Cambridge: Cambridge University Press.

Ballard, R. (ed.) (1994), *Desh Pardesh: the South Asian presence in Britain*, London: Hurst and Co.

Ballard, R. (1994), 'Differentiation and Disjunction among the Sikhs', in *Desh Pardesh*, London: Hurst and Co.

Ballard, R. (1996) (a), 'Negotiating Race and Ethnicity: Exploring the Implications of the 1991 Census, *Patterns of Prejudice*, Vol. 30, No. 3, London: Sage Publications.

Ballard, R. (1996) (b) 'Islam and the construction of Europe', in Shadid, W.A.R. and van Koningsveld, P.S. (Eds.), *Muslims in the Margin*: Kampen The Netherlands: Kok Pharos.

Ballard, R. (1997), 'The construction of a conceptual vision: 'Ethnic Groups' and the 1991 U.K. Census', *Ethnic and Racial Studies*, Volume 20, No. 1, Routledge.

Banks, M. (1996), *Ethnicity: anthropological constructions*, London and New York: Routledge.

Baumann, G. (1996), *Contesting Culture: discourses of identity in multi-ethnic London*, Cambridge: Cambridge University Press.

Barth, F. (1969), *Ethnic groups and boundaries: the social organization of culture difference*, London: George Allen and Unwin.

Basham, A.L. (1976), 'The Practice of Medicine in Ancient and Medieval India' in Leslie C. (ed.), *Asian Medical Systems*, California: University of California Press: 18–43.

Baumann, G. (1992), 'Ritual implicates 'Others': rereading Durkheim in a plural society, in D. De Coppet (ed.), *Understanding Rituals*, Routledge: London and New York.

Bhachu, P. (1985), *Twice Migrants: East African Sikh settlers in Britain*, London: Tavistock.

Bhachu, P. (1988), 'Aapni Marzi Kardhi. Home and Work: Sikh women in Britain', in Westwood, S. and P. Bhachu (eds.), *Enterprising Women: ethnicity, economy, and gender relations*, London: Routledge, pp. 76–102.

Bhopal, (1986), 'The inter-relationship of folk, traditional and western medicine within an Asian community in Britain', *Social Science and Medicine*, Volume 22, No. 1:99–105.

Blunt, E.A.H. (1931), *The Caste System of Northern India*, Oxford: Oxford University Press.

Boddy, J. (1989), *Wombs and Alien Spirits: Women, Men and the Zar Cult in Northern Sudan*, Madison: University of Wisconsin Press.

Brooks, D. (1975), *Black Employment in the Black Country*, London: Runnymede Trust.

Brown, C. (1984), *Black and White Britain: The Third PSI survey*, Aldershot: Gower.

Cambridge University Asian Expedition (1962), *The Budhopur Report: a study of the forces of tradition and change in a Punjabi village in the Gujranwala District, West Pakistan*, Lahore: University of the Punjab, Social Sciences Research Centre.

Castles, S. and Kosack, G. (1973), *Immigrant workers and class structure in western Europe*, London: Oxford University Press for the Institute of Race Relations.

Castles, S. (1995), 'How nation-states respond to immigration and ethnic diversity', *New Community*, Vol. 21, No. 3.

Clarke, A. and Parson, E. (eds.), (1997), *Culture, Kinship and Genes: towards crosscultural genetics*, London: Macmillan.

Cohen, A. (1969), *Custom and politics in urban Africa: a study of Hausa migrants in Yoruba towns*, London: Routledge and Kegan Paul.

Coleman, D. and Salt, J. (1996), *Ethnicity in the 1991 Census, Volume One: Demographic characteristics of the ethnic minority populations*, London: H.M.S.O.

Currie, P.M. (1978), *The shrine and cult of Mu'in al-Din Chishti of Ajmer*, Oxford University: Unpublished D. Phil thesis.

Dahya, B. (1972–3), 'Pakistanis in England', *New Community*, Vol. 2, No. 1.

Dahya, B. (1973), 'Pakistanis in Britain: transients or settlers?, *Race*, Vol. XV1, No. 3.

Dahya, B. (1974), 'The nature of Pakistani ethnicity in cities in Britain', in A. Cohen (ed.), *Urban ethnicity*, A.S.A. Monographs 12, London: Tavistock, pp. 77–118.

Daniel, W.W. (1968), *Racial Discrimination in England*, Harmondsworth: Penguin.

Darling, M.L. (1928), *The Punjab peasant in prosperity and debt*, London: Oxford University Press.

Darling, M.L. (1949), *At freedom's door*, London: Oxford University Press.

Darr, A. and Modell, B. (1988), 'The frequency of consanguineous marriage among British Pakistanis', *Journal of Medical Genetics*, Vol. 25, pp. 191–194.

Das, V. (1873), 'The Structure of Marriage Preferences: An Account from Pakistani Fiction, *Man*, 8, 30–45.

Davis, K. (1951), *The population of India and Pakistan*, Princeton: Princeton University Press.

Dawood, N.J. (1974) (trans.), *The Koran*, Harmondsworth: Penguin Books, 4th edition.

Deakin, N. (1970), *Colour, citizenship and British society*, London: Pantheon Books.

Desai, R.H. (1963), *Indian immigrants in Britain*, London: Oxford University Press for the Institute of Race Relations.

De Souza, A (ed.) (1975), *Women in Contemporary India*, Delhi: Manohar.

Donnan, H. (1985), 'The rules and rhetoric of marriage negotiations among the Dhund Abbasi of Northeast Pakistan', *Ethnology*, Vol. 24:183–196.

Donnan, H. (1988), *Marriage among Muslims: Preference and Choice in Northern Pakistan*, Leiden: E.J. Brill.

Douglas, M. (1966), *Purity and Danger: an analysis of concepts of pollution and taboo*, London: R.K.P.

Dumont, L. (1980), *The Caste system and its implications*, Chicago: University of Chicago Press.

Eade, J. (1989), *The Politics of Community: The Bangladeshi Community in East London*, Aldershot: Gower.

Eaton, R. (1984), 'The Political and Religious Authority of the Shrine of Baba Farid' in B.D. Metcalf (ed.), *Moral Conduct and Authority: the place of Adab in south Asian Islam*, Berkeley.

Eglar, Z. (1960), *A Punjabi village in Pakistan*, New York: Columbia University Press.

Eriksen, T.H. (1993), *Ethnicity and nationalism: anthropological perspectives*, London: Pluto Press.

Ewing, K. (1985), 'The Sufi as Saint, Curer, and Exorcist in Modern Pakistan', in *Contributions to Asian Studies,* Vol. XVIII:106–114.

Fischer, M. (1991), 'Marriage and power: tradition and transition in an urban Punjabi community' in H. Donnan and P. Werbner (eds.), *Economy and Culture in Pakistan: migrants and cities in a Muslim society*, London: Macmillan.

Gardner, K. (1995), *Global migrants, local lives: travel and transformation in rural Bangladesh*, Oxford: Clarendon Press.

Gellner, E. (1983), *Nations and nationalism*, Oxford: Basil Blackwell.

Gibson, M. (1988), *Accommodation without assimilation: Sikh immigrants in an American high school*, Ithaca: Cornell University Press.

Gillespie, M. (1995), *Television, Ethnicity and Cultural Change*, London and New York: Routledge.

Griffith, J.A.G. and Henderson, J. (1960), *Coloured immigrants in Britain*, London: Institute of Race Relations.

Helweg, A.W. (1979), *Sikhs in England: the development of a migrant community*, Delhi: Oxford University Press.

Hershman, P. (1974), 'Hair, Sex and Dirt', *Man*, 9:274–298.

Hiro, D. (1971), *Black British, White British*, London: Eyre and Spottiswoode.

Holmes, C. (1991), *A Tolerant Country? Immigrants, Refugees and Minorities in Britain*, London: Faber and Faber

Holy, L. (1989), *Kinship, Honour and Solidarity: Cousin Marriage in the Middle East*, Manchester: Manchester University Press.

Hutton, J.H. (1946), *Caste in India*, Cambridge: Cambridge University Press.

Ibbetson, D. (1883), *Punjab Castes*, Lahore: Government Printing Press.

Imran, I. and Smith, T. (1997), *Home from Home: British Pakistanis in Mirpur*, Bradford: Bradford Heritage Recording Unit.

International Social Services (1976), *Immigrants at London airport and their settlement in the community*, London.

Jacobson, J. (1998), *Islam in Transition: Religion and identity among British Pakistani youth*, London: Routledge.

Jeffery, P.M. (1976), *Migrants and Refugees*, Cambridge: Cambridge University Press.

Jeffery, P.M. (1979), *Frogs in a Well: Indian women in Purdah*, London: Zed Press.

Johnson, M. (1986), 'Inner city residents, ethnic minorities and primary health care in the West Midlands', in T. Rathwell and D. Phillips (ed.) *Health, Race and Ethnicity*, London: Croom Helm.

Kalka, I. (1991) (a), 'The politics of the "community" among Gujarati Hindus in London', *New Community*, 17(3), pp. 377–385.

Kalka, I, (1991) (b), 'Striking a bargain: political radicalism in a middle-class London borough', in P. Werbner and M. Anwar, (eds.), *Black and Ethnic Leaderships: the Cultural Dimensions of Political Action*, London: Routledge.

Khatana, R.P. (1976), 'Marriage and kinship among the Gujar Bakarwals of Jammu and Kashmir', in I. Ahmad, (ed.), *Family, kinship and marriage among Muslims in India*, Delhi: Manohar Book Service.

Kleinman, A. (1977), 'Depression, somatization and the "new cross-cultural psychiatry"', *Social Science and Medicine*, 11:3–10.

Kleinman, A. (1995), *Writing at the Margin: discourse between anthropology and medicine*, Berkeley: University of California Press.

Krause, I. -B., (1989), 'Sinking Heart: a Punjabi Communication of Distress', *Social Science and Medicine*, 29:563–575.

Lomas, G.B. (1973), *The coloured population of Great Britain: preliminary report*, London: Runnymede Trust.

Lee, S. (1990), *The Cost of Free Speech*, London: Faber and Faber.

Lewis, C. and Young, A. (1992), *Paths to Asian Medical Knowledge*, California: University of California Press.

Lewis, P. (1994) (a), 'Being Muslim and Being British', in R. Ballard, (ed.), *Desh Pardesh: the South Asian Presence in Britain*, London: Hurst and Company.

Lewis, P. (1994) (b), *Islamic Britain: Religion, Politics and Identity among British Muslims: Bradford in the 1990s*, London: I.B. Taurus.

Lyon, W. (1991), 'Competing doctors, unequal patients: stratified medicine in Lahore' in Donnan and Werbner, (eds.), *Economy and Culture in Pakistan: Migrants and Cities in a Muslim Society*, London, Macmillan.

Mandelbaum, D.G. (1970), *Society in India, Volume 1: Continuity and Change; Society in India; Volume 2: Change and Continuity*, Berkeley: University of California Press.

Mauss, M. (1954), *The Gift: Forms and Functions of Exchange in Archaic Societies*, London: Cohen and West Ltd.

Mays, N, (1981), 'The health needs of elderly Asians', *Geriatric Medicine*, 11:37–41.

McNeill, 1985, 'Reassertion of the Polyethnic Norm since 1921', in *Polethnicity and National Unity in World History: the Donald G. Creighton Lectures*, Toronto: University of Toronto Press.

Mernissi, F. (1975), *Beyond the Veil: male-female dynamics in a modern Muslim society*, Cambridge, Massachusetts: Schenkman Publishing Company.

Modell, B. and Kuliev, A.M. (1992), *Social and Genetic implications of Customary consanguineous marriage among British Pakistanis*, London: Galton Institute, Occasional papers, second series, No. 4.

Modood, T. (1990), 'British Asian Muslims and the Rushdie Affair', *Political Quarterly*, April 1990, pp. 143–160.

Modood *et al.*, (1997), *Ethnic Minorities in Britain: diversity and disadvantage*, London: Policy Studies Institute.

Minocha, A. (1980), 'Medical Pluralism and Health Service in India, *Social Science and Medicine*, 14B.

Mumford, D.B. (1993), 'Somatization: a transcultural perspective', *International Review of Psychiatry*, 5:231–242.

Nair, K (1961), *Blossoms in the dust*, London: Duckworth.

Naveed-I-Rahat (1981), 'The role of women in reciprocal relations in a Punjab village', in T.S. Epstein and R. Watts (eds.), *The Endless Day: some case Material on Asian Rural Women*, 47–81, Pergamon.

Nichter, M. (1996), *Anthropology and International Health: South Asian Case studies*, (2nd edition), Chapter 3, Gordon and Breach Publishers.

Oxford City Council, 1975, *East Oxford preliminary local plan policies*.

Papanek, H. (1973), 'Purdah: Separate Worlds and Symbolic Shelter', *Comparative Studies in Society and History*, 15:289–325.

Parry, J. (1979), *Caste and Kinship in Kangra*, London: Routledge and Kegan Paul.

Peach, C., *(date), details to follow*.

Pehrson, R.N. (1966), *The Social Organization of the Marri Baluch*, Chicago: Aldine Press.

Pettigrew, J. (1975), *Robber noblemen: a study of the political system of the Sikh Jats*, London: Routledge Kegan Paul.

Pocock, D. (1973), *Mind, Body and Wealth: a study of belief and practice in an Indian village*, Delhi: Oxford University Press.

Qureshi, B. (1990), 'Alternative/complementary medicine' in B. McAvoy and L. Donaldson, *Health Care for Asians*, Oxford Medical Publications, General Practitioner Series 18, Oxford: Oxford University Press.

Rack, P.R. (1982), *Race, Culture, and Mental Disorder*, London: Tavistock.

Rai, S.M. (1965) *The Partition of the Punjab*, London: Asia Publishing House.

Rex, J. and Moore, R. (1967), *Race, Community and conflict: a study of Sparkbrook*, London: Oxford University Press for the Institute of Race Relations.

Robinson, V. (1986), *Transients, Settlers, and Refugees: Asians in Britain*, Oxford: Clarendon Press.

Rose, E.J.B. *et al.*, (1969), *Colour and citizenship: a report on British race relations*, London: Oxford University Press for the Institute of Race Relations.

Roy, S. (1979), *Status of Muslim women in north India*, Delhi: B.R. Publishing Corporation.

Russell, R. (1969), 'The Pursuit of the Urdu *Ghazal*', *Journal of Asian Studies*, 29:107–124.

Russell, R. (1985), 'South Asian Radicals and Britain's South Asian languages', Published by the author.

Russell, R. (1995), 'Love Poetry: the *ghazal*s of Mir and Ghalib' *in Hidden in the Lute: two centuries of Urdu Literature*, Manchester: Carcanet: 127–176.

Russell, R. (1999), 'Salman Rushdie, Islam and Multiculturalism', in *How not to write the History of Urdu Literature, and other essays on Urdu and Islam*, New Delhi: Oxford University Press.

Ruthven, M. (1990), *A Satanic Affair: Salman Rushdie and the Rage of Islam*, London: Chatto and Windus.

Saifullah-Khan, V. (1976) (a), 'Pakistanis in Britain: perceptions of a population', *New Community*, Vol. 5, No. 4.

Saifullah-Khan, V. (1976) (b), 'Purdah in the British Situation', in D.L. Barker and S. Allen, *Dependence and exploitation in Work and Marriage*, London: Longman.

Saifullah-Khan, V. (1977), 'The Pakistanis: Mirpuri villagers at home and in the city of Bradford' in J.L. Watson (ed.), *Between two cultures: migrants and minorities in Britain*, Oxford: Basil Blackwell.

Scott, D. (1972–3), 'West Pakistan in Huddersfield: aspects of race relations in local politics', *New Community*, Vol. 2, No. 1.

Shami, S.A. (1982), 'Study of consanguineous marriages in the population of Lahore, Punjab, Pakistan', *Biologia*, Vol. 28, pp. 1–15.

Shaw, A. (1988), *A Pakistani Community in Britain*, Oxford: Basil Blackwell.

Shaw, A. (1991), 'The making of a Pakistani community leader' in Vertovec, S. (ed.), *Oxford University papers on India, Vol. 2, Part 2: Aspects of the South Asian Diaspora*, Delhi: Oxford University Press.

Shaw, A. (1994), 'The Pakistani Community in Oxford', in Ballard (ed.), *Desh Pardesh: The South Asian presence in Britain*, London: Hurst and Co.

Shaw, A. (1997), 'Women, the household and family ties: Pakistani migrants in Britain' in Donnan, H. and Selier, F. (eds.), *Family and gender in Pakistan: domestic organization in a Muslim society*, New Delhi: Hindustan Publishing Corporation.

Schimmel, A. (1975), *The Mystical Dimensions of Islam*, North Carolina Press.

Sherani, S.R. (1991), 'Ulema and *Pir* in the politics of Pakistan', in Donnan and Werbner (eds.), *Economy and Culture in Pakistan: migrants and cities in a Muslim society*, London: Macmillan: 224–6.

Simpson, S. (1997), 'Demography and ethnicity: case studies from Bradford', *New Community* 23 (1) January.

Smith, D.J. (1976), *The Facts of Racial Disadvantage*, London: Political and Economic Planning.

Smithies, B. and Fiddick, P. (Eds.) (1969) *Enoch Powell on Immigration*, London: Sphere.

Srinivas, M.N. (1968), 'Mobility in the Caste System' in M. Singer and B.S. Cohn (eds.), *Structure and Change in Modern India*, Chicago: Aldine.

Srinivas, M.N. (1976), *The Remembered Village*, Delhi: Oxford University Press.

Srinivasan, S, (1995), *The South Asian petty bourgeoisie in Britain: an Oxford case study*, Aldershot: Avebury.

Tambs-Lyche, H. (1980), *London Patidars: a case study in urban ethnicity*, London: Routledge and Kegan Paul.

Tapper, R. and Tapper, N. (1972/3), 'Marriage, Honour and Responsibility: Islamic and local models in the Mediterranean and the Middle East, *Cambridge Anthropology*, 16:2.

Taylor, J.H. (1976), *The half-way generation: a study of Asian youths in Newcastle upon Tyne*, London: N.F.E.R. Publishing Company Ltd.

The Runnymede Trust and the Radical Statistics Race Group, (1980), *Britain's Black Population*, London: Heinemann Educational Books.

Ullah, I. (1958), 'Caste, Patti and Faction in the Life of a Punjab Village', *Sociologus*, New Series, 8:170–186.

Vatuk, S. (1972), *Kinship and urbanization: white collar migrants in north India*, Berkeley and Los Angeles: University of California Press.

Vatuk, S. (1982), 'Purdah Revisited: a comparison of Hindu and Muslim interpretations of the cultural meaning of Purdah in South Asia', in Papanek, H. and Minault, G. (eds.), *Separate Worlds: Studies of Purdah in South Asia*: 54–78, Delhi: Chanakya Publications.

Vreede de Stuers, C. (1968), *Parda: a study of Muslim women's life in northern India*, Assen: Van Gorcum & Co.

Watson, J.L. (1977), Between Two Cultures: *Migrants and Minorities in Britain*, Oxford: Basil Blackwell.

Weiner, A. (1976), *Women of Value, Men of Renown, New Perspectives in Trobriand Exchange*, Austin: University of Texas Press.

Weldon, F. (1989), *Sacred Cows*, London: Chatto and Windus.

West, J. and Pilgrim, S. (1995), 'South Asian women in employment: migration, ethnic origin and the local economy', *New Community*, 21(3):357–378.

Werbner, P. (1980), 'Rich Man, Poor Man, or a Community of Suffering: Heroic Motifs in Manchester Pakistanis' Life Histories', *Oral History Journal*, 8:43–8.

Werbner, P. (1998), 'Taking and giving: working women and female bonds in a Pakistani immigrant neighbourhood', in Westwood, S. and P. Bhachu (eds.), *Enterprising women: ethnicity, economy and gender relations*, London: Routledge, pp. 176–202.

Werbner, P. (1990), *The Migration Process: capital, gifts and offerings among British Pakistanis*, Oxford: Berg.

Werbner, P. (1991) (a), 'The fiction of unity in ethnic politics: aspects of representation and the state among British Pakistanis', in P. Werbner and M. Anwar (eds.), *Black and Ethnic Leaderships: the Cultural Dimensions of Political Action*, London: Routledge.

Werbner, P. (1991) (b), 'Shattered bridges: the dialectics of progress and alienation among British Muslims', *New Community* 17(3), pp. 331–341.

GLOSSARY

GLOSSARY of Urdu, Arabic or Panjabi words that appear more than once in the text

ādmī	person
afsos	condolences, sorrow
āmil	exorcist, someone with power over jinn
'aqīqa	sacrifice made for a child, traditionally when the first head hair is shaved.
ashraf	respectable, noble
baithak	sitting room
baraka	spiritual power
bakrā	goat
bāraī	groom's 'party' at a wedding
barā	big, great
birādarī	relatives, patrilineage
bhaī	brother
bahin	sister
burqā	a garment which conceals the face and body
chachā	father's younger brother
chādar	shawl
chārpāi	wooden-framed string bed
chulhā	hearth
chapātī	round flat unleavened bread
chaudharī	honorific form of address; headman
dāi	midwife
desī	home-made
desī gorī	literally 'home-made English girl'.
dupattā	headscarf
fakīr	wandering holy man
garmī	heat
gāon	village
ghī	clarified butter
ghusal	major ablution; bath
gorā	white
hajj	pilgrimage to Mecca
halāl	lawful
halwā	a traditional sweet dish
hakīm	practitioner of Unani (Greek) medicine
hasab	addition
imām	priest
īdu'l-fitr	the festival at the end of Ramzan, the month of fasting

īdu'l-zohā	also called *īdu'l-qurbān*: the festival commemorating Abraham's offering of Isaac, held on the tenth day of the month of hajj
īdī	pocket money given to children at Id
izzat	honour, respect
jādū	magic
jorā	a pair, a suit
jinn	a capricious spirit
jum'ā	congregation, Friday
kachchā	raw, uncooked, mud-built
kālā	black
kammī	artisan castes
kametī	committee, rotating credit association
khāndān	family
khatmī-Qur'ān	the 'completion' or 'sealing' of the *Qur'ān*
khūn	blood
khushī	happiness
laddū	large round sweet
lenā-denā	taking-giving
log	people
lotā	jug
mannat	vow
mahr	payment by groom to bride at marriage
mangnī	engagement
maulvī	priest
menhdī	henna
mubārak	congratulations
nahānā	to wash
namāz	prayers
nāpāk	impure
nasbandī	sterilization, literally 'tube-closing'
nazar	a gaze, the evil eye
nikāh	marriage contract
niyat	intention
nuskhā	prescription
palang	bed
pakkā	cooked, firm, brick-built
parāthā	chapati cooked with ghi
pīr	saint, spiritual guide
plīt	impure (Panjabi)
qurbānī	sacrifice
qaum	people, nation
rukhsatī	a bride's 'send-off'
sādqā	a sacrifice to avert misfortune
sāl girāh	birthday (literally 'year-knot')
samosā	triangular pastry filled with meat or vegetables
sawāb	religious merit
seviān	sweet vermicelli
sharīf	respectable

sipārā	one of the 30 sections of the *Qur'an*
salāmī	gift of money at marriage
shalwār-qamīs	loose trousers and long shirt/blouse
taubā	forgiveness
tā'wīz	amulet
tel	oil
tandūr	an earthen oven
thand	cold
vaid	a practitioner of Ayurvedic medicine
valāyatī	from abroad
vūzū	minor ablution
ylāj	remedy
zakāt	alms
zamīndār	landowner
zāt	caste

INDEX